The
BUSINESS
VALUATION
Book

The
BUSINESS
VALUATION
Book

Proven Strategies for Measuring a
Company's Value

Scott Gabehart
and
Richard Brinkley

AMACOM

American Management Association

New York • Atlanta • Brussels • Buenos Aires • Chicago • London • Mexico City
San Francisco • Shanghai • Tokyo • Toronto • Washington, D.C.

This publication is designed to provide accurate and authoritative information in regard to the subject matter covered. It is sold with the understanding that the publisher is not engaged in rendering legal, accounting, or other professional service. If legal advice or other expert assistance is required, the services of a competent professional person should be sought.

Library of Congress Cataloging-in-Publication Data

Gabehart, Scott, 1961–
    The business valuation book : proven strategies for measuring a
company's value / Scott Gabehart, Richard Brinkley.
      p. cm.
    Includes index.
    ISBN 0-8144-0642-4
    1. Business enterprises—Valuation—United States—Handbooks,
manuals, etc. I. Brinkley, Richard, 1956– II. Title.
    HG4028.V3 G3 2002
    658.15—dc21   2002007796

Pratt's Stats™, www.BVResources.com℠, www.Marketdata.com℠, www.BVLibrary.com℠ and variations thereof are all trade and service marks of Business Valuation Resources, LLC. BIZCOMPS® is a trademark of Jack Sanders.

Printing number

10 9 8 7 6 5 4 3 2

Contents

5 Business Valuation Through the ARM Approach, Part II   131

7 Fractional Interests and Discounts   231

8 ARM Approach Case Study and Words of Wisdom   255

Foreword

I have been an interested observer of Scott Gabehart and his career from the time he pursued and completed his Masters Degree at Thunderbird (The American Graduate School of International Management), through his international auditing career and management positions with Motorola and Schering-Plough, and now as a licensed business broker and Certified Business Appraiser with VR Business Brokers. During this period, Scott took the time to complete many of the course requirements for a Ph.D. in Economics at Arizona State University. He has also taught at several of the schools and universities in the Phoenix area – as well as Thunderbird.

For this publication, Scott has teamed up with Richard Brinkley, currently the Managing Director of Brinkley & Gutta, P.A., a middle-market M&A and business consulting firm with offices in Miami, Ft. Lauderdale, and Boca Raton Florida. I first became aware of Richard when he served as the Chief Executive Officer of VR Business Brokers and took the franchise to number one in the *Entrepreneur* magazine ratings (2000 rankings). VR is by most measures the leading business brokerage organization in the nation with over sixty offices. Richard has personally bought and sold four different businesses since 1978, helping to provide the book with a well rounded valuation perspective that includes the results of a comprehensive valuation survey that was distributed to business brokers across the country.

Many business brokers do not take the time or make the effort to develop expertise and secure accreditation in their area. Both Richard and Scott have obtained not only the required licenses (real estate and securities) but also an impressive collection of designations, certifications, and memberships. Richard is an active member of the International Business Brokers Association, Florida Business Brokers Association, Business Brokers of Florida, Society of Commercial Realtors, and is a lifetime member of the Institute of Business Appraisers (IBA). Scott is a Certified Business Appraiser and member of the IBA, the National Association of Certified Valuation Analysts, National Center for Employee Ownership, Valley Board of Business Brokers, and has made application toward the American Society of Appraisers.

The innovative *Business Valuation Book* focuses on valuation of the small to medium-sized business that would be of most interest to the entrepreneur. It covers all of the recognized techniques used in obtaining the fair market value (FMV) of such a business. The authors' "ARM approach" to business valuation offers a clever, user-friendly format for both the novice valuator and professional that will help ensure a credible, useful valuation result.

It's practical, easy to read, yet contains all of the essential required information for the professional as well as the owner with the desire to determine those factors that influence the worth of his or her business entity. The dozens of Web sites referred to throughout this book are extremely useful for those readers who wish to expand their valuation knowledge in a targeted manner. The questionnaire included on the CD offers valuators of all backgrounds an incredible tool for sizing up the value of any type of business in a customizable format.

> Dr. Paul R. Johnson
> Distinguished Professor of Global Entrepreneurship
> The American Graduate School of International Management

Abbreviations

The following abbreviations are used throughout *The Business Valuation Book* and are provided here for your convenience.

ACF	adjusted cash flow
AICPA	American Institute of Certified Public Accountants
AMEX	American Stock Exchange
A/R	accounts receivable
ARM	adjusted cash flow, rules of thumb, and market comparables
ASA	American Society of Appraisers or Accredited Senior Appraiser
B.I.	beginning inventory
BIG	built-in gains
BV	book value
CAM	common area maintenance
cap	capitalization rate
CBA	Certified Business Appraiser
C-corp	Subchapter C corporation
CEO	chief executive officer

CGS	cost of goods sold
comp	comparable
CPA	Certified Public Accountant
CPI	consumer price index
CRT	charitable remainder trust
CVA	Certified Valuation Analyst
DCF	discounted cash flow
DMDM	direct market data method
EBIT	earnings before interest and taxes
EBITC	earnings before interest, taxes, and owner's compensation ("annual earnings" in the IBA database)
EBITDA	earnings before interest, taxes, depreciation, and amortization
EBT	earnings before taxes
E.I.	ending inventory
EPA	Environmental Protection Agency
ESOP	employee stock ownership plan
FASB	Financial Accounting Standards Board
FF&E	furniture, fixtures, and equipment
FIFO	first-in, first-out (inventory accounting)
FMV	fair market value
FV	fair value
GAAP	generally accepted accounting principles
GAAS	generally accepted auditing standards
GAVP	generally accepted valuation principles
GDP	gross domestic product
GP	general partnership
IBA	Institute of Business Appraisers
IPO	initial public offering
ISP	Internet service provider
IV	investment value
LESOP	leveraged employee stock ownership plan
LIFO	last-in, first-out (inventory accounting)
LLC	limited-liability company
LP	limited partnership
LV	liquidation value
M&A	mergers and acquisitions
MVIC	market value of invested capital
NACVA	National Association of Certified Valuation Analysts
NAICS	North American Industrial Classification System

NASDAQ	National Association of Securities Dealers Automated Quotations
NYSE	New York Stock Exchange
OSHA	Occupational Safety and Health Administration
OTC	over-the-counter
P/E ratio	price to earnings ratio
QMDM	quantitative marketability discount model
R&D	research and development
R/E ratio	revenue to earnings ratio
RMA	Robert Morris Associates
ROA	return on assets
ROE	return on equity
R.R.	IRS Revenue Ruling
SBA	Small Business Administration
S-corp	Subchapter S corporation
SDC	seller's discretionary cash
SDCF	seller's discretionary cash flow
SEC	Securities and Exchange Commission
SEP	Simplified Employee Pension
SIC	standard industrial classification
SP	sole proprietorship
SWOT	strengths, weaknesses, opportunities, and threats
T&E	travel and entertainment
VBBB	Valley Board of Business Brokers
VR	Venture Resources
VRBB	Venture Resources Business Brokers
WACC	weighted average cost of capital

Introduction

Entrepreneurs, business brokers, accountants, bankers, consultants, and many other professionals who are routinely involved with buying and selling privately held companies know that many books have been published about business valuation and business appraisal from a variety of perspectives and frameworks. Each author purports to be different or superior in one way or another in the battle for market share. This book is no exception in regard to its attempt to carve out a niche in this market and to strive for an innovative and unique approach to business valuation.

It is our honest belief that we have succeeded in bringing the often convoluted and seemingly complex realm of business valuation to a user-friendly, standalone platform that will allow you to credibly and quickly estimate the fair market value (FMV) of businesses on a going-concern basis. In short, you will be able to generate an FMV estimate for the subject company on your own. Depending on surrounding circumstances and the reason for the valuation, you will be able to customize the depth and breadth of the review, ranging from a quick-and-dirty, single-flash estimate to a rigorously detailed assessment based on a weighted average of multiple valuation approaches and methods (or any level in between).

The business valuation process has long been considered mysterious and nebulous. Many entrepreneurs have been forced to rely on either the false sense of security that comes from a popular rule of thumb or on the costly assistance of well-paid business appraisers. Understanding the finer points of valuing a business, especially a privately held company, is a skill that takes time to perfect.

The major difficulties and challenges in business valuation are not a result of the many seemingly complicated formulas or techniques one must choose from in a given situation.

They are also not a result of the need to learn to use one or more of these valuation methods. It is certainly not a matter of understanding which methods make the most sense for a specific valuation or learning how to weigh the results obtained from different techniques. These areas do present a challenge to the novice valuator, but it is our belief that an entrepreneur who can run a business profitably can figure out how to interpret a business valuation formula and derive a value estimate.

The typical entrepreneur can easily learn and apply these procedural or quantitative tools. The primary difficulty seems to lie in understanding how to assess, interpret, and apply the various subjective components of the dozens of potential valuation methods.

Certain professional valuators intentionally mystify the valuation process, but the basic yet powerful valuation techniques presented in this book can be understood and properly used by any entrepreneur, with one major caveat: The entrepreneur must be able to independently, credibly, justifiably, and reasonably assess and interpret the overall pluses and minuses of a given business. This is where the science turns to art and the objective turns to the subjective.

Every valuation technique contains at least one component that is primarily subjective. For example, should the applied multiple against adjusted cash flow be 1, 2, or 3? Should the capitalization rate be 20 percent or 33 percent? Should the discount rate be 25 percent or 40 percent? What are the primary considerations for a given type of business that will affect the pertinent valuation multiple?

It is ultimately the owner of a business who has the clearest insights into these questions, making the entrepreneur the most capable of all when it comes to valuing a business. Only the entrepreneur knows the intimate details of a particular company's history and the intricacies of the subject industry. If business owners are supplied with basic tools and perspectives and choose to learn about business valuation, credible value estimates are within their grasp. Professional appraisers have the advantage of having mastered the universe of valuation techniques, which allows them to focus on gathering the specifics of a particular company and industry before making a formal estimate of the company's value. However, the professional appraiser often relies on the business owner to share detailed knowledge about the company and industry in making a value estimate.

Other subjective components besides the proper multiple or capitalization rate demand attention as well. Should the tangible fixed assets be valued at one-half the distance between original cost and current depreciated book value, or should they be valued using "blue book" or similar data? Should a discounted cash flow analysis contain a terminal value? Which valuation method makes the most sense for a given type of business, and how are such methods applied in practice? Given the importance of understanding business value for a variety of reasons, the entrepreneur should be versed in the related processes.

This last sentence captures the essential justification for this book. It is in the business owner's best interest to understand the business valuation process. Even if you decide to rely on a professional appraiser, it is important to recognize and understand the factors that affect business value and the tools that are used to formally estimate that value. This is precisely the goal of this book.

How will you learn to recognize and understand the factors that affect business value and the tools that are used to formally estimate that value? By becoming familiar with the contents of this book, particularly the ARM Approach Questionnaire and the Five-Page Tool, you will gain the foundation and support needed to generate a credible estimate of business value. After reading this book and the CD-ROM materials, you will have the framework you need to master the business valuation process and apply it to a variety of situations.

After an initial reading, you will be able to choose the particular sections of the book that are most helpful in a given situation.

Chapter One

Every good how-to book contains a user-friendly overview. Beginning with a definition of the ARM approach to business valuation, Chapter One provides a roadmap for a journey into the realm of business appraisal. The important link between classical business valuation approaches and the ARM approach is presented after a useful disclosure about the practical nature of the book's content. This book is written to allow the reader to understand and apply basic yet powerful valuation techniques as used by professional business brokers and other valuation professionals who operate in the trenches of dealmaking.

If the ultimate goal is to maximize company value at the time of sale, an obvious subgoal should be to understand the key facets of the business valuation process. Specifically, we shall try to understand the finer points behind business valuation as related to the ARM approach. The many facets of adjusted cash flow, rules of thumb, and market comparables (comps) play an important role in this journey.

After clarifying the relationship between classic business valuation and the ARM approach to business valuation, Chapter One presents an overview of other book materials.

Finally, an overview of the important CD-ROM materials is provided in the appendix to Chapter One. It is necessary to note that the CD-ROM materials are a critical component of this book and should be used in conjunction with the printed text.

Chapter Two

The second chapter is a formal introduction to business valuation. After a discussion of the many reasons why businesses are valued, the business valuation process is clarified in terms of three distinct market segments: business brokerage, middle market, and mergers and acquisitions (M&A) transactions. Each of these market segments is characterized by different valuation approaches, varying multiples, and differing availabilities of company and industry information.

What follows is an overview of generally accepted valuation principles (GAVP) that apply to all business valuation assignments. Appraisal designations and certifications are presented along with the major sections of a typical business appraisal. The important concepts related to standard of value and premise of value are covered briefly before the initial steps of a typical valuation assignment are listed.

Finally, the basics of classic business valuation methods are addressed to round off the analysis of generally accepted valuation principles. The income, cost or asset, and market approaches to business valuation are reviewed as a prelude to the next chapter's journey into the ARM approach. It is important to understand the ARM approach is essentially a reorganization and extension of classic business valuation principles and methods, an attempt to simplify and focus the valuation process on the techniques most often used in the trenches of the buying and selling of privately held companies. Choosing appropriate valuation methods and weighting various valuation results complete this chapter.

Chapter Three

In this chapter the ARM approach to business valuation is spelled out in greater detail. Generally speaking, Chapters Three, Four, and Five are the focal chapters of the book because they delve into the specifics of the ARM approach. The essence of the ARM approach is analyzed through discussion of each of the three major components: adjusted cash flow, rules of thumb, and market comparables.

The ARM Approach Questionnaire and the Five-Page Tool are introduced in chapter three. The actual questionnaire is presented in this chapter (note that there are two versions to the questionnaire, one full-length and one condensed) so you can familiarize yourself with it. As noted earlier, once you have read the book and CD-ROM materials, the ARM Approach Questionnaire and Five-Page Tool should be sufficient for purposes of conducting business valuations. In other words, the questionnaire and Five-Page Tool are stand-alone valuation tools that can be used to generate business value estimates. You may want to return to the material contained in the book or CD-ROM, but ultimately you will be able to complete business valuations using the ARM Approach Questionnaire and Five-Page Tool alone. How quickly you reach this skill level is a function of individual capability and effort. Once you attain a certain understanding of generally accepted valuation principles and classic business valuation approaches, it will become nearly second nature to rely on the questionnaire alone.

Chapter Four

Chapters Four and Five (and parts of the CD-ROM material) dig deeply into the specifics of the three main components of the ARM approach. Chapter Four focuses entirely on the first ARM component, adjusted cash flow (ACF), and Chapter Five focuses on the remaining two components: rules of thumb and market comps.

An entire chapter is devoted to ACF for several reasons. The overwhelming reason is that cash flow and other measures of income are the primary indicators of business success. In short, people buy businesses for one major reason: to make money. Generating cash flow and cash-equivalent benefits is the primary goal of most businesses and entrepreneurs. Generally speaking, entrepreneurs do not purchase companies because they have substantial assets or because they provide a valuable service to the public. They purchase businesses to provide financially for themselves and their families.

Analysis of a company's ACF is not important just because it is the primary indicator of business value. From a business valuation perspective, ACF is also important for the role it plays in the three ARM approach valuation components. The first component, of course, is ACF itself. One of the pertinent rules of thumb (the second component) in an evaluation often is a multiple of ACF. Finally, the use of market comparable sales data (the third component) also often involves ACF. Thus, ACF is used either directly or indirectly in each of the three major ARM approach components. Note that gross revenues may be more significant for many rules of thumb and for the assessment of market data, with each specific situation calling for a careful analysis and interpretation of data to make the optimal comparison with the norm.

Once the importance of ACF is established, a practical and detailed analysis of how to calculate ACF is presented. In general, ACF is the amount of cash-equivalent benefits accruing to a single owner working the business on a full-time basis. From the buyer's point of view, it can be interpreted as the amount of cash-equivalent resources available to service debt, pay an owner's salary, and yield a positive return on invested cash. Regardless of the perspective, ACF is calculated as the sum of pretax income and a series of addbacks including owner's salary and perks, depreciation and amortization expense, interest expense, and any one-time or unusual expenses.

To avoid confusion over terminology, a detailed discussion of the various uses of the term *cash flow* is provided. ACF is not the only measure of cash flow, and care must be taken to use the several different terms related to cash flow properly. The chapter concludes with an appendix that contains a sample application of an income approach valuation method called the Snowden technique. This technique is based on an analysis of several pertinent factors that affect business value via a quantification of the factors into a derived multiple. In short, this technique links the qualitative and quantitative assessments of a given company to a derived multiple to be applied against the company's ACF.

Chapter Five

This is the final book chapter that introduces the finer points of the ARM approach. Chapter Five covers the two remaining ARM components: rules of thumb and market comps.

Rules of thumb are covered first in introduction and overview sections. A general classification of rules of thumb is presented along with detailed examples involving accounting and tax practices and restaurants. Such businesses (like many others) are routinely valued based on a rule of thumb. Accounting and tax practices specifically and professional companies generally often are valued based on a multiple of gross revenues (as are restaurants and other food service companies).

Although many professional appraisers tend to dismiss rules of thumb as invalid for business valuation purposes, many businesses are bought and sold based on such rules of thumb. Furthermore, these rule-based sales become the market comp data used by these same professional appraisers. A list of general factors that tend to push rule of thumb multiples up or down is presented, as are general rules of thumb that apply to larger businesses (after-tax multiples).

The second portion of Chapter Five deals with the use of market data. The classic valuation method includes the market approach, which is incorporated into the ARM approach for obvious reasons. Although the proper way to use market data has always been a matter of great debate, there is no doubt that actual market-driven sales statistics are an incredibly productive tool for valuing most privately held companies. The coverage is broken down into two distinct market-based valuation methods: the comparable sales method and the guideline public companies method.

The comparable sales method is recommended over the guideline public company method for most smaller privately held companies. The larger a business is, the more attractive the guideline method becomes. Whereas the comparable sales method is based on the collection and review of sales data resulting from the brokerage of similar privately held companies, the guideline public company method relies on current publicly traded share data.

The final portions of the chapter include applications of the comparable sales method and a detailed grid overviewing the major market comp databases and their differences. To round off the analysis of accounting and tax practices via a rule of thumb, market comp data are applied to this type of business before the chapter's concluding remarks.

Chapters Six and Seven

Although it is not recommended, it would be possible to skip Chapters Six and Seven. Chapters Six and Seven are more advanced applications and insights that may or may not be necessary for a given valuation assignment. Because Chapter Six highlights the importance of various terms and conditions that are negotiated between buyer and seller in terms of their impact on final deal prices, this material is, practically speaking, potentially important. In other words, the final deal price that ultimately becomes a market comp statistic may vary depending on the normal give and take that occurs in the negotiations process. A final deal price will be higher rather than lower under the following conditions:

Low cash down payment

Long payback period

Low interest rate

Less collateral

Corporate guarantee only (no personal guarantee)

Longer and broader covenant not to compete

Fewer and less valuable tangible assets

Asset sale rather than stock sale

Longer rather than shorter lease

Longer rather than shorter training and transition phase

Clearly, the final deal price is a function of many factors beyond the normally considered factors such as the amount and trend of revenues and cash flow, degree of competition, reliance on key employees, etc. Each of these factors affects the final deal price. It is precisely because of the wide variation in terms and conditions that a large sample size is needed for the comparable sales valuation method. The rest of Chapter Six includes a practical discussion of the differences between the sale of company stock and the sale of company assets (stock versus asset sale) and a basic overview of certain tax minimization strategies.

Chapter Seven deals with sales of less than 100 percent of a company's assets or stock. If the valuation assignment involves a minority interest, then the valuation process and results must be adjusted accordingly. The value of a 20 percent interest in a business is not equal to 20 percent of the company's value as normally estimated. In fact, a 20 percent share is worth less than 20 percent of the company's value on a controlling, 100 percent basis because of the combination of a minority interest discount and a marketability discount. Depending on circumstances, each of these discounts could easily reach 25 percent or more, dramatically reducing the value of a minority interest.

Chapter Eight

The final chapter brings our discussion of the ARM approach to a fitting end in the form of a generic case study. The unique aspect of this case study is that it does not involve an actual business. Rather, this chapter walks through the five sections of the ARM Approach Questionnaire and the use of the Five-Page Tool.

Before tracking the valuation process from start to finish, this chapter explains how to best use the questionnaire and Five-Page Tool. As mentioned earlier, we have tried to create a flexible, practical valuation tool that you can use to estimate the value of any company of interest. It is not necessary to complete every question or section of the questionnaire; the analysis can be as detailed as desired. For example, Sections One, Four, and Five alone might suffice. Alternatively, the condensed version might be more adaptable to your plan of attack. Because the questionnaire is presented on the CD-ROM as well you can selectively cut and paste the areas of relevance to a given valuation situation.

In the chapter's final comments, a list of valuation facts, concepts, tips, and other quips is included as a refresher.

CHAPTER 1

Overview

Introduction to the ARM Approach to Business Valuation

Regardless of the specific reason you are reading this book, you are about to take an enlightening journey through the basics of practical business valuation. This is not a typical valuation book, however, for one primary reason. This book will teach you to understand and apply basic yet powerful valuation techniques as used by professional business brokers and other valuation professionals who operate in the trenches of dealmaking.

The goal of this book is to provide entrepreneurs, business brokers, bankers, accountants, management consultants, and others who are not full-time business valuators with the knowledge, insights, and tools to credibly estimate the fair market value of a given company for an array of reasons. By studying the information presented in this book (and the attached CD-ROM) and using the ARM Approach Questionnaire in conjunction with the Five-Page Tool, you are well on your way to generating realistic and credible estimates of fair market value.

There is nothing wrong with the high-powered, complex, and often math-intensive valuation approaches and techniques that make up the professional appraiser's toolkit. Topics such as the capital asset pricing model, betas, expected values, arbitrage pricing theory, compound option valuation, arithmetic versus geometric means, regression analysis, and midyear discounting all play an increasingly important role for the professional business appraiser in a variety of circumstances. However, in most circumstances, such as evaluating companies for purchase or for sale, they are unnecessary in terms of estimating fair market value on a going-concern basis.

As illustrated throughout this book, most businesses can be valued through the use of fairly straightforward techniques. These techniques make up the focal point of our efforts, captured in the ARM approach to business valuation. The acronym *ARM* refers to

Adjusted cash flow (adjust the cash flow and apply the proper multiple)

Rules of thumb (determine which rules apply to a given type of business)

Market comparables (modify these results via review of market comp statistics)

After learning about the fundamentals behind these three components, you can use the ARM Approach Questionnaire and the Five-Page Tool productively. Almost every type and size of business can be valued credibly by determining and balancing the three components of the ARM approach.

The material on the attached CD-ROM is in many cases as important as the material presented in the book. In particular, the "Asset or Cost Approach to Business Valuation," "SBA Business Valuation," and "Accounting Primer" (especially the subsection titled "Use of the Income Statement") sections of the CD-ROM are direct extensions of the material in the book; you must read them to fully appreciate the breadth and depth of the ARM approach to valuation.

To appreciate the big picture, you may want to skip ahead and preview the ARM Approach Questionnaire before moving further into the book. At first glance, the questionnaire may appear overwhelming (note that a condensed version is presented in addition to the full-length version on the CD-ROM). Once you recognize the nature of each of the five major sections and complete your initial study of the material presented in the next few chapters, you will see the logic behind it.

You will also see that it is possible to perform the valuation without completing Sections II and III; they may be skipped without compromising the overall valuation results. You may also want to preview the section titled "Words of Wisdom" at the end of Chapter Eight. To help gauge your progress, it might be interesting to read the numerous statements included in the "Words of Wisdom" section now, then reread them after you have finished the rest of the book. You will be pleasantly surprised at how much you have learned and how much deeper and broader your understanding is.

Even if you find yourself needing professional or independent valuation assistance (e.g., when valuing employee stock ownership plans or obtaining Small Business Administration [SBA] financing), your newfound knowledge will allow you to optimize these valuation outcomes by understanding the key factors that affect business value and directing the professional to the relevant facts and considerations that may otherwise be overlooked.

There are a number of reasons why you may need to evaluate a given business. Therefore, it is in your best interest to recognize and understand the key value determinants and related valuation perspectives. In addition, a business often is the largest single asset on an individual's personal balance sheet (or in a person's retirement plan). Therefore, the owner should devote the time and effort needed to understand the concepts and procedures behind the business valuation process.

What Are the Goals of Our Journey?

Modern financial theory holds that the goal of the firm is to maximize shareholder value. Although this typically refers to larger, publicly traded companies, this goal applies to the privately held company as well. If you understand the nature of the valuation process, your ability to maximize business value increases dramatically. For example, once an entrepreneur realizes that each additional dollar of cash flow creates as much as four or five incremental dollars upon sale of the business, his or her efforts to maximize profits take on increased meaning.

If the ultimate goal of the business owner is to maximize company value at the time of sale, an obvious subgoal is to understand the key facets of business valuation. Specifically, this book describes the finer points behind business valuation as related to the ARM approach. As implied by the *ARM* acronym, the many concepts and tools related to adjusted cash flow, rules of thumb, and market comparables play an important role in this journey.

As you will appreciate as you read this book, the single most important determinant of business value is the company's ability to generate cash flow for the owner's benefit. In general, the more the cash flow, the greater the value. The more stable and less risky the cash flow, the greater the value. There is no way to overstate the importance of these relationships in the realm of business valuation.

How Will We Reach Our Goals?

Our journey begins with an overview of traditional or classical business valuation. The business valuation community has evolved over the past decades to a point where there are in effect a series of generally accepted valuation principles, similar to the accounting world's generally accepted accounting principles (GAAP). An example of the increasing cohesion among valuation experts is found in the glossary presented at the end of this book. The bulk of this glossary is the result of discussion and coordination between several major organizations involved with business valuation. Many of the generally accepted valuation principles and concepts can be found in or are related to the classical business valuation trio:

> Income approach
>
> Asset or cost approach
>
> Market approach

To those who have a real estate license or have been involved in real property valuation, this trio may be familiar. Real estate valuation principles and procedures have been around for much longer than business valuation principles. The American Society of Appraisers (ASA), the primary certification-granting authority in the United States for real estate appraisers, recently extended its formal coverage to business valuation. The ASA now certifies business appraisers as well as real estate appraisers (as do the Institute of Business Appraisers and the National Association of Certified Valuation Analysts). In short, the bulk of classical business valuation methods revolves around the same three approaches as developed and used by real estate appraisers.

To fully understand the ARM approach, it is necessary to be familiar with classical income, cost, and market perspectives. Therefore, our first task is to work through the three major approaches in the context of typical valuation assignments. In other words, we must not only learn about these three valuation approaches and their related valuation techniques but also discuss the valuation environment in which they will be applied.

Once the valuation date or "as of" date is determined, issues such as defining the specific interest to be valued (e.g., stock or assets) and choosing the relevant standard of value (e.g., fair market value or liquidation value) and premise of value (e.g., going concern or assemblage of assets basis) must be addressed. These types of issues arise from the environment within which valuation techniques from the three major approaches are applied.

From Classical Valuation to the ARM Approach

After carefully covering the classical valuation methods, we will turn to the ARM approach. It is important to realize that the ARM approach and the traditional valuation perspective are not mutually exclusive. In fact, each of the three ARM components (adjusted cash flow, rules of thumb, and market comps) is rooted in classical valuation theory and practice. The primary difference is that the ARM approach to business valuation is practical and has been developed from years of combined experience as a business broker and business appraiser.

In other words, the ARM approach is driven by the reality behind business sales between real buyers and sellers as opposed to academic theory and hypothetical buyers and sellers. For example, many professional appraisers scoff at the idea of using a rule of thumb in valuing a company, claiming that they are imprecise, overly simplistic, and inconsistent with professional valuation standards. However, many businesses are bought and sold almost exclusively based on the application of a given rule of thumb. If the goal of a valuation is to estimate fair market value, one cannot ignore the tool that is responsible for the bulk of actual market comparable deal prices.

Although the ARM approach is practical, it does not ignore economic or finance theory to the extent that theory is an attempt to model reality. For example, financial theory holds that the greater the risk associated with an asset and its cash flows, the less the asset is worth (higher risk, lower value). The ARM approach directly and indirectly incorporates this important relationship in a variety of ways without couching it in overly theoretical terms. The ARM approach captures this link, for example, via evaluation of the company and industry for purposes of estimating the proper multiple to apply against cash flow or revenues. If the subject company is overly dependent on the owner's efforts and the owner will depart from the business upon sale, the relevant multiple of cash flow is substantially depressed (higher risk, lower value).

The best way to become a reliable and credible business appraiser is through real-world experience in facilitating the buying and selling of companies. It is through such experience that one learns first hand the relative importance of transactional issues such as the percentage down payment in cash, the amount of collateral and guarantees, and a wide range of other terms and conditions that have almost nothing to do with theoretical business valuation. Thus, it is the practical experience combined with the theoretical training of the author that has led to the development of the ARM approach to business valuation. It combines the best of both worlds in a manner that nonappraisers can understand and use.

The Journey Expands and Deepens

After we have completed our discussion and analysis of the three components of the ARM approach (adjusted cash flow, rules of thumb, and market comps), we will have the benefit of understanding both the classical approach to business valuation and the refined, practical ARM approach. Then we will be prepared to move on to other related discussions and applications that expand and deepen our understanding of the valuation arena. Specifically, we will address the following topics:

> Importance of terms and conditions for pricing or valuing businesses (Chapter Six)
>
> Fractional interests and discounts or premiums (Chapter Seven)

These chapters broaden your knowledge of business valuation concepts and procedures. Depending on your specific needs regarding business valuation, you may skip Chapter Seven with no loss of continuity. However, Chapter Six is essential for a complete understanding of the ARM approach in general and the market comp component in particular.

Importance of Terms and Conditions

As we shall learn, to use market comp data effectively, one needs a sufficiently large sample size to account for the wide divergence in these terms and conditions from one deal to the next. In addition, understanding the central role of the relationship between all-cash and seller financing is a necessary condition of credible valuation analysis.

Evaluating the many terms and conditions found in the typical purchase contract will also give the new valuator a deeper understanding of the role played by negotiations between buyer and seller in determining actual, final deal prices (which subsequently become market comp statistics for use in valuing other companies). In general, the lower the down payment, the lower the interest rate, the longer the payback period, the less the collateral, the narrower the guarantee, the longer and deeper the covenant not to compete, the less generous the employment contract to the seller, and the longer the transition period, the greater the purchase price or business value (all other things being equal).

Each of these elements influences the final deal price; recognizing this fact is important for purposes of valuing the typical business (particularly when it comes to using and interpreting market comp statistics from one of the major databases). Thus, Chapter Six is an integral extension of the ARM approach to business valuation.

Chapter Seven will take you to the next level of valuation knowledge and skills (if desired) through exposure to additional realms of generally accepted valuation principles.

Fractional Interests and Discounts or Premiums

In most business valuations, issues related to fractional interests (minority shareholdings) are absent from discussion and analysis. The fact that most business valuations involve an entire company (100 percent of the shares or assets) means that fractional interests are largely irrelevant. However, if the valuation environment includes the presence of minority holdings, whether 1 percent or 49 percent, the valuation perspective changes dramatically.

In short, the presence of minority shareholders necessitates a change in perspective. In such cases, it becomes necessary to evaluate the following two distinct types of discounts that apply in almost every minority shareholder scenario:

Minority interest discount (lack of control discount)

Marketability discount (illiquidity discount)

The result of these discounts is that a given minority stake (e.g., 10 percent) is worth less than 10 percent of the whole company (control) value. The minority interest discount is taken first, reflecting the fact that a noncontrolling interest is worth less than a controlling interest. Stated differently, there is value in control over important company decisions such that controlling shareholders are worthy of a premium as compared to noncontrolling shareholders.

The second discount is then applied to the reduced value resulting from the minority interest discount. The so-called marketability discount is applied to reflect the greater difficulty in selling the ownership rights of a noncontrolling interest (i.e., the lesser liquidity of such rights). Although it is true that the market for buying and selling privately held companies is less liquid than that of publicly traded shares, a marketability discount is not directly applied when valuing the entire privately owned company (as it is for minority shareholdings). The relative illiquidity of 100 percent privately owned companies is evidenced by the generally lower multiples paid for such companies as compared with 100 percent publicly traded companies.

The major consideration at this juncture is to recognize that when minority shareholders exist, discounts generally must be applied to these noncontrolling shares to reflect the lack of control and relative illiquidity. Chapter Seven will demonstrate techniques that are used to estimate the proper level of these discounts, which generally range between 20 and 40 percent each. In practice, this means that a 10 percent stake in a company worth $1 million will be worth substantially less than $100,000 (or 10 percent of $1 million). For example, if each discount turned out to be equal to 33 percent, the discount would be calculated as follows:

$100,000 minus 33 percent (minority discount) = $67,000
$67,000 minus 33 percent (marketability discount) = $44,890

Thus, a 10 percent stake worth $100,000 on a pro rata basis is worth only about $44,890 after the minority shareholder discounts (a 55 percent reduction overall).

The Final Stretch

Chapter Eight is an attempt to analyze the actual process of using the ARM approach (through the ARM Approach Questionnaire and Five-Page Tool) and refine our understanding of business valuation. The questionnaire and Five-Page Tool are discussed in a manner that reflects the actual valuation process. Even the case study is presented in a way that explains the role of the questionnaire and Five-Page Tool on a section-by-section basis. When reviewing the case study, it is more important for you to understand the ARM valuation process than to understand the specifics of the subject company and its value. In other words, your goal is to learn to implement the ARM approach to a business of interest with relative ease and general understanding. Chapters Six through Eight will formalize your knowledge and valuation skills to a degree that will prove beneficial in your real-world applications. Business valuation is half art and half science. Alternatively, "valuation is an art to be learned, not a science to be practiced." (Dr. Ken Ferris, author of *Valuation: Avoiding the Winner's Curse*, published by Prentice-Hall in 2002.) When you complete your studies, you should be ready to meld the art and the science and thereby promote your self-interest in a variety of valuation scenarios. To gauge your new level of understanding, review the "Words of Wisdom" section in Chapter Eight to see how many of these statements make better sense than when you first set out on this important journey.

Appendix: Overview of CD-ROM Materials

Given the importance of the material on this CD-ROM, it is critical to be familiar with its content. The CD-ROM materials are not optional reading but an integral component of the publication. For example, the "Asset or Cost Approach to Business Valuation" section and the information related to cash flow contained in the "SBA Business Valuation" and "Accounting Primer" sections of the CD-ROM are essential if one wants exposure to the complete realm of business valuation techniques.

Do not hesitate to return to relevant sections of the CD-ROM to formalize and strengthen your general understanding of business valuation techniques and principles. If convenient, make a printout of the more important sections of the CD-ROM and use as a physical attachment to the book.

The following sections are included on the CD-ROM:

Asset or Cost Approach to Business Valuation

Rules of Thumb

Accounting Primer

SBA Business Valuation

Case Study Analysis

ARM Approach Questionnaire

Condensed ARM Approach Questionnaire

You are encouraged to read the book chapters first, before reading the CD-ROM materials. As noted earlier, the most important information on the CD-ROM for maximizing your valuation skills and knowledge is found in three different sections ("Asset or Cost Approach to Business Valuation," "SBA Business Valuation," and the "Accounting Primer"). These three sections will facilitate greater understanding of the valuation processes related to the ARM approach.

Once again, note that the material on the CD-ROM is integral to the study of business valuation presented throughout this publication. Each section contains important information and insights into various aspects of the ARM approach. Before reading these sections, review the following summary commentaries.

Asset or Cost Approach to Business Valuation

This material is part and parcel of classical business valuation and is a must for even novice valuators. This section should be read in conjunction with

Chapter Two and reviewed upon completion of all book chapters. In addition to traditional asset-based valuation insights, the practical and often relevant excess earnings method is presented with examples. The discussion of the relationship between assets and cash flow is also quite useful, as are the several perspectives on goodwill.

Rules of Thumb

This list was generated primarily via survey of participating business brokers throughout the Venture Resources (VR) Business Brokers franchise network of approximately seventy offices across the United States. The actual rules are contained on the CD-ROM to save space in the book, not because they are considered of secondary importance. Each category contains a description, two to four actual rules of thumb with corresponding ranges, standard industrial classification (SIC) codes, and related Web site addresses for additional information. This section is a direct extension of the material found in the first half of Chapter Five.

Accounting Primer

This section primarily provides more detail on how to assess a company's income statement for purposes of calculating adjusted cash flow or (ACF). Before the important and practical segment called "Use of the Income Statement," an overview of the accounting process and procedures is presented along with an introduction to financial statement analysis. The final portion of this primer provides extended coverage of various intangible assets such as goodwill, which should be read as an extension of the related coverage in the "Asset or Cost Approach" section of the CD-ROM.

SBA Business Valuation

The information presented here is much more than a discussion of SBA loans and relevant valuation procedures recommended by the SBA. The analysis begins with a review of SBA loan programs, approval criteria, advantages and disadvantages of seller versus bank (SBA) financing, and insights into recent developments at the SBA in regard to change-of-ownership or business acquisition financing.

It is the detailed review of discount rates, capitalization rates, and discounted cash flow (DCF) analysis that makes this essential material for those interested in grasping the full depth and breadth of business valuation. DCF analysis is becoming the valuation method of choice for advanced valuation professionals, so grasping its essence (the time value of money) is ever more important.

In addition to covering DCF and time-value-of-money analysis, this section will refine your understanding of the relationship between multiples and discount or capitalization (cap) rates. Furthermore, the exact relationship between discount and capitalization rates is derived and techniques for estimating or establishing a discount or capitalization rate are presented. In short, one must estimate the discount rate before establishing a cap rate (i.e. capitalization rate = discount rate minus growth rate, or $c = d$ minus g).

Other coverage in this section includes insights into how banks measure cash flow and what amount of cash flow in relation to the proposed debt service is necessary to pass the "smell test" and move toward approval.* Finally, the four primary SBA-sanctioned business valuation techniques (gross revenue multiplier, discounted future earnings, capitalized earnings, and adjusted book value) are covered in detail, with a commentary regarding each method and the SBA's overall approach to valuing businesses.

Case Study Analysis

Quite different from the case study presented in the book, this analysis is intended to illustrate the wide range of potential valuation procedures and presentation formats found in the real world. It is also meant to stimulate your insights and perspectives as to what a valuation might entail. You are encouraged to perform your own valuation based on the financial information presented in the initial part of the case study.

ARM Approach Questionnaire

The full questionnaire can be copied and used in actual valuation projects. The condensed version is provided to facilitate customization of the questionnaire to your specific needs under various circumstances.

---

*The smell test refers simply to a test of reasonableness. Does the result make sense intuitively or in relation to the facts at hand? Is it a realistic multiple or estimate of value? Could the value be substantiated by use of normal repayment schemes (market interest rates over 3 to 7 years, etc.)?

Useful Valuation–Related Web Sites

To further your knowledge of business valuation, consider visiting one or more of the following Web sites now or as you read this book. They vary in their content and sophistication, but the brief description for each site should give you enough information to understand their general nature.

Whenever possible, free sites were selected to minimize costs. However, certain important Web sites (particularly those containing market comparable sales data) charge fees. The ARM Approach Questionnaire in Chapter Three contains advice on how to minimize the cost of tapping into market comp data. Note also that the questionnaire contains numerous additional Web sites of interest to business valuators of all backgrounds (as does Chapter Five, covering market comp analysis).

BIZCOMPS   www.bizcomps.com
One of three major market comp databases available to the public. They maintain two databases by SIC code (the second database is for larger entities that sold for more than $500,000).

Business Valuation Resources   www.bvresources.com
Perhaps the most complete business valuation Web site in the world. Newsletters, special reports, court case reporting, and access to four sources of market comp data help to make this a one-stop valuation Web site.

Institute of Business Appraisers   www.go-iba.org/
Another market comp database available to the public. Contains tutorials on how to use the comp data with their direct market data method.

VR Business Brokers   www.vrbusinessbrokers.com
The nation's leading business brokerage company. This site contains tips on buying, valuing, and selling businesses of all types. Their agents have access to perhaps the largest database of market comps (thousands since 1979).

Mercer Capital   www.bizval.com
This site is home to two pragmatic newsletters dealing with business valuation topics and carries a wide selection of professional valuation-related articles that are both user-friendly and practical. This site is home of the newly developed quantitative marketability discount model (QMDM) approach to estimating marketability discounts.

American Fact Finder   http://factfinder.census.gov
Developed by the U.S. Census Bureau, this site contains useful demographic data, community profiles, and industry data from the current economic census.

American Society of Association Executives [ASAE]   www.asaenet.org
This trade association for trade associations contains links to all major trade associations. These associations can provide useful insights into their respective industries as well as valuation guidelines and rules of thumb.

Manufacturing Marketplace   www.manufacturing.net
This self-proclaimed "Online Resource for Manufacturing Solutions" contains useful valuation-related information applicable to all manufacturing companies.

Valuation Resources   www.valuationresources.com
Another Web site that attempts to be a one-stop solution for business valuation needs. Articles that explain business valuation methods, industry reports, links to market comp data, an online bookstore, and much more help make this one of the best sites available for business valuation purposes.

Companies Online   www.companiesonline.com
Provided by Lycos and Dun and Bradstreet, this site will take you to information covering more than 90,000 public and private companies (searchable by SIC code, geographic location, Web address, and stock symbol). Importantly, most entries contain a link directly to the listed company.

CorporateInformation   www.corporateinformation.com
This site contains information on more than 350,000 companies and houses more than 15,000 industry reports. Each research report contains information concerning valuation, sales, profitability, and research and development, typically presented in a ten-year format.

Northern Light   www.northernlight.com
This is a hybrid search engine and information source presenting licensed materials from important valuation-related publishing companies such as Thomson Financial. Excellent tool for researching public companies.

Goldman Sachs Research on Demand   www.gsnews.com
Exceptional industry analyses are available from one of the world's leading investment banks.

Salary.com   www.salary.com
This site will help you gauge what the typical wages and salaries are for particular occupations in particular industries (can aid in reconstructing income statements for certain valuation methods and in determining whether a company's salaries are too high or low).

NVST.com   www.nvst.com
On this site, which focuses primarily on mergers and acquisitions, one can search three powerful M&A databases (BIZCOMPS, Done Deals, and the Corporate Growth Deal Retriever) or access other industry publications via sample issues and subscription information.

The Intellectual Property Mall   www.ipmall.fplc.edu

A comprehensive collection of intellectual property resources assembled by the Franklin Pierce Law Center in Concord, New Hampshire. The "Tools and Strategies" section can help educate anyone on how to assess various intellectual property tasks and concerns. In addition, a wealth of pertinent links make this a good place to begin your analysis of intellectual property.

Richard Brinkley's Web Site   www.bg-consultants.com

Describes his firm's services from M&A consulting to business plan development, including affiliations and useful links to other relevant Web sites. Mr. Brinkley's e-mail address is *rb@bg-consultants.com*.

Scott Gabehart's Web Site   www.scottgabehart.com

Contains numerous articles related to buying, valuing, and selling businesses as well as access to his first book, *The Upstart Guide to Buying, Valuing, and Selling Your Business* from Dearborn Financial Publishing. Mr. Gabehart's e-mail address is *sgabe57806@ aol.com*.

CHAPTER 2

Introduction to Classical Business Valuation

As mentioned in Chapter One, the diverse participants of the business valuation community have developed a broad collection of generally accepted valuation principles (GAVP). Although there is no formal collection of such principles, there is a great deal of overlap between the principles, terminology, definitions, procedures, and applications recommended by the major valuation-related organizations, such as the Institute of Business Appraisers, the American Society of Appraisers, and the National Association of Certified Valuation Analysts, and the leaders of the valuation community, such as Shannon Pratt (author of several books that form the basis of study for most organizations that grant appraisal certifications), Ray Miles (director of the Institute of Business Appraisers and author of *Basic Business Appraisal*) and Tom West (publisher of the *Business Reference Guide* and author of often-cited articles and books related to business valuation). The focus of this chapter is to present the concepts that make up the foundation of GAVP.

Before delving into these concepts, a few comments about the general valuation environment are in order. In particular, it is worthwhile to discuss the following issues in some detail before moving into valuation concepts and techniques:

Why is it necessary to value a business?

Are there differences between valuing smaller and larger companies?

Why Value a Business?

Most experienced entrepreneurs and business professionals are aware that dozens, if not hundreds, of books have been written on business valuation. They are aware of this fact because from time to time they are called on to understand why and how businesses of all types are valued. Whether one is trying to sell a business for top dollar (or buy for bottom dollar) or attempting to settle a divorce proceeding or estate tax dispute, the estimated fair market value of a business can play a major role in the final outcome of such events. Simply put, understanding how to value a business is an important and often necessary tool for entrepreneurs and professionals of all backgrounds.

As you review the following list, try to imagine who the audience will be and what special factors or considerations may be relevant in performing the valuation.

Reasons for Attempting to Value Businesses

To establish asking price and terms before listing a business for sale

To evaluate a company's value before making an offer to purchase a business

To plan for or settle an estate tax dispute with the IRS or other family members

To generate a settlement in divorce proceedings

To fulfill the requirements of a buy–sell agreement between partners of a business

To assist a buyer in obtaining bank financing to purchase a business

To aid an owner in obtaining bank financing to grow a business

To help ownership effectively implement strategic planning or exit strategy steps

To satisfy the curiosity of a business owner about the company's value

To estimate the level of insurance needed to protect the company's assets

To implement an employee stock ownership plan (ESOP)

To guide the sale of a minority interest to employees or other parties

To facilitate restructuring the corporation via a tax-free reorganization

To establish proper tax deductible charitable contributions of the company's stock

To promote a fair settlement during eminent domain proceedings

Every business owner will face one or more of these situations over the course of his or her entrepreneurial dealings. The relevant techniques and processes will vary depending on the purpose of the valuation. For example, valuing a company in preparation for sale calls for a different approach from attempting to negotiate a settlement with the IRS regarding estate taxes. Not only might the relevant valuation approach (e.g., income, cost or asset, market) and specific techniques (e.g., excess earning method or DCF analysis) differ, but the desired valuation results are diametrically opposed: When valuing to sell a company, a higher valuation is sought, and when settling with the IRS, a lower valuation is sought. Cynics will note that the value of a business should be the same regardless of why the valuation is taking place. Although this may be theoretically or ethically correct, in practice the results will be quite different.

To summarize, there are many reasons why one may need to evaluate a business, and the purpose of the valuation directly affects the relevant valuation approach and techniques.

Different Market Segments Related to Business Valuation

For purposes of clarification, it is possible to break down the market for buying and selling companies into the following segments:

Business brokerage

Middle market

Mergers and acquisitions

These segments differ in many ways, including company size. Also, the relevant due diligence steps differ. The scope and depth of the purchase contract and related documents vary substantially and become increasingly complex as the company size increases. Most importantly for our purposes, the proper valuation techniques can be dramatically different. The following table compares these three segments.

	Business Brokerage	Middle Market	Mergers and Acquisitions
Revenues	Up to $5 million	$5 million to $50 million	More than $50 million
Typical staffing	1 to 10	10 to 100	More than 100
Measure of earnings	Adjusted cash flow*	Earnings before interest and taxes (EBIT), earnings before interest, taxes, and depreciation and amortization (EBITDA) to after-tax earnings	After-tax earnings
Range of earnings**	Up to $500,000	$500,000 to $5 million	More than $5 million
Earnings multiples***	1 to 3	3 to 15	10 to 200+
Deal terms	40% cash + seller's note Possible Small Business Administration financing	2 times earnings + bank note and owner financing to 100% cash at closing	Cash, assumed debts, stock for stock (any combination thereof)
Financial statements	Compiled only	Typically reviewed	Always audited
Ownership role	Active management Key employee	Management in place to support owner role	Management appointed by board of directors
Valuation methods	Multiple of adjusted cash flow	Multiple of EBITC	Discounted cash flow (DCF) analysis

*Adjusted cash flow (ACF) multiples can reach 4 for certain types of businesses; they average approximately 2.3 times ACF.

**As noted earlier, there is an empirical relationship between the amount of earnings and the relevant multiple (all other things equal). Middle market earnings include adjustments for excessive owner's compensation.

***The historical average price-to-earnings (P/E) ratio for the Dow Jones Industrials has hovered around 24. Recent company multiples and average multiples in many stock indices such as the NASDAQ were "irrationally exuberant," according to Federal Reserve chair Alan Greenspan, and fell dramatically in 2001.

Naturally, these are approximations only, and the three segments can overlap depending on the specific industry and other relevant characteristics. Although some companies that are handled like business brokerage listings may have revenues and cash flow that exceed the amounts presented in the table, most businesses listed by business brokers generate less than $500,000 in ACF. Other common definitions for various market segments include the following.

Criteria Used by the Small Business Administration (SBA):

Very small: any business with fewer than 20 employees

Small: any business with 20 to 100 employees

Medium: any business with 101 to 500 employees

Large: any business with more than 500 employees

Criteria Used in the **Business Reference Guide***:*

Small: any business priced at less than $1 million

Midsize: any business priced between $1 million and $20 million

Large: any business priced at more than $20 million

Criteria Used in the **M&A Handbook for Small and Mid-Sized Companies:**

Small: any business with less than $1 million in annual sales and fewer than 10 employees

Midsize: any business with $1 million to $20 million in annual sales and 10 to 249 employees

Large: any business with more than $20 million in annual sales and more than 249 employees

As can be gleaned from these guidelines, there is no precise definition of a small to midsize business. Chapter Five also contains comparisons of smaller, privately held companies and larger, publicly traded companies in connection with the use of market comparable statistics via the ARM approach.

Whatever the precise breakdown between segments may be, it is important to understand that companies in each general category are subject to differing approaches regarding due diligence, contract preparation, and valuation issues. As explained in Chapter One, as the amount of cash flow (however defined) rises, so does the multiple one must apply to arrive at an estimate of value. For example, businesses with ACF less than $250,000 typically sell for one to three times ACF, whereas businesses with $250,000 to $500,000 typically sell for two to four times ACF.

A recent edition of the BIZCOMPS market comp database showed that businesses selling for more than $500,000 generated a multiple of cash flow approximately 88 percent higher than for transactions under $500,000. These larger businesses also received a greater percentage of the asking price than their smaller counterparts (87.5 percent versus 74.5 percent). Overall, larger businesses are more profitable, pay less rent per dollar of sales, and sell for higher multiples (lower overall risk).

In conclusion, it is important to bear in mind that different-sized businesses (and different types of businesses, as discussed later) are subject to differing valuation techniques. Therefore, both the purpose of the valuation and the size and type of business affect the relevant valuation techniques. When conducting a business valuation for any purpose, it is also important to periodically remind yourself who the intended audience is for your report. Business valuation reports and conclusions are important only when they are used to reach an objective of some type, such as to maximize the sale price on the open market or to minimize estate taxes during an IRS audit or review.

Generally Accepted Valuation Principles

Just as GAAP consists of various authoritative documents and sources, GAVP is also found in diverse locations (as opposed to a single document or source). For example, GAAP includes principles that range from the double-entry bookkeeping system developed in Italy hundreds of years ago to the latest Financial Accounting Standards Board (FASB) promulgation on accounting for derivatives.

All valuation professionals recognize many fundamental truths. For example, all valuators agree on the basic definitions surrounding key concepts such as fair market value (FMV) or discount rate. They may disagree on whether FMV is the relevant standard of value in a divorce setting or on how to estimate a discount rate, but not on the essential components of each of these concepts.

Our goal now is to introduce and explain the most fundamental and important principles and concepts related to business valuation as part of our effort to understand both classical business valuation and the ARM approach. The following discussions are equally applicable to both the classical valuation world and the ARM approach.

Valuation Versus Appraisal

Different circumstances influence the type of analysis best suited to meet the needs of the valuation recipient. A wide range of possibilities exist in terms of the type and content of information available from valuation specialists. One key distinction is between valuation and appraisal. There is a tendency to use these terms interchangeably despite the important differences. The primary distinction between the two is that anybody can complete a business valuation, whereas only licensed or certified professionals can complete a business appraisal.

Only business brokers who have earned a designation such as Certified Business Appraiser can produce business appraisals. Business appraisals are more detailed and standardized, requiring the certified party to follow prescribed rules and guidelines in preparing and distributing the appraisal reports. Because of the higher qualifications and the generally greater work requirements of business appraisers, business appraisals almost always cost more than business valuations. Generally speaking, an appraisal of similar length and content will cost two to four times more than a valuation prepared by a noncertified party. The primary appraiser designations are as follows:

Certified Business Appraiser (CBA; granted through the Institute of Business Appraisers after a lengthy examination process and preparation, review, and correction of two full-blown, formal appraisal reports)

Certified Valuation Analyst (CVA; granted through the National Association of Certified Valuation Analysts to Certified Public Accountants (CPAs) with college degrees and full-time experience in performing valuations)

Accredited Senior Appraiser (ASA; granted through the American Society of Appraisers upon passing an exam, providing written appraisals, and demonstrating five years of appraisal experience)

The common thread between these designations is that the appraiser must meet or exceed requirements that demonstrate his or her expertise in valuing companies. Each group also maintains a "uniform standards of practice" element, consistent with the Uniform Standards of Professional Appraisal Practice (USPAP) as promulgated by the U.S. Congress as a result of the savings and loan crisis of the 1980s.

Whether an entrepreneur needs to obtain a business valuation or business appraisal is a function of many factors, including the following:

Purpose of obtaining value estimate

Willingness and ability to devote financial and time resources to completion of the report

Availability of qualified valuators or appraisers

In most cases, third parties reviewing the results of valuations and appraisals will give more credence to the appraisal than to the valuation. However, a business valuation can be just as accurate in estimating a company's FMV as an appraisal. This situation may arise when one compares the work of a business broker who has been evaluating businesses for more than two decades with that of a certified appraiser who has valued primarily residential or commercial real estate and is just beginning to value companies. In short, it is critical to assess the exact skills and experience of the evaluators to make the best choice.

In other instances it may be mandatory to obtain an appraisal. In a tax set-tlement case, the courts will look more favorably on a report from a certified appraiser. In a divorce settlement, the opposing counsel may be less likely to challenge the results from an appraiser rather than a noncertified evaluator. A formal appraisal is legally required in some instances, as when one is determin-ing an employer's annual contributions to an ESOP or when an appraisal is re-quired under the terms of a buy–sell agreement between two or more partners in the case of dissolution. Although not a legal requirement, many participating SBA lenders now rely on independent third-party business appraisals in support of their loan approval process.

The choice between an appraisal and a valuation may boil down to cost. Many business owners shudder at the thought of spending $3,000 or more for a report. If the party preparing the valuation is competent, a valuation may be most cost-effective. However, is important to seek the advice of your legal coun-sel or CPA before making a decision.

Key Components of an Appraisal

Each of the following components is required by most appraisal certification-granting bodies:

Client information and appraiser's name and background

Precise definition of the legal interest to be appraised

Official as-of date for the appraisal assignment

Purpose of appraisal assignment

Definition of appropriate standard of value

Definition of appropriate level and premise of value

Complete description of subject property interest to be appraised

Description of type of report

Statement of limiting conditions and key assumptions

Statement of qualifications

A brief analysis of a few of these components is worthwhile in our pursuit of understanding GAVP. To begin with, note that in terms of the legal interest to be appraised, there is a distinct difference between valuing a company's stock and valuing its assets. Therefore, typically a different value is placed on 100 percent of the company's stock and 100 percent of the company's assets. The obvious differ-ence between the two is that owning the stock carries liabilities (known and unknown) as well as assets, thus affecting valuation. Furthermore, the value of a 10 percent minority interest stake in a company is not worth 10 percent of the entire company's stock because of a lack of control. Minority interests are subject to a discount because of this lack of control. Conversely, a controlling block (e.g., 51 percent of the shares) is worth much more than a 49 percent minority share because it includes the ability to control the operations of the business. As discussed in Chapter Seven, a marketability discount may also be relevant under certain valuation scenarios, reflecting the relative illiquidity of selling a minority block of shares in a privately held company. The so-called "level of value" refers to the difference between a "control value" and a "nonmarketable minority-interest value," whereby valuation results are obtained either directly or indirectly via assessments of control and liquidity (or lack thereof).

Every appraisal (and every valuation, for that matter) must contain an effective date, commonly called an as-of date, on which the valuation result is based. The value of a company theoretically changes every hour of the day as the business activities that affect cash flows unfold. As described earlier, there are many purposes for which appraisals (valuations) are undertaken. The purpose of the appraisal helps determine the standard of value and premise of value. *Standard of value* refers to the choice among one of many value concepts, including the following:

Fair market value (FMV)

Liquidation value (LV)

Book value (BV)

Investment value (IV)

Fair value (FV)

Other standards of value include insurance value and replacement value (cost). In most appraisal and valuation assignments, FMV is the focal point. Most people are familiar with the basic concept, but the following definition will clarify the concept for our purposes:

The fair market value (FMV) of an asset or company is the price at which the company would change hands between a willing buyer and willing seller, each acting with complete information about the company and under no unusual duress, allowing for ample time on the market to expose the business to a sufficient number of prospective buyers.

All appraisals must contain an adequate definition of the applicable standard of value, similar to the preceding paragraph. Liquidation value is the value of the company upon disposition of all tangible and intangible assets. There are two levels of liquidation value, as follows:

LV as part of a planned liquidation

LV as part of a forced liquidation

As described later, when one is valuing a company based on liquidation value, the difference between a planned and forced liquidation becomes evident in the percentages applied to each category of assets. For example, accounts receivable as of less than ninety days will be discounted at around 80 percent for a planned liquidation and at around 50 percent for a forced liquidation. The general idea is that with time and planning, more effective marketing will generate more qualified buyers and higher prices.

Book value is an interesting but fairly useless valuation concept in evaluating going concerns. Book value is the difference between a company's assets and liabilities, as evidenced by the so-called accounting equation:

Assets (A) − Liabilities (L) = Owner's equity (OE) = Book value (BV)

Note that *owner's equity* is synonymous with *book value, net worth, shareholder's equity, net assets,* and other terms. Although this may be confusing, each of these terms refers to the relationship between a company's assets and liabilities. Book value is an accounting measure as opposed to a market-based measure of value. In most cases, the FMV of a company is greater than its BV. In fact, there is an investment strategy used by certain stock market professionals that calls for investing in companies wherein their FMV is less than their BV. The logic is that the assets must be "undervalued" or a source of "hidden value."

Book value also can refer to a particular asset; for example, the book value of a piece of equipment is equal to the original cost minus accumulated depreciation. Therefore, book value is partly a function of the depreciation method used by companies. A company that accelerates depreciation for book purposes will show lower book values than a company that uses only straight-line depreciation. The book value of a company is determined by the sum of all accounting transactions and methods used by the company, so this concept is unimportant in business valuation. (The "Accounting Primer" on the CD-ROM attached to this book will also shed some light on the relevance of book value.)

There is a type of valuation method known as "adjusted book value" or "net assets" (or known by other names) that attempts to value a company by adjusting the book value of its assets and liabilities to their respective FMV. Although there is some merit to this approach in certain cases (e.g., a company that carries many assets but has recently been or is currently shut down and not generating revenues or cash flow), it is not typically necessary in most business valuations. One of the primary challenges of methods such as "adjusted book value" or the "sum of the assets" lies in the need to estimate the value of goodwill and other intangible assets. Although this is possible, such valuation processes are filled with difficult subjective determinations and assumptions that often are more trouble than they are worth. Certain versions of those methods typically ignore goodwill altogether on the basis that it cannot be liquidated or sold separately from the company's other assets.

Investment value (IV) is an important standard of value from a buyer's point of view. Specifically, investment value is the value of a particular company to a particular buyer under particular circumstances. As opposed to FMV, which is based on a hypothetical buyer or an amalgam of all buyers, IV is based on the unique conditions facing a particular buyer.

The practical effect of this measure of value is that it illustrates the notion that a given business is worth different amounts to different buyers. For example, an accounting or tax practice is worth more to an experienced CPA than to an inexperienced entrepreneur. A more dynamic example is an Internet service provider (ISP): The value of an established ISP is higher for another ISP than for a buyer outside the industry. The higher value is generated by synergism and economies of scale and scope. One can double the number of customers through a purchase without doubling the number of customer service reps, salespeople, accounting clerks, and other personnel. Other synergistic effects might include a broadening of the customer base to smooth out future revenues (e.g., if an ISP focusing on individual consumers acquires an ISP that caters primarily to business customers). Additional savings in rent, phone line expense, and other overhead items also increase the value for another ISP.

Another situation that illustrates the importance of investment value involves construction and contracting businesses active in special trades such as painting, electrical work, or plumbing. Experience has shown how difficult it is to sell such contractors to people who are not already active in the same industry. One factor that contributes to this difficulty lies in the often significant tangible asset values included in the sale. No matter how small a company's cash flow is, the owners are unlikely to sell for anything less than the value of the tangible assets plus an amount for goodwill.

The problem here is that the asset value alone may take the asking price to a seemingly exorbitant multiple of cash flow, thus making the deal unattractive to the typical financial buyer (as opposed to a strategic buyer with experience and current involvement in the industry). Therefore, it is often the case that only other contractors active in the industry can feasibly afford such an asking price. The reason that they can pay the higher price is that they can reduce overhead, diversify their customer base, and take advantage of other synergistic benefits that a financial (individual) buyer could not. Thus, because the investment value to a competitor or similar company is higher than to a financial buyer, the majority of special trade contractors are sold to other special trade contractors based on investment value.

In fact, it is the presence of high investment values that leads to the consolidation of industries, often through execution of multiple roll-ups by different parties. A roll-up effort calls for a lead company to actively pursue and purchase similar companies for purposes of combining all operations into one single, competitive company. The typical goal of a roll-up is to engineer an initial public offering (IPO), that is, to take the business public. It is often industries in which IV exceeds FMV that are subject to the roll-up process. In regard to business valuation, it is important to note that businesses in industries currently subject to consolidation will tend to sell for high multiples relative to recent pricing trends. Recently, dozens of industries have been subject to this type of consolidation, including the following:

Funeral homes (HBO's series *Six Feet Under* shows the darker side of roll-ups)

ISPs

Computer repair and service companies

Telecommunication and networking businesses

Electrical contractors

Waste management companies

Corporate training companies

Advertising agencies

Industrial distribution companies

Courier or delivery companies

In short, the value of a company to a particular buyer is a function of the buyer's individual preferences and characteristics. One buyer may already operate in the subject industry, whereas another may not. One buyer may choose to pay all cash, whereas another buyer will seek 100 percent financing. One buyer may choose to work the business full-time, whereas another buyer will be absentee. One buyer may be able to enjoy tax loss carryforwards to minimize future taxes, whereas another buyer may not carry such a shield. Each of these differences affects the future cash flows of a given business and therefore its value. Remember, valuation is chiefly a prophecy as to the future, i.e., it is a type of prediction regarding the future performance of a business. The primary indicators of value are the amount, timing, and risk of the future cash flows associated with the investment. Larger, quicker, less risky cash flows generate more value than smaller, slower, more risky cash flows.

Our final standard of value is known as fair value (FV). FV is a concept founded in equity and typically is associated with various state laws that are designed to protect the interests of dissenting or minority shareholders. In general terms, state statutes protect minority shareholders from being taken advantage of by majority shareholders who sell their companies. In other words, minority shareholders are entitled to fair value when they are involved in the sale of their shares in conjunction with a merger, takeover, or other sale of the company's stock or assets. Fair value is close to FMV, but it is much more fluid and subject to interpretation by the court officials overseeing the transaction. FV is in essence a statutory standard that varies from state to state and is applicable to dissenting or minority shareholders and their rights relating to takeovers, dissolutions, or similar events. Chapter Seven addresses various issues related to minority shareholdings such as minority interest discounts (lack of control discount) and marketability discounts.

In states that have adopted the Uniform Business Corporation Act (UBCA), the following definition for fair value is presented:

> Fair value, with respect to a dissenter's shares, means the value of the shares immediately before the effectuation of the corporate action to which the dissenter objects, excluding any appreciation or depreciation in anticipation of the corporate action unless exclusion would be inequitable.

The bottom line here is that if you find yourself involved in such a situation, it is critical to obtain qualified legal counsel to take account of the applicable legal precedents.

Premise of Value Concepts

Every business appraisal must set forth both the selected standard of value and premise of value. As just noted, most readers of this book (entrepreneurs seeking to buy or sell a business) will be interested in determining a company's FMV on a going-concern basis. In other words, most readers will be entrepreneurs who are contemplating or evaluating the possible purchase or sale of a business. Therefore, in most cases, the relevant standard of value is FMV and the relevant premise of value is "on a going-concern basis." For comparison, consider another combination: "liquidation value (LV) as a collection of assets."

The standard of value (LV) and the premise of value (collection of assets) both differ here from the norm just described. A standard of value is one of several well-defined value concepts that differ in terms of the perspective and method used to estimate its magnitude. A premise of value is the background against which the standard of value is applied. The major premise of value choices include the following:

Value as a going concern

Value as a collection or assemblage of assets

Value as a planned liquidation

Value as a forced liquidation

Value as a Going Concern

Value as a going concern is the primary premise of value, wherein the subject company is operating at or near capacity and has an active customer and supplier base served by a complete array of employees. Most business valuation assignments concern a company that has its doors open and is conducting business in an ordinary fashion. As defined by Shannon Pratt in his widely cited *Valuing a Business* (4th edition, published by McGraw-Hill), value as a going concern is "value in continued use, as a mass assemblage of income producing assets, and as a going concern enterprise"

Value as a Collection or Assemblage of Assets

This term refers to the assets of a company that were previously engaged on a going-concern basis but are now idle. For example, a restaurant owner may have suffered from a major illness and was forced to shut down for a while. Eventually, the owner decides that the best option is to sell the restaurant on the open market despite the fact that the business is not currently operating. Some goodwill still exists because the company recently enjoyed an active customer base and a collection of employees and suppliers. The primary distinction between this premise and the prior premise of value is that no income is being produced by the assets at present.

Value as a Planned Liquidation

This premise of value is almost self-explanatory. In this situation, the valuation environment is characterized by a complete lack of the going-concern element. The proper description here is "value in exchange," as opposed to "value in use" or "value in place." Rather than selling all assets together, as in the case of the first two premise of value concepts, in a liquidation the assets typically are sold separately or on a piecemeal basis. The "planned" element implies that the subject assets will be available for inspection by would-be purchasers with ample time to evaluate the quality and condition of the assets and ultimately allow the seller to receive maximum liquidation value.

Value as a Forced Liquidation

The only difference between this liquidation scenario and the prior one is that no planning is involved. The liquidation occurs quickly and without a great deal of marketing and exposure for the subject assets. As a result of the "forced" element, the valuation results are the lowest here.

Initial Steps in the Valuation Process

Before attempting to value any business of any type or size, the valuator should carefully and precisely clarify the framework within which the valuation analysis will take place. The purpose, standard of value, and premise of value should be clarified within the scope of the entity to be valued. Such clarifications will establish the foundation on which information is collected and applied to pertinent valuation techniques. The ARM Approach Questionnaire will lead you through these initial steps, helping to ensure a proper framework and credible valuation outcome.

The initial steps in the valuation process should include use of the Five-Page Tool. As you will see, this tool calls for a careful review of the company's income statement and the components of the company's adjusted cash flow (ACF). This same tool is incorporated into the ARM Approach Questionnaire for use in reviewing all aspects of the subject business.

Describe the Purpose and Define What Is to Be Valued

It is critical to determine whether one is attempting to value all or only a portion of a company's assets or stock. Describing the purpose of the valuation and defining exactly what is to be valued are the first steps in performing any valuation or appraisal.

There is a substantial difference between valuing a company for purposes of marketing it to the public for the highest price possible and valuing a company for estate or divorce purposes. There is also a vast difference between valuing all of a company's assets (ignoring liabilities if the business is being purchased or sold as an asset sale) and valuing a portion (minority interest) of a company's stock. The former is the most common scenario, but occasionally a buyer seeks to purchase only a portion of a business, such as a share of a medical practice, through the purchase of stock. The medical practice situation often is called a buy-in, facilitating a partnership effort of several doctors in an office (perhaps on the way to a complete buy-out of all shares by one of the participating doctors). The main point here is that the precise scope of the valuation analysis must be determined at the beginning of any valuation effort. In short, defining exactly what is to be valued is the first step in estimating the value of the subject entity.

Determine the Standard of Value

As discussed earlier in this chapter, several potential standards of value exist, ranging from the most common FMV to the state-specific, statute-oriented standard known as fair value. In short, a determination must be made regarding the relevant standard of value, whether it be FMV or some other standard such as LV.

Establish the Premise of Value

The next determination in this framework-building effort is to establish the relevant premise of value. In general, the premise of value is the environment within which the standard of value-based valuation result is sought. As noted earlier, "on a going-concern basis" is the most common premise of value, meaning that the valuation result is based on a business that is up and running and active in its pursuit of revenues and profits (as opposed to an assemblage of assets, in which the company exists but no revenues are being generated).

Although the theoretical underpinnings of determining the relevant standard or premise of value for a business appraisal may seem very different from the nuts and bolts of estimating the value of a business, there is something to be gained by understanding the general thought processes behind the various measures involved.

Collect and Analyze Relevant Company and Industry Information

After these important conceptual valuation tasks are completed, the valuator can begin to collect and analyze the relevant company and industry information needed to execute the valuation techniques. This is a good time to briefly discuss the key company documents and other information sources that are necessary to ensure that a credible and accurate valuation result will result from the valuation process. At a minimum, the following documents and data sources are needed to properly evaluate a company's value:

Financial statements (balance sheet, income statement, others if available)

Federal and state tax returns (including all related forms)

Company policies, procedures, and organizational chart

Complete list of all tangible assets (from inventory to buildings)

Valuation questionnaire (e.g., the ARM Approach Questionnaire, adjusted to fit subject company and industry)

Reviewing this information is a useful starting point for the valuation analysis. The financial statements should be obtained for at least the past three years and preferably the last five years. In most cases, the current operating results are the most important, so if the analysis is being completed during the middle of a fiscal or calendar year, a current interim statement must be obtained and reviewed. Regarding what might be considered current, the SBA requires a set of financial statements (balance sheet and income statement at a minimum) that are no more than ninety days old.

Most privately held businesses' financial statements are "compiled," which means that the accountant has not made any meaningful effort to evaluate the accuracy of the account balances or to ensure that they are completed in accordance with generally accepted accounting principles (GAAP). "Reviewed" statements lie between "compiled" and "audited" statements, wherein certain key account balances are checked for accuracy and GAAP compliance. Importantly, reviewed (and audited, but not compiled) statements typically include a well-developed set of footnotes that detail the company's chosen accounting policies (often important for calculating ACF or for comparing with other companies).

Federal and state tax returns also are an important component of the valuation analysis in that certain information is contained on the tax returns that is not contained in the financial statements. For example, a complete list of all assets acquired by the company with cost and book value information is found on federal tax returns. Federal returns also include a section that explains the difference between the "net income" figure found on the tax returns and the company's financials. Remember that accounting for tax purposes is different than accounting for book purposes.

Another important role played by the tax returns is one of insurance. In most cases, if a company declares revenues and pays taxes on the profit, you can rest assured that the sales were actually generated, that is, they are verified in part by their presence on the tax return. It is rare for a company to create phantom income and then pay tax on it. In fact, the opposite typically is the driving force behind tax return preparation: Most business owners will do everything in their power to minimize their tax liability. It is common for owners to accelerate recognized expenses and postpone recognized revenues.

On the other hand, there are several documented cases in which companies that were being sold via SBA financing had submitted doctored or false tax returns along with false financial statements. The SBA has solved this problem by requiring all relevant tax returns to be checked against originals filed with the IRS. There is an IRS form that allows anyone to obtain original tax returns with the permission of the relevant party (IRS Form 4506), and any lender will exercise this option when evaluating a proposed loan.

During the valuation process, additional questions arise that may necessitate additional documents or direct feedback from the business owner or the owner's advisers. Depending on the nature of the valuation assignment, it may be prudent to obtain various source documents within the company, such as sales tax reports, payroll records, accounts receivable and accounts payable ledgers, and work in progress tables (for manufacturing companies). In addition, a wide variety of external information sources should be reviewed, including the following:

Current industry analysis for subject company (Internet search)

Robert Morris Associates financial data (or other sources) for subject standard industrial classification (SIC) code

Valuation-related insights for subject industry

Market comparable data from one or more sources

These information sources should be considered only a starting point for the valuation analysis. Not only is business valuation one part art and one part science, but it is also a fluid, sometimes wandering process that requires a case-by-case judgment on the part of the valuator as to what is or is not important. It is practically impossible to know before executing the valuation everything that is relevant in estimating the FMV of a particular going concern. Nonetheless, these materials will provide the information needed to complete a substantial portion of the analysis. Chapter Five contains several useful references available to the public for purposes of conducting company and industry research.

In conclusion, the initial steps in the valuation process are as follows:

1. Describe the purpose of the valuation and define what is to be valued.
2. Determine the standard of value.
3. Establish the premise of value.
4. Collect and analyze relevant company and industry information.

The Basics of Classical Valuation Methods

Having addressed the background concepts of business valuation procedures, we can begin a formal discussion of the valuation approaches and techniques that make up classical valuation methods. For the sake of perspective, it is proper to consider the information just presented (e.g., standard of value, premise of value, defining interest to be valued, differences between valuations and appraisals) on an equal footing with the following discussion of classical valuation methods to the extent that both areas make up GAVP.

Remember that our ultimate goal is to understand and apply the ARM approach (using multiples of ACF, rules of thumb, and market comp data) to business valuation. However, we must not forget that the foundation of the ARM approach is the classical valuation methods incorporated into the three major valuation approaches (income, cost or asset, and market) and the other concepts, issues, and definitions presented earlier, which together represent GAVP.

Each valuation approach has an entire family of related techniques or methods that differ in both subtle and substantial ways. For example, the income approach has perhaps the most diverse collection of specific techniques that vary primarily in terms of how income is defined and measured. In this sense, there are at least as many income-based methods as there are measures of income (e.g., pretax income, after-tax income, ACF, EBIT, EBITDA, or net free cash).

In addition, the relevant measures of cash flow are applied differently depending on the particular technique. In general, the cash flow or earnings of a company can be multiplied, capitalized, or discounted.

The ARM approach relies primarily on the use of multiples, which calls for applying the derived multiple against the chosen measure of cash flow (ACF). The derived multiple reflects the unique circumstances facing the subject company and industry. A number of options exist for estimating the appropriate multiple (e.g., the Snowden method presented at the end of Chapter Four). It is interesting to note that the average business in the VR Business Brokers network has consistently sold for about 2.3 times ACF (i.e., a multiple of 2.3 is the average, taking into account all businesses of all types under all conditions over time; the VR database features primarily smaller businesses with sales of less than $3 million and ACF less than $500,000). It is critical to understand that as the size of the ACF rises, so does the average multiple; for example, when the ACF is $250,000 to $500,000, such businesses sell for two to four times ACF (as opposed to one to three times ACF for the smaller companies).

Other useful valuation techniques exist that depend not on multiples but on capitalizing or discounting the relevant cash flows. The capitalization process involves deriving the appropriate capitalization rate, which is applied to some measure of historical cash flow (as opposed to future cash flows). The discounting process involves deriving the appropriate discount rate, whereby the estimated future net cash inflows are converted to present value dollars.

Both capitalizing and discounting are processes for converting income or cash flow streams into business value. As described in the "SBA Business Valuation" section of the CD-ROM, cap rates are derived from discount rates (i.e., cap rates can be calculated only after discount rates are estimated). Cap rates are more closely related to multiples than to discount rates because both cap rates and multiples are applied to either historical or normalized levels of cash flow (as opposed to exclusively future-based cash flows, as in the case of discounting).

It is important to realize that cap rates can be considered the inverse of multiples. For example, a multiple of 3 is similar to a cap rate of 33 percent, and a multiple of 5 is similar to a cap rate of 20 percent. For the sake of consistency and the use of market comp databases (presented in terms of multiples), we shall use multiples when implementing the ARM approach.

The market approach, on the other hand, has only two major techniques or methods that differ in terms of which collection of similar companies is used (primarily private transactions or publicly traded companies). The comparable sales method relies on the historical sale of similar privately held companies, whereas the guideline public company method relies on the current share prices of similar company stocks.

Rules of thumb are the most plentiful and diverse of all, reflecting the incredible array of company types and industries. Most industries are associated with one or more rules of thumb that industry participants use to gauge company value. Common value indicators include cash flow, assets, and revenues in addition to industry-specific measures such as the number of commercial versus residential customers (e.g., for ISPs) or the number of active meters (e.g., for water utilities).

Income Approach Basics

This approach is based on a review and analysis of a company's income-generating capability. As just noted, the diversity of techniques within this broad approach is primarily a result of the various measures of income that can be used. These measures range from broad-based indicators such as gross revenues used in a gross revenue multiplier (e.g., convenience stores often are valued at 15 to 25 percent of annual gross revenues, plus inventory) to detailed and complex figures such as net free cash flow, which is the integral component of discounted cash flow (DCF) analysis and accounts for all expenses, taxes, working capital needs, and capital expenditures.

Measures of Income

Specific measures of income include the following:

Gross revenues (gross sales; can be measured on a cash or accrual basis)

Gross profit (net sales less cost of goods sold)

EBITDA

EBIT (or operating income)

ACF (as used by business brokers, also known as net or seller's discretionary cash flow)

Normalized income (similar to ACF, but various versions exclude an owner–operator's salary and include a typical manager's salary or may address annual expenditures on capital equipment or an average of the past several years or reflect probable future income)

Net free cash flow (an all-inclusive measure that accounts for income tax, working capital infusions, capital expenditures, and other mandatory payments such as preferred stock dividends or sinking fund payments)

The value of most going-concern entities is a function primarily of income or cash flow. The ability of a company to generate positive cash flows (however defined) accruing to the owner into the future is the most influential determinant of value. In lay terms, the value of a business generally is a function of its ability to create or generate income for the owner. The importance of "income" is highlighted in the often-cited IRS Revenue Ruling 59-60, which calls for the evaluation of eight specific factors when estimating business value (including two income-oriented considerations related to "earnings" and "dividend-paying capacity)."

Depending on the specific method being used, the given measure of income or cash flow may be monthly, quarterly, or annual, historical or future-oriented, single-period or an average of several periods. The most commonly applied multiple is applied to the previous year's cash flow or an average of prior years, but some situations call for different time periods (e.g., ISPs may be valued as a multiple of the anticipated gross revenues over the next year based on the current quarter's activity or as a multiple of the past four quarters or trailing revenues).

The various methods or techniques that make up the income approach should always be given serious consideration when estimating the value of any operating entity. For companies that are shut down or operating at less than capacity, the income approach is less relevant. In these situations, an asset approach typically is more appropriate.

To conclude our introductory comments on the income approach, consider the following valuation insights:

> Valuation is a prophecy as to the future.
>
> The value of any asset is the sum of all discounted future, net cash inflows to the owner.
>
> The greater and more stable or predictable the future cash flows, the more they are worth.

The essence of the income approach thus is found in the evaluation of a company's historical and probable future ability to generate income or cash flow for the owners in light of the actual or perceived riskiness of the company's future operations. Stated succinctly, the income approach attempts to estimate the value of a going concern in terms of the commonly understood risk-versus-reward paradigm (i.e., less risk means greater value and vice versa). Chapter Four contains additional details and insights into the important role of cash flow or income in the valuation process. In addition, the "SBA Business Valuation" section on the CD-ROM contains an introduction to the derivation and application of discount rates and capitalization rates, both of which are key components of various income approach valuation techniques.

Cost or Asset Approach Basics*

This approach focuses on a company's assets and liabilities, so it is sometimes called a balance sheet approach (as opposed to the income approach, which

---

The CD-ROM contains a thorough review and analysis of the cost or asset approach to business valuation. This coverage is an integral component of classical business valuation and is directly related to the ARM approach. It is suggested that the reader review this portion of the CD-ROM in conjunction with material found in Chapters Three and Four.

would be called an income statement approach). This approach is generally based on the process of adjusting a company's asset and liability book values to their corresponding FMVs. The key to successfully applying the cost approach lies in being able to determine the existence of and FMV of all assets and liabilities, including intangible assets and those that are not listed on a typical balance sheet.

Assets such as accounts receivable and inventory, for example, are almost always present on a balance sheet (perhaps with the exception of service companies, which typically carry no inventory) and can be analyzed without any great challenge. However, both assets must be restated at their respective current fair market value (as opposed to their current book value). Depending upon the specific technique being utilized, there is a school of thought that holds that only "nonoperating" assets should be adjusted to FMV (whereas operating assets are to be assessed at their respective, and typically lower, BVs.)

Receivables for most companies have an FMV less than their BV, depending on how frequently they are "written down" by the company's accountant. GAAP requires that receivables be carried at their net realizable value, which means that the total amount of receivables must be adjusted to reflect the probability of bad debts or uncollectible revenues. Because most financial statements for smaller, privately held companies are compiled (not reviewed or audited to ensure compliance with GAAP), the need to adjust the receivables to their realizable value (synonymous in this case with FMV) is common. It is up to the valuator to determine what the precise adjustment will be, but deductions of 5 to 15 percent are not uncommon.

Similarly, inventory must be carried at the lower of cost or market, which means that theoretically the carrying value of inventory should reflect current market values (if they are lower than original cost). In addition to reflecting current market values, accounting for obsolete and damaged inventory may also reduce the current book value to a lower figure. Other assets must also be similarly adjusted to reflect current FMV (e.g., marketable securities; furniture, fixtures, and equipment; and real estate). As illustrated in the "Asset or Cost Approach to Business Valuation" section of the CD-ROM, the liability side of the balance sheet must also be adjusted to reflect FMV. The amount of such adjustments for liabilities typically is less than the adjustments for assets.

Hidden Assets and Liabilities

A major difficulty in this approach (regardless of which specific technique is used) is found in the search for and recognition of assets and liabilities that are not listed on the balance sheet and the act of excluding assets and liabilities that are of a personal nature or that will be excluded from the sale (in the event that the valuation assignment is related to buying or selling the company). Examples of hidden assets include fixed assets that have been fully depreciated or were fully expensed at the time of acquisition (e.g., Section 179 deductions) or any relevant intangible asset such as a customer list, a trade name, or goodwill.

An example of an asset on the balance sheet that should be excluded is a personal automobile or artwork purchased by the business that will be retained by the owner after the closing. On the liability side, the existence of unknown or contingent liabilities must be investigated (often called off-balance-sheet liabilities). For example, a retail company that sells computer systems may have a substantial unrecorded liability associated with returns and allowances or possibly warranty repairs. Companies that are in the middle of a lawsuit that might lead to a monetary judgment owed to a former employee or customer are subject to a contingent liability. Under the cost approach to valuing such a company, the probability and amount of such a liability should be evaluated and incorporated into the valuation. Other liabilities, such as loans from the company's owners, may be excluded from the adjusted balance sheet when applying one of the techniques associated with the cost approach.

This approach is particularly useful or relevant for companies that are shut down or are not earning profits or generating positive cash flow from operations. If a business is not functioning properly or operating at only a portion of capacity, its value typically is diminished to a point where the market value of the tangible assets is the primary source of value. Overall, this approach gives the valuator a low-end result for the typical business that is actively generating revenues and profits.

Miscellaneous Considerations

Recall that the value of a company generally differs when one is evaluating corporate stock as opposed to corporate assets. The majority of privately held business sales are "asset" transactions rather than "stock" transactions. The typical asset sale is made under specific conditions, as follows:

The buyer is purchasing all assets, tangible and intangible, unless specifically excluded.

The seller will keep the cash, accounts receivable, and other liquid financial assets, such as deposits and prepaid expense balances, as of the closing date or any other mutually agreed date.

The seller will deliver the business free and clear of all debts as of closing unless specifically agreed otherwise.

These asset sale conditions emphasize the importance of clarifying what is being valued (e.g., stock or assets, all or some). Under the ARM approach, it is assumed that we are valuing the company under the terms of an asset sale. If the conditions differ from those listed earlier (e.g., the sale includes the receivables), then an adjustment must be made. Furthermore, if a stock sale is contemplated, several adjustments should be made in the valuation approach.

When one considers the steps involved in the adjusted book value method, it is obvious that the way in which the cash, receivables, and debts of the company are handled in a sale affects the valuation results. Under the typical asset sale conditions, the estimated FMV of the company using the ARM approach must be interpreted in conjunction with the disposition of the cash, receivables, and debts to capture the big picture. If the cash and receivables are greater than the debts to be paid off at closing, this positive difference represents additional value to be received by the seller as a result of the sale.

Market Approach Basics

The third major approach can provide the most reassuring and grounded estimates of FMV if the related techniques are applied properly and consistently. When the typical business owner reviews a valuation report or appraisal performed by a so-called expert, the owner often takes great comfort in reviewing the section on market comps. These comps are supposed to reflect what similar businesses have sold for in the recent past or what they might sell for today.

The general theory behind the market approach is that companies deemed to be similar in terms of revenues, cash flow, and assets and operating in the same industry should react the same way to market forces and enjoy a definite if not strong correlation in business value. If the stock market punishes a certain stock from a certain industry, the message is ultimately that the risk associated with this investment has increased. For example, if the value of publicly traded Internet-based retailers plummets because of the increased chance that an Internet sales tax is forthcoming, a similar impact should be expected on the value of a privately held Internet-based retailer.

In general, this approach should be used in all valuation assignments. At a minimum, the results here will serve as a valuable cross-check against other valuation results. The use of this approach may expose the valuator to insights that would not be apparent through other approaches and techniques. Despite the strong appeal of these valuation data, tremendous caution must be exercised in locating and evaluating the information related to the sale of similar companies. For example, very small or unique privately held companies may not allow meaningful comparison to other companies.

Wanted: Similar Companies

Generally speaking, the key to proper application of market comp data is consistency. In other words, the valuator must be able to use truly comparable statistics for this approach to provide useful results. The subject company must be similar not only in terms of obvious characteristics such as industry, niches served within general industries, geographic territory served, and company size (in revenues, assets, and employees) but also in terms of deal structure (e.g., stock versus asset sale, all-cash versus seller financing, payback period and interest rate, amount and strength of collateral and guarantees). For example, a smaller company always sells for a lower multiple than a larger company (all other things equal), reflecting what is known as the size factor or size premium. The logic here is that smaller, private companies are riskier than larger, public companies.

Another example is the difference in price or value of a company that is sold as a stock sale as opposed to an asset sale. Almost invariably, the price of a stock sale is less than the price of an asset sale, primarily because of the lower tax burden associated with the sale of stock versus assets (all capital gains instead of a combination of capital gains and ordinary income, amounting to as much as a 15 percent difference) and the inheritance of all liabilities, known and unknown. Everyone is familiar with the notion of a cash discount, which applies equally to the sale of almost any asset or product, including whole companies. On average, a company sold for all cash sells for 10 to 30 percent less than a company sold (purchased) on terms.

Although there will be no truly identical companies to evaluate, it is important to find and use the most similar companies for these techniques. At a minimum, considering the following factors will help you ensure optimal comparisons:

Type and category of business (similar SIC codes are important)

Size of business (e.g., in terms of revenues, assets, profits, cash flow, and employees)

Other features (e.g., geographic markets served, capital structure of companies, depth of management, growth rates, competitive forces, and accounting methods)

This introductory discussion should make it clear that the valuator must be careful in applying any technique associated with the market approach. Despite these caveats, the use of the market approach is an essential element of a well-rounded, practical, and credible estimate of company value. Because this approach is grounded in actual, historical sales, its importance cannot be overemphasized. Even in the situation where the valuator must reply on a large sample of only generally similar businesses, e.g., all account-based service companies, the resulting data can be quite enlightening.

When valuing a company for purposes of estate tax settlement or divorce proceedings, great care must be taken to apply the techniques in a manner that is expected by the courts. If there is any way to determine which judge will be overseeing a case, it is worthwhile to investigate the results and findings of this judge in recent, similar situations. Some judges dismiss the use of market comps if there is not a thorough, clearly presented analysis supporting the choice of companies. Other judges allow a wide range of company types to satisfy the market comp requirements, particularly if there are no truly comparable companies to analyze. Valuation analysis must always be adapted to the needs or expectations of the audience.

Different Techniques

Depending on the specifics of the company being valued, two major techniques from the market approach are available:

Market comparable technique

Guideline publicly traded company technique

To determine which technique is preferable, a case-by-case analysis is warranted; it is common to use both techniques. A third technique is also applicable when there is a history of buying and selling shares in the company; that is, when past transactions in the company's shares have already taken place, this information can be useful in estimating the company's current stock value. A fourth method is based on evaluating recent public company takeovers in industries similar to the subject company (because of its difficulty and questionable accuracy, this method is not discussed here).

The most commonly used method is a "basket" technique, which calls for the collection and analysis of pertinent financial and operational information for a handful of similar companies (typically all privately held companies). Relevant data on each sale are collected and averaged, with the goal of applying this average information to the subject company. For example, it may be determined that the average company in the basket sold for 45 percent of gross revenues or three times the adjusted cash flow. These figures must then be properly applied to the subject company. The key question becomes, "Is the subject company average, above average, or below average?" Furthermore, if the company is found to be above or below average, a sufficient analysis must be made in support of this conclusion. One must determine whether the subject company is above or below average and by how much. This is not a straightforward or necessarily objective determination.

Whatever the framework used to make such a determination, it is important to apply it consistently across the board in attempting to value businesses. When establishing the position of the subject company relative to the average, all relevant characteristics should be considered (or as many as are feasible, depending on your time and resources).

Factors ranging from the quality of the lease to the importance of the owner in sustaining future profits should be considered when establishing the relative value of a given company to the norm. Experienced acquisition specialists and valuation professionals develop their own list of key factors to evaluate a subject company for purposes of determining both a proper multiple of cash flow and the company's standing relative to the average when assessing market comps. In terms of the ARM Approach, the first page of the Five-Page Tool is used specifically to capture these "pros and cons" and "pluses and minuses."

As discussed fully in Chapter Six, the many terms and conditions included in a purchase contract affect the final deal price that eventually ends up in a database representing market value. Some terms have an obvious and material impact on price, such as stock sale versus asset sale or all-cash versus seller financing. Such terms can change a deal price by 25 percent or more. It is important to gather as large a sample size as possible to even out these diverging terms and conditions. A large collection of market comps will help ensure that the average is truly an average in terms of both price and all other terms and conditions.

A second technique in the market approach is also worthy of consideration. The publicly traded or guideline company method calls for the same process of locating similar companies, but in this case the companies are all publicly traded on a securities exchange with an active market for trading the company's stock. In general, this technique is more applicable to middle-market companies (which are less reliant on any one owner–operator and generally have more reliable financial statements) than to smaller companies.

In this technique, the relevant publicly traded companies are located and relevant statistics are calculated and analyzed, with the end result a function of adjusting the market data toward the reality of the subject company. Both objective and subjective adjustments are needed (e.g., adjusting the company's income statements to reflect similar accounting procedures is an objective adjustment, and adjusting the publicly traded multiples downward to reflect a size premium is a subjective adjustment). This technique is more complicated than the comparable sales method, but for certain companies it is preferred for several reasons.

To prevent confusion in regard to the so-called size effect, it is necessary to clearly distinguish the two distinct uses of this term in business valuation. As just discussed, use of the guideline public company method as part of the market approach to business valuation may entail a downward adjustment to the average multiples of the larger, publicly traded comps to allow comparison with the typically smaller, privately owned subject company. This type of size effect is similar to the second usage of the term, but distinct in its application. The second size effect refers to the empirical fact that as the subject company's ACF rises, the corresponding multiples also rise. As noted elsewhere, common break points are at $250,000 and $500,000 (as below):

ACF Amount	Typical Multiples
ACF under $250,000	1 to 3 times ACF
ACF between $250,000 and $499,999	2 to 4 times ACF
ACF between $500,000 and $999,999	3 to 5 times ACF
ACF between $1 and $2 million	4 to 7 times ACF

Regardless of which method is used for the market-based component of the ARM approach, the importance of multiples is clear. Although individual transaction prices may vary from the normal pattern for a given type of company, a sufficiently large enough number of transactions should be a fair indicator of overall fair market value. Every valuation effort should include the review of market data because such sales tend to reflect the informed judgment of parties active in the buying and selling of companies in a particular market.

What About Rules of Thumb?

Rules of thumb are at the same time the most intriguing, abused, contradictory, critical, irrelevant, silly, practical, general, specific, diverse, useful, questionable, and reliable valuation tools available to entrepreneurs and practitioners alike. Note that rules of thumb are not a direct component of classical valuation methods (i.e., there is not a fourth approach called rules of thumb). The inclusion of rules of thumb in the ARM approach is one of the major differences between classical methods and the ARM approach. For reasons explained elsewhere, rules of thumb often are essential for obtaining a credible valuation result.

According to the American Society of Appraisers, a rule of thumb is "a mathematical relationship between or among a number of variables based on experience, observation, hearsay, or a combination of these, usually applicable to a specific industry."

There are two primary keys to properly using rules of thumb in business valuation:

Determine the availability and evaluate the relevance and frequency of use of rules of thumb for the subject company and industry.

Learn and understand the intricacies of each rule of thumb and apply them properly, cautiously, and consistently.

In general, the goal here is to determine which, if any, rules of thumb apply to a particular size and type of business and then apply them as they are used by professionals or other parties active in the relevant industry. Regardless of how appealing a particular rule may appear, if it is not actively used by valuation professionals or industry participants, it should be avoided. Chapter Five and the CD-ROM describe the most commonly used rules of thumb in practice today. A comprehensive survey of participating VR Business Brokers agents from across the country was used to support the information presented in the book and on the CD-ROM.

VR Business Brokers is the leading business brokerage firm in the nation, having sold thousands of businesses of all types and sizes since 1979. In addition to providing examples of common rules of thumb through the survey, VR also has given the authors access to some of the market comp data used in Chapter Five and elsewhere. Detailed company information can be found on their corporate Web site at *www.vrbusinessbrokers.com*.

Rules of thumb run the entire spectrum from essential to irrelevant. They may be general, such as a multiple of cash flow (e.g., two to three times ACF), or specific (e.g., $300 to $400 per dial-up account in a commercially oriented ISP). Chapter Five and the CD-ROM include segments covering rules of thumb and provide much more insight and numerous examples of the use of this often important valuation tool.

Which Approach Is Best?

There is no single best approach or technique that always stands out above the crowd. However, under specific circumstances there may be a better approach or technique or even a required approach or technique. As noted throughout Chapters One and Two, the purpose of the valuation helps determine the relevant standard of value and the relevant premise of value, which in turn helps determine the most relevant and important valuation approach and techniques:

> Purpose of business valuation → Standard or premise of value →
> Valuation approach → Specific valuation techniques

For example, most business owners are interested in determining the transaction value of their company for purposes of selling to the highest bidder. This task, along with attempting to value a company for purchase (naturally, they both occur at the same time if a company is being sold), is the most common purpose of valuing a business. Accordingly, the most commonly used standard of value is FMV, and the most common premise of value is on a going-concern basis. The appropriate valuation approach and the techniques for establishing FMV ultimately depend on the type and size of the company involved. In general, it is wise to use at least one technique from each approach (commonly more than one technique per approach is advisable). The attractiveness of the ARM approach to business valuation derives partly from its ability to incorporate methods from each approach in a practical, user-friendly manner.

Weightings Within a Basket

Many valuation professionals believe that a basket of approaches and techniques best serves the interests of creating a credible, accurate estimate of FMV. To ensure optimal use of this basket of techniques, it is necessary to weight each technique according to its relative importance or accuracy, defined as the likelihood of reflecting the current FMV of the particularly size and type of company. For example, you may settle on the use of five different techniques, weighted at 35, 20, 20, 15, and 10 percent, respectively. The weightings should be applied in a format similar to the following hypothetical valuation results:

Technique 1	$500,000	(35%)	$175,000
Technique 2	$720,000	(20%)	$144,000
Technique 3	$660,000	(20%)	$132,000
Technique 4	$435,000	(15%)	$ 65,250
Technique 5	$600,000	(10%)	$ 60,000
Overall weighted value			$576,250

Note that there is not absolute agreement that weighting valuation results according to the valuator's assessment of relevance and reliability is the proper way to finalize valuation estimates. For example, the IRS has long held that there is no reasonable justification for such weightings. Opponents of weighting argue that such a process only adds more subjectivity to an already nebulous environment. Others believe that to the extent that one or more methods are more reliable or relevant than others, mathematical weighting is the logical solution; the majority of practitioners agree. For example, Shannon Pratt typically uses weightings but places a disclaimer in the report stating that there is no empirical basis for exact weightings.

CHAPTER 3

Overview of the ARM Approach

Now that we have concluded our introduction to basic business valuation principles and procedures (including the three major classical valuation methods), we can turn our focus to the primary target of our efforts: the ARM approach to business valuation. Although the foundation of the ARM approach is the classical valuation methods and GAVP, there are substantial differences in orientation and content. The ARM approach is intended to give the novice valuator the tools needed to value any type or size of business in a practical and credible fashion.

The focal point of this approach is the ARM Approach Questionnaire and the Five-Page Tool. This step-by-step process will guide the entrepreneur or novice valuator through the necessary considerations and determinations that ultimately generate a value estimate. The questionnaire is practical, thorough, and user-friendly, and it can be streamlined if desired. Once you attain a certain degree of familiarity with the approach, you can choose which sections and which specific questions are most important in a given situation.

Depending on the circumstances, you may choose to skip the questionnaire altogether. If a quick-and-dirty estimate is all you need, use of a fairly simple technique (e.g., the Snowden Technique, as described at the end of Chapter Four) may prove sufficient. This efficient technique calls for evaluation of several major valuation factors, with the results recorded on a scale (higher numbers represent more favorable valuation outcomes) and then averaged into a single number. This final, averaged number is the multiple to be applied to the subject company's adjusted cash flow (ACF) figure.

A more robust shortcut might include the use of a relevant rule of thumb along with the Snowden result, whereby the average of these two valuation results provides a quick estimate of value. The more important the valuation, however, the less appealing such shortcuts are. As noted elsewhere, the more thorough and detailed the valuation analysis becomes, the more credible the results will be.

In most valuation circumstances, using the full questionnaire (or at least a customized derivation thereof) is worth the effort. It directs buyers to key due diligence issues (in addition to key valuation factors) and sellers to insights that will help defend the asking price (in addition to steps to take in the future that may improve the company's value).

Essence of the ARM Approach

Consider the following brief overview as an introduction to the details presented in Chapter Four. The ARM approach to business valuation is based on the premise that any company can be valued using a combination of the following three valuation components:

Adjusted cash flow (ACF)

Rules of thumb

Market comparables

The ARM approach holds that the value of any business can be estimated by weighting the results from three distinct valuation methods. First, calculate the company's ACF and then derive and apply the proper multiple against the ACF (e.g., three times ACF) to obtain the first estimate of value. Second, determine whether a particular rule of thumb (or two) is commonly used to value the subject company and, if so, use the formula as necessary (e.g., one times ACF plus tangible assets). Third, compile as many recent market comparable sales results as possible and calculate the average multiple of ACF or multiple of gross revenues (or other measures) for comparison with the subject company. If the subject company is better than the average, a higher-than-average multiple should be applied against the company's ACF or gross revenues (and vice versa).

Once these three related yet separate results have been estimated, it is now up to the valuator to determine which, if any, of the three valuation results is more reliable or credible for the subject company and weight these results accordingly (e.g., 50 percent, 30 percent, and 20 percent, respectively). In addition, it may be wise to check your results using the payback method. This method allows you to back into the purchase price (value) based on the amount of cash flow available to service a typical debt load.

Finally, it is up to the discretion of the valuator to manipulate all these results into a final estimate of fair market value. If you can properly perform these three practical valuation techniques, the resulting value estimate will be realistic, credible, and helpful in meeting your valuation objective (whatever it may be).

Valuation Process of the ARM Approach

The actual valuation process of the ARM approach begins with the Five-Page Tool, an essential supplement to the questionnaire. This tool is as simple as it is productive, calling for the use of five blank sheets of paper (or more if necessary). At the beginning of your valuation analysis, take out five blank sheets and title them as follows:

Key Valuation Factors (Plus and Minus)

Adjusted Cash Flow

Balance Sheet

Major Assumptions

Questions

The Five-Page Tool will focus the valuator on the more critical aspects of valuing the subject company. Key valuation factors can include any fact, event, insight, idea, trend, or issue (favorable or not) that will affect the valuation outcome. For example, if you notice that the company's sales have risen steadily for five years, make a note to this end in the "Plus" column. If you realize that family members are active in the business, jot it down. If you are unsure of the role played by family members, write a question on the fifth sheet and ask for more details.

In most cases, the best place to begin your analysis is with the company's income statement and the company's ACF. Many of the important questions and answers that influence the final valuation result stem from the analysis of the income statement. On the "ACF" page, analyze the income statement by listing the ACF components for the most current complete year and the most recent interim statement available. Leave enough space to the right of the current year analysis to make similar calculations for the prior year and perhaps the year before this.

As you work your way down the income statement and build the cash flow estimate (Chapter Four describes the key components of cash flow in detail, with additional insights found on the CD-ROM in the "Accounting Primer"), you will undoubtedly have many questions. List these questions on the "Questions" page as they arise. The ACF page is a good place to list the revenue figures over the past three to five years, possibly including gross profit figures and percentages and pretax income figures and percentages (percentage of sales). If you spot any trends at this time, list them on the "Key Valuation Factors" page under "Plus" or "Minus." If you have a computerized spreadsheet program, you can analyze the income statement and the balance sheet on your computer as well. For that matter, you could create five different computer files to represent the pages of the Five-Page Tool.

Do the same thing for the balance sheet by listing the key assets and key liabilities and writing down questions regarding their amount and nature onto the fifth page as they arise. In addition to breaking out the assets and liabilities into key groupings (e.g., current versus noncurrent assets), prepare the worksheet in a manner that facilitates comparisons over time in preparation for a more thorough financial statement analysis later in the valuation process (trend and common size analysis, defined in the questionnaire). Any trend or red flag should be transferred to the "Key Valuation Factors" page as a plus or minus depending on its nature. Liabilities and equity accounts should also be analyzed for purposes of understanding the full nature of the business, even if the valuation is based on an asset sale in which all liabilities are excluded (paid in full by the seller at closing). Operationally speaking, it is necessary to evaluate working capital needs, so liabilities must be evaluated accordingly.

Key assumptions should be listed on the "Major Assumptions" page (e.g., the furniture, fixtures, and equipment [FF&E] are valued at halfway between original cost and current book value; or a replacement salary for a family member working the business without compensation was estimated to be $35,000 per year). Given the common usage of the "halfway rule" for estimating FMV of a company's FF&E (fixed assets), carefully monitoring book value and original cost upon first review of the balance sheet is recommended.

It is preferable to prepare these five pages and complete as much groundwork as possible before you begin working through the questionnaire. The actual questionnaire will lead you back to the various pages of the Five-Page Tool, including in particular the "Key Valuation Factors" page, listing pluses and minuses. This page eventually will prove to be pivotal in determining the ultimate valuation result because the balance of pluses and minuses will dramatically influence the chosen multiple to apply against cash flow, the relevant range for a given rule of thumb, and the relationship between the average market comp results and the subject company. It is essential to write down every thought that arises as it relates to the attractiveness of the subject company. It is important to immediately write down such thoughts while they are fresh in your mind. Whether it is seemingly trivial (e.g., the customer service area needs painting) or obviously critical (e.g., the business obtains more than 50 percent of its revenues from one customer), write it down as soon as possible.

If at First You Don't Succeed

Most entrepreneurs have only a limited understanding of business valuation. However, their business experience typically provides them with exceptional insights and intuition about the key determinants of value for their particular business. This book provides the bridge between the entrepreneur's natural business acumen and the details of the valuation process. Such a bridge takes time and effort to build properly, so do not be alarmed if you find yourself returning to key sections of the book during your valuation analysis.

As you will shortly see, the questionnaire is filled with references to Web sites that should prove beneficial in evaluating a given component of the questionnaire. You should freely seek out these Web sites and their content, and you should not hesitate to return to the corresponding portion of this book to strengthen your general knowledge of the valuation process. For example, it is to be expected that you will need to return to the section describing the nature of ACF and presenting insights into how it is best calculated. Furthermore, you should visit some of the many valuation-related Web sites listed at the end of Chapter One. Such visits are an important part of your educational experience as you seek to improve your business valuation skills. Given the importance of valuation for the entrepreneur, such effort is a wise investment that will eventually pay handsome dividends.

The ARM Approach Questionnaire

Before proceeding into the finer points of the valuation procedures associated with the ARM approach (Chapter Four), it seems prudent to present the ARM Approach Questionnaire now for a preliminary review. As you read the questionnaire, you will become aware of many of the considerations that are discussed in Chapter Four. For now, observe the general flow of the questionnaire to appreciate the big picture and visualize the valuation process. Return to the questionnaire after you have read Chapter Four to evaluate your progress.

The five sections of the questionnaire are presented in the order of a typical business valuation:

Section One: Begin with the five-page tool (general questions about the valuation assignment, such as what is being valued, standard of value, premise of value, and minority interests).

Section Two: Fill in the blanks for the subject company (major questions about the owner, company, and industry, such as history, performance trends, organizational format, owner's duties and compensation, role of family members, reliability of books and records, working capital needs, recent changes, unique characteristics of business, and strengths and weaknesses).

Section Three: Provide a brief overview of important features and characteristics (detailed questions covering all company operations and industry background, such as product or service offered, customer base, product differentiation, advertising, competition, suppliers, key employees, lease data, fixed assets, fixed and variable costs, breakeven analysis, contracts, economic conditions, capacity constraints, and environmental concerns).

Section Four: Answer questions that relate directly to the ARM approach (e.g., actual valuation analysis using ARM components, such as calculation of ACF, list of pluses and minuses, financial statement analysis, managerial evaluations, industry research, assessment of relevant multiple, derived multiple to apply to ACF; list revenues, assets, and ACF over last five years; determine applicability of rules of thumb and use pluses and minuses accordingly, conduct payback method analysis, determine proper SIC code for market comp analysis, locate market comp data from proper source, and assess subject company relative to average comp data).

Section Five: Weight your findings and prepare the final value estimate (e.g., list results from three major ARM components and take arithmetic average, check results, assign weightings based on reliability and credibility, compare straight average with weighted average and choose most proper result, and adjust value to all cash terms if desired).

This summary should help you visualize the ARM approach before reading the complete version. The essence of the ARM approach is that the typical business can be valued credibly using ACF, rules of thumb, and market comp data if the necessary information is processed correctly through a careful evaluation of the subject company and industry.

Note Regarding Web Sites Listed in the Questionnaire

The Web sites listed in the ARM Approach Questionnaire were selected for their practical nature and relevance to the valuation process. Many of these sites are free of charge, but some Web sites recommended in the questionnaire charge fees for information. It is generally possible to complete a valuation without incurring substantial costs (other than time), with the notable exception of the use of market comp data. In this case, it is difficult to find suitable complimentary data related to the historical sale of privately held companies because there are no mandatory reporting requirements.

In the case of BIZCOMPS, buying a current study (which contains all historical sales to date) will provide benefits for at least a year or two. Annual membership dues for the IBA will provide exposure to exhaustive market data and other useful valuation-related information. You can purchase market comp data on the Business Valuation Resources Web site (*www.BVResources.com*) on a more selective basis, thus reducing the initial costs but providing minimal future benefits. You can also obtain data from agents who belong to your local state business brokers association, VR, or USBX. An advantage of the Pratt's Stats data is that a membership to their Web site allows simultaneous access to BIZCOMPS data. The choice made by the valuator is primarily a function of how many times and how many different businesses will be valued over the course of the year. If more than one company is involved, either a BIZCOMPS study or a membership to Business Valuation Resources is recommended. If only a single valuation effort is planned, one-time fee options would make the most sense. Prices for such services vary over time, so it is prudent to contact each potential source before making a decision.

ARM Approach Questionnaire

Section One

Begin with the Five-Page Tool described in detail earlier in the chapter:

1. Take out five blank sheets of paper and title them with the following terms:

   Key Valuation Factors (Pluses and Minuses)
   Adjusted Cash Flow
   Balance Sheet
   Major Assumptions
   Questions

If you need additional space, simply label each extra page in such a manner as to tie the additional analysis back to the questionnaire.

2. After receiving the subject company's income statement in accordance with the next section, review it line by line with an eye toward calculating the company's ACF on the first sheet. If you are unsure about a particular entry, write a question that includes the account name on the fifth sheet. As you calculate the ACF during this initial phase, address any uncertain items through questions and record any major assumptions. Conduct a similar line-by-line review of the balance sheet and again record questions related to accounts that need explaining and major assumptions (e.g., if a business is being valued as an asset sale, certain accounts are excluded or certain assets are subject to lease–purchase conditions and will be bought at the end of the lease). The best time to list the uniquely positive or negative features of the business or industry is when the related thought is fresh and easily put on paper.

3. Continue to use the five pages as you move forward with the valuation. It is important to write down important thoughts as they occur, including major insights into the unique surroundings and nature of the company or industry such as the winning of awards, ownership of patents, lease information, or possible new regulation. Jotting down the pluses and minuses as you think about them is a simple yet critical step. The Five-Page Tool will help you focus on what is important generally and specifically in regard to business valuation. Valuation done properly is a dynamic process that takes a certain amount of time and feedback, so don't hesitate to ask questions of the owner and the owner's broker or CPA. The Five-Page Tool will support this important discovery process.

Before beginning analysis, request copies of the following items:

Financial statements including balance sheet, income statement, and statement of cash flows (if available) for at least the past three years (five years preferable)

Federal tax returns for subject company for at least the past three years (five years preferable), including all supporting schedules (especially depreciation schedules)

Copy of operating lease (premises or equipment)

Descriptive company information such as brochures, pamphlets, advertising copy, mission statement, previous appraisals of the business or real estate, and other descriptive information about the subject company or industry

(if available, the company's business plan and any type of forecast would
be helpful)

Additional financial information such as equipment lists, accounts receivable and accounts payable aging reports, sales analysis reports, and cost
analysis reports

If the subject business is a franchise,* also request all franchise documents
including but not limited to the following:

Franchise agreement
Uniform offering circular

Other information will be requested as the review proceeds, but at a minimum it is necessary to obtain financial statements and tax returns to begin
the analysis. Outside sources of data and insights should be reviewed as well,
including industry data and the company's and competitors' Web sites. Any
questions that arise as you review the income statement and balance sheet
should be written down and submitted to the owner for feedback. Ideally, the
owner would fill out this questionnaire to the best of her ability. If this is not
feasible, then questions must be submitted piecemeal over time.

Regarding the valuation assignment, answer the following questions:

**1. What is the purpose for the valuation (e.g., potential purchase or
sale of company, divorce settlement, estate taxes)? Who is the intended
audience?**

_____

_____

_____

**2. What specifically is being valued (e.g., the entire company in re-
gard to an asset sale, 100 percent of the stock in regard to a stock sale,
50 percent of the entire company in regard to a stock sale, 10 percent
minority interest)? Sole proprietor, S- or C-corporation, limited liability company, or partnership?**

_____

_____

_____

See Addendum 2 for franchise-related questions.

3. What are the relevant standard and premise of value (e.g., most commonly valuation of the company on a fair market value or going-concern basis, possibly investment value on a going-concern basis)?

_____

_____

_____

4. Describe the overall valuation effort in one sentence (e.g., "The goal is to estimate the fair market value on a going-concern basis of an Internet service provider for purposes of selling the business as a sale of assets to the highest bidder").

_____

_____

_____

5. If the valuation assignment concerns a minority interest, complete Addendum 1, found at the end of this questionnaire. Describe the minority interest briefly:

_____

_____

_____

Section Two

Fill in the blanks for the subject company.

If the owner of the subject company cannot or will not fill in the portions of this questionnaire that are best answered by ownership, use the list of questions from the Five-Page Tool to add new questions that arise as you work through the questionnaire. One way or another, many questions can be answered only by the owner, key employees, or company advisers, so this list is a critical determinant of valuation credibility.

1. Name, location, and general lease information for subject business:

_____

_____

_____

2. Owner's name, phone number, and e-mail address (also provide name and number for agent if applicable):

_____

_____

_____

3. Nature of operations and hours open for business:

_____

_____

_____

4. Years in business:_____

5. Years owned by current owner:_____

6. Type of entity (e.g., S-corporation, limited-liability company):

_____

7. If corporation or limited-liability company, number of shareholders and their percentage ownership. Also, are all shareholders or partners willing to sell?:

_____

_____

_____

8. Do family members or partners actively work for business?_____

9. If answer is yes to question 8, describe their hours worked, duties performed, and annual salary or wages (plus payroll taxes) plus benefits (e.g., car payments, auto insurance, personal travel and entertainment, any other personal or discretionary expenses).

_____

_____

_____

10. Describe owner's work schedule, duties performed, annual salary, and payroll taxes plus benefits (e.g., car payments, insurance, personal travel and entertainment, any other personal or discretionary expenditures).

_____

_____

_____

11. How important is the owner to the success of the company? How would the business fare if the current owner departs?

_____

_____

_____

12. If business is run on an absentee basis (owner does not actively work at business), describe the manager's work schedule, duties performed, annual salary, and payroll taxes plus benefits (e.g., car payments, insurance, personal travel and entertainment, any other personal or discretionary expenditures).

_____

_____

_____

13. In general, what has been the trend in gross revenues and ACF for the company over the past five years?

_____

_____

_____

14. Are there additional revenues earned by the subject company that are not shown on the income statement? Query the owner and broker (if applicable) and report results here. Are the additional revenues verifiable?

_____

_____

_____

15. Is the business capital-intensive? If yes, what dollar amount of expenditures will be needed during the first year of new ownership and each year thereafter?

_____

_____

_____

16. How much working capital does the company carry on average (current assets minus current liabilities)? To estimate the amount of future working capital needs under different scenarios, use the working capital calculator found at *www.dinkytown.net/java/Capital.html*.

_____

_____

_____

17. Add the results of questions 15 and 16 to gauge the amount of additional cash the new owner will need to maintain operations at their current level (in addition to any down payment, if applicable).

_____

_____

_____

18. Can all sales revenue be verified or otherwise proven? What percentage of sales are made for cash? In addition to financial statements, are other source documents readily available such as sales tax receipts or reports, customer invoices, credit card statements, and bank deposit slips or statements? Answer the same questions for expenses.

_____

_____

_____

19. Ask the owner whether anything has recently changed or is likely to change in the future that would have a negative or positive impact on the business, its profitability, or its cash flow generation (e.g., lease rate will rise soon, electricity rates will double, new customer is coming on board, key competitor is entering the market or depart-

ing via bankruptcy, access to business will be restricted by upcoming construction).

Note: Question 19 is asked again in Section Four in relation to an updated "plus and minus" factor analysis.

20. Has the business used the services of an outside consultant for any purpose during the past several years? If so, what was the nature of the investigation and the corresponding findings? Is a copy of the report available?

---

21. What are the unique features of the subject company and industry as they relate to profitability and business value (include a general assessment of the local and national economy)?

Section Three

For each of the following areas, provide a brief overview of the important features and characteristics that might affect the future success of the company (revenues, expenses, profits, cash flows) and business value. Note that it is not necessary to answer every single question to complete the valuation effort. Note also that the Web sites listed with certain question areas generally are different from those listed elsewhere in the book (e.g., at the end of Chapter One). Therefore, feel free to return to Chapter One and review the recommended Web sites to maximize your exposure to useful and credible Web sites. If a particular issue is extremely important to you, a fresh Internet search may be productive.

An excellent one-stop Web site for conducting company and industry research is called Researching Companies Online, compiled by Debbie

Flanagan of Fort Lauderdale, Florida. Not only is this site efficient and logical in its layout, but all the major links are to free sites. Of course, there are also sublinks that increase the exposure to hundreds of pertinent sites. This tutorial-based site is found at *http://home.sprintmail.com/~debflanagan/index. html*.

Product or Services Offered

Key products or services (include SIC or NAICS codes from *www.naics. com*):

_____

_____

_____

Sales volume for each year over past five years (compare financial statement with tax returns and explain the difference):

_____

_____

_____

Inventory balance during the middle of the year and at year-end? Percentage of current inventory that is obsolete or unsalable? For inventory level analysis under future sales levels scenarios, go to *www.dinky town.net/java/Inventory.html* and use the free calculator (see Section Four for in-depth financial statement analysis).

_____

_____

_____

Future potential of products or services? (Review and select from the eighteen steps associated with industry research at the exceptional Web site found at *www.virtualpet.com/industry/howto/search.htm# general.*):

_____

_____

_____

Possible new products or services?

_____

_____

_____

Are there proprietary or unique products or services, such as patents or registered trademarks? (If applicable, verify at the U.S. Patent and Trademark Office Web site at _www.uspto._)

_____

_____

_____

What pricing strategy does the company follow? Price leader? Low cost? Cost plus profit?

_____

_____

_____

Have company sales followed industry trends?

_____

_____

_____

What is the forecast for future industry sales (use industry source, Internet search with _industry_ as keyword, or _www.industryresearch.com_)?

_____

_____

_____

How are sales made (e.g., inside salesperson, outside salesperson, distributors)?

_____

_____

_____

Is the owner directly responsible for new sales? What percentage of all sales?

_____

_____

_____

Does the company operate a Web site? If so, review for content and general usefulness. Go to *www.websitegarage.netscape.com/* for a quick and thorough effectiveness review and more.

_____

_____

_____

What would current owner do to increase sales in the future? Ask more than once for full impact.

_____

_____

_____

Who is primarily responsible for sales promotion and advertising? For insights into advertising for a specific type of business or a particular industry, conduct an Internet search using a specific descriptor (e.g., "retail bicycle advertising").

_____

_____

_____

Are the advertising, promotion, and marketing effective? Why or why not? For a practical analysis of how to increase sales through advertising that culminates in a useful worksheet for evaluating a company's advertising budget, go to *www.muextension.missouri.edu/xplor/miscpubs/ mp0660.htm* (also includes average advertising expenditures as percentage of sales for many business types).

_____

_____

_____

Customer Base

How many customers are served each week, month, or year? _____

What percentage of sales come from the top one, three, five, and ten customers?

_____

_____

_____

Who are the most important customers, and why do they return?

_____

_____

_____

What potential major customers could be approached for adding to the customer base?

_____

_____

_____

What percentage of business could be considered repeat sales? One-time only?

_____

_____

_____

What is the geographic breakdown of past sales? Local versus regional versus national?

_____

_____

_____

What seasonal effect applies to this company's products or services? Describe.

_____

_____

_____

In regard to seasonal fluctuations, is now a favorable time to buy or sell the company?

_____

_____

_____

What percentage of current customers might leave if the current owner suddenly departs? What could be done to minimize this fallout (don't forget the difference between investment value and fair market value in regard to the valuation assignment and perspective)?

_____

_____

_____

What is the typical markup or range in markup percentages (retail, wholesale, and manufacturing only)? For service companies, what is the markup over labor and materials?

_____

_____

_____

How large is the backlog (if any) now?

_____

_____

_____

What is the breakdown in sales between cash, credit card, check, and company financing?

_____

_____

_____

What is the bad debt experience of the company? Describe briefly in dollars and as a percentage of sales.

_____

_____

_____

What are the typical financing terms offered to customers? Do the majority pay early and take the discount (if offered)?

_____

_____

_____

What steps would the owner take to increase sales volume over the next year or longer?

_____

_____

_____

If the owner had an additional amount of funds equal to 5 percent of sales to spend on advertising, where would the owner invest this money?

_____

_____

_____

Is there a seasonal nature to working capital needs (see question 16 in Section Two)? When might additional cash be needed to sustain operations that cannot be supported by operational cash flow?

_____

_____

_____

Are any of the customers served based on written contracts? If yes, for what amount and over what period of time? Are such contracts easily transferred?

_____

_____

_____

Product or Service Differentiation

How does the company distinguish itself from the competition?

_____

_____

_____

Are company products or services and trade name readily recognizable in key markets?

_____

_____

_____

Is the company known as a leader in quality, price, or service?

_____

_____

_____

In regard to pricing, where does the company stand relative to the competition? See *www.pricingsociety.com* for pricing basics.

_____

_____

_____

What is the nature of the company's service or warranty reputation?

_____

_____

_____

What is the most distinctive feature of the company overall?

_____

_____

_____

Advertising

What percentage of sales are devoted to advertising? For comprehensive information related to advertising (e.g., statistics, industry trends, case studies) go to the Web site of the Direct Marketing Association at *www.the-dma.org/index.shtml*.

_____

_____

_____

According to the owner or company salespeople, which advertising works best and worst? For interesting statistical information about advertising by type and by industry, go to *www.census.gov/prod/2001 pubs/statab/sec18.pdf.*

If the owner had an extra 5 percent of sales for new advertising, how would it be allocated or prioritized from greatest to least? For advertising tips and full coverage of retail businesses, go to *www.retail industry.about.com/mbody.htm.*

What improvements could or should be made to the company's Web site? At what cost and benefit?

Are there any recent press releases, articles about the company or industry, or ad copies available for review? Is a press agent or public relations company involved?

Key Competitors

List and describe the top three to five competitors. This information ideally will come from the current owner or a quick look at the yellow pages (for retail and service companies, try driving around a 3- to 5-square-mile radius to spot competitors).

Who is the market leader? Why are they the market leader? Go to *www.babson.edu/library/indcontents.htm* for a guide to industry research.

_____

_____

_____

Which competitor charges the lowest prices? Highest prices?

_____

_____

_____

What are the pluses and minuses of each top competitor? For a review of competitive intelligence issues, go to *www.management.miningco. com/smallbusiness/management/library/weekly/aa111598.htm.*

_____

_____

_____

In regard to reputation, which competitor excels and why?

_____

_____

_____

Supplier Base

Who are the key suppliers, and how long have they served the company? For information regarding supply chain management, go to *www.manufacturing.net/scm/index.asp.*

_____

_____

_____

What are the key raw materials or inventory items purchased for use in manufacturing or resale?

_____

_____

_____

Are any raw materials or inventory items difficult to locate or purchase (e.g., tight supplies or sole-source suppliers)?

_____

_____

_____

Does the company have access to ample backup suppliers for key items? Go to the Thomas Register of American Manufacturers at *www.thomas register.com* for complete lists of suppliers.

_____

_____

_____

Is there a seasonal nature to purchasing the necessary inventory? Is there a specific trade show that is important to the industry? Go to *www.ipl.org/ref/AON/* for a list of trade associations on the Internet.

_____

_____

_____

What percentage of the inventory on the books is obsolete, in poor condition, or otherwise unsalable?

_____

_____

_____

Is the inventory pledged as collateral for any type or amount of financing?

_____

_____

_____

What are the standard industry payment terms?

_____

_____

_____

Are supplier relationships based on personal guarantees from the owner?

_____

_____

_____

Are any supplier relationships deteriorating or in danger of being lost altogether?

_____

_____

_____

Does the owner believe that all supplier relationships would survive the sale of the company?

_____

_____

_____

Ask owner or determine independently whether other potentially advantageous suppliers are available (e.g., located nearby, favorable pricing, wide availability).

_____

_____

_____

Does the owner believe it possible for a new owner to renegotiate existing debts downward in exchange for a pledge of continued purchasing (contractual pledge)?

_____

_____

_____

Employee Base and Key Employees

How many full-time and part-time employees work for the company?

_____

_____

_____

Is an organizational chart available?

_____

_____

_____

Which employees does the owner consider to be key employees? Why?

_____

_____

_____

What are salary and wage levels for employees? Are they considered high or low by industry or competitive standards (see _www.salary source.com_ or access labor statistics through _www.dbm.com/jobguide/ salary.html_)?

_____

_____

_____

What are the sales per employee and gross profit per employee statistics over the past few years? Go to _www.saibooks.com/fin.html_ to find such statistics by industry in the _Workforce Ratios and Forecasts_ publication from Schonfeld & Associates.

_____

_____

_____

What is the annual turnover rate for all employees? What amount of unemployment benefits are paid each year on average (if any)?

_____

_____

_____

Does owner believe employees will leave immediately after sale of company? Specifically who?

_____

_____

_____

Is payroll handled by an outside company such as Paychex, Paymaster, or ADP? Go to *www.adp.com* for information on payroll-related issues and costs.

_____

_____

_____

How and where are new employees located?

_____

_____

_____

Are special bonuses or other enticements necessary to attract needed personnel?

_____

_____

_____

What is the standard benefit package for new employees? For comprehensive information about human resource issues and concerns including benefit-related discussions, analyses, tips, forms, and worksheets, go to *www.atyourbusiness.com/public/content/benefits/default.asp*.

_____

_____

_____

What is the company's worker's compensation rating? Rising or falling? See *www.lawguru.com/faq/22.html* for answers to related questions.

_____

_____

_____

Have there been any worker's compensation or claims (past, present, or upcoming)?

_____

_____

_____

Are labor unions active in the subject industry or for the subject
company?

_____

_____

_____

Besides labor union activity, are any employees hired based on negotiated and signed contracts?

_____

_____

_____

Are any key employees under contract? Would they consider signing a
long-term contract with the new owner?

_____

_____

_____

Are any employees paid cash instead of through normal payroll
channels?

_____

_____

_____

Which employees, if any, are paid more than market wages or less
than market wages (commonly family members)? If so, by how much
on an annualized basis?

_____

_____

_____

Lease and Premises

What is monthly rent (including common area maintenance
charges) and square footage of facility? For a thorough analysis of

commercial leasing, including the top ten mistakes made in this area, go to *www.leasesmart.com/tenantguide.htm* for the Tenant's Guide to Leasing.

_____

_____

_____

Are there provisions that call for rental rate acceleration (e.g., consumer price index increases each year or percentage of sales clauses that may arise with higher sales revenue)?

_____

_____

_____

Is the per-foot rental rate above average, average, or below average in regard to similar premises in the area?

_____

_____

_____

When does the current lease expire, and are there renewal options? How many and how long? For an overview of leasing procedures and analysis of major leasing issues and pitfalls (and a free newsletter called **Real Estate Leasing Tips**), go to *www.centerforcommercialrealestate.com/newsletter.htm.*

_____

_____

_____

Will there be difficulties in transferring the lease? (Review applicable lease forms and ask owner, other tenants, or landlord)?

_____

_____

_____

Is there a security system in place? Has there been any recent theft, robberies, or vandalism in the immediate area, including the subject business?

_____

_____

_____

If real estate is also available, how does price compare with market levels?

_____

_____

_____

If real estate is included in deal or valuation assignment, will the seller fill out and sign a seller's disclosure statement?

_____

_____

_____

Are there visible or known problems with the real property of any type or magnitude (e.g., deferred maintenance, environmental concerns)? For information on Phase I, II, and III environmental audits and links to environmental-related Web sites, go to *www.primenet. com/~gwr/phases.htm.* Or, for the U.S. Environmental Protection Agency's resource guide, *Environmental Assistance Services for Small Business,* go to *www.epa.gov/sbo/ea-resourceguide.pdf.*

_____

_____

_____

Are there any peculiar, unusual, or noncustomary terms or conditions in the existing lease?

_____

_____

_____

Are there any problems or concerns in areas such as parking, zoning, allowable activity per the lease terms, or ownership of building (is it for sale on the open market)?

_____

_____

_____

Fixed Assets (furniture, fixtures, equipment, and vehicles)

Describe the type, age, and condition of major furniture, fixtures, and equipment (FF&E) categories (see the Five-Page Tool "Balance Sheet" page) as found on the most recent balance sheet and federal tax return:

_____

_____

_____

Are the company's operations automated or computerized to a substantial degree (note type and cost of software and hardware)?

_____

_____

_____

What is the original cost of the company's fixed assets on the most current balance sheet (see the Five-Page Tool for earlier analysis)?

_____

_____

_____

What is the current depreciated book value of the company's fixed assets? (To verify accuracy of depreciation figures, go to *www.fixedassetinfo. com/calculator.htm.*)

_____

_____

_____

What is the current estimated FMV of the company's fixed assets? If no other means exist to make this estimate, add the original cost to the current book value and divide by two (also compare financials with tax returns).

_____

_____

_____

Are vehicles included in these asset figures (if so, find current *Kelly Blue Book* values at *www.kbb.com*)? Which vehicles will not be included in the sale of business (their corresponding value must be backed out if they are not part of the sale)?

_____

_____

_____

How much is spent each year on maintenance? As a percentage of sales? Compare with industry average by SIC code (now or later, as part of the financial statement analysis in Section Four) via Internet search with the following keywords listed after the industry name: "maintenance repairs percentage of sales".

_____

_____

_____

Inspect the premises and ask the owner whether there is any substantial deferred maintenance that should be addressed, such as roofing or air conditioning. See *www.collegehouses.org/deferred.htm* for an overview.

_____

_____

_____

What is the dollar cost of assets that are being leased that can be purchased at lease-end? What are current payoff amounts? Are they all subject to lien? For complete leasing coverage, see *www.leaseassistant. org/basics/*.

_____

_____

_____

If the owner had additional funds available to invest in fixed assets, what would the owner purchase? Assume an amount equal to 25 percent of the original cost of existing FF&E.

_____

_____

_____

What is the FMV of equipment, machinery, and tools that have been fully depreciated and are no longer on the books or were immediately expensed rather than capitalized? (This value must be added to the balance sheet–based calculations made as part of the Five-Page Tool). For self-constructed assets, make sure to add an appropriate "labor" component.

_____

_____

_____

How would you characterize the rate of technological development in the subject company's industry? How important is it to have the latest technology to remain competitive? See *www.marketresearch.com* for current technological developments by industry.

_____

_____

_____

Fixed Costs, Variable Costs, and Breakeven Analysis

What costs must be paid regardless of sales volume per month?

_____

_____

_____

What is approximate breakeven level of sales on a monthly and annual basis? See *www.innovationworks.org/resources/library/be.html* for basic insights and *www.dinkytown.net/java/BreakEven.html* for a user-friendly breakeven calculator.

_____

_____

_____

What can the new owner do to reduce fixed costs? For tips on controlling overhead and other costs, see *www.synrgistic.com/busplan/tip index.htm*. This guide was written for entrepreneurs who own businesses experiencing financial distress.

_____

_____

_____

What are key variable costs (e.g., labor, raw materials, utilities, T&E)?

_____

_____

_____

What are the percentage of sales figures for labor and raw materials or inventory? Either now or later during the financial statement analysis, compare with industry averages from Robert Morris Associates data (or other sources such as *IRS Corporate Financial Ratios*).

_____

_____

_____

Which variable costs are subject to potential reduction?

_____

_____

_____

Ask the owner how he might reduce costs in the future to increase profits. For a thorough analysis of fixed costs, variable costs, breakeven analysis, fixed asset analysis, and seventy-two ratios compiled from IRS tax information for reporting businesses, go to *www.saibooks.com/fin.html* to purchase the *IRS Corporate Financial Ratio* book (excellent for financial statement analysis overall).

_____

_____

_____

Contractual Relationships

Ask owner to list all current contractual relationships (all types).

_____

_____

_____

Are contracts signed or guaranteed by the owner, the company, or both?

_____

_____

_____

Which contracts are or should be transferable?

_____

_____

_____

Will key employees sign employment agreements for one year or more? Will the owner consider an employment contract or consulting agreement in conjunction with the sale?

_____

_____

_____

Economic Conditions

Describe the recent, current, and probable state of the economy on a local or regional basis as well as nationally. What is the general outlook for the economy as it relates to the subject company and industry? (See *www.federalreserve.gov/FOMC/BeigeBook/Current/*.**)**

_____

_____

_____

Locate and list the following interest rates and yields found in the *Wall Street Journal* **or online: prime rate, SBA rate (equals prime + 2.5**

percent), 10-year Treasury note (see *www.bankrate.com* or *www.bloom berg.com*).

_____

_____

_____

Are interest rates rising or falling at the present time? Over the next one to two years?

_____

_____

_____

How are consumer sentiments and consumer sentiment indices trending? (See *www.mier.org.my/csi.html* or enter these keywords, e.g., "consumer confidence survey," "consumer sentiments," or "consumer confidence trends," with name of relevant state.)

_____

_____

_____

Assess the local and regional economic conditions by conducting an Internet search with the name of the state and keywords "economic conditions," "statistics," "trends," and "forecasts."

_____

_____

_____

What are the most substantial links between the general economy and the subject company (e.g., interest rate sensitive, recession-proof, local layoffs)?

_____

_____

_____

Financing Issues

What have been the traditional sources of financing for the company? What is the current debt-to-equity ratio? (For industry averages, go to *www.bizstats.com*.)

_____

_____

_____

What have been the major hurdles in seeking bank financing?

_____

_____

_____

Are there any existing loan covenants that would be violated upon sale of the company without making prior arrangements?

_____

_____

_____

Other Areas of Concern

Ask the owner for a copy of the business plan, mission statement, or list of goals and objectives.

_____

_____

_____

Are there any required or recommended licenses, permits, or certifications?

_____

_____

_____

Can the necessary licenses, permits, or certifications be easily and quickly transferred? How much time is needed for such transfers if outside approval is necessary? Costs?

_____

_____

_____

Are there any health-related or environmental-related concerns or problems? Any historical or expected concerns or problems?

_____

_____

_____

What types of capacity constraints does the business face (e.g., floor space, seating capacity, labor supply, equipment)? How much could sales be increased without the need for additional "space" or major asset acquisitions?

_____

_____

_____

Based on the current state of affairs (size of premises, labor, and access to raw materials), how much could sales increase without substantial changes in the resource base?

_____

_____

_____

What are the most important trade associations and publications for the subject industry? For links to major trade associations, go to *http://info.asaenet.org/gateway/OnlineAssocSlist.html* (American Society of Association Executives' Gateway) or *www.ipl.org/ref/AON* for Associations on the Net from the Internet Public Library.

_____

_____

_____

Are there any past, present, or anticipated legal actions related to the company (e.g., pending lawsuits of any type, potential liabilities related to product liability, or warranty repairs)? If so, please describe. Ask this question more than once and request that the owner "sign" any such disclosures.

_____

_____

_____

Will owner agree to complete and sign a seller's disclosure statement regarding the company's operations? (Go to *www.scottgabehart.com* to purchase the *Upstart Guide to Buying, Valuing, and Selling Your Business* from Dearborn Financial Publishing, which contains comprehensive disclosure statements for both businesses and real property.)

_____

_____

_____

To the best of the owner's knowledge, is the relevant industry currently subject to the efforts of consolidators or roll-up specialists?

_____

_____

_____

Section Four

Answer these questions that relate directly to the ARM approach.

Adjust the Cash Flow and Apply the Multiple

1. Using the last few year-ending accounting statements, finalize the company's calculated ACF by completing the Five-Page Tool results:

	1998	**1999**	**2000**	**2001**	**2002**
+/– Pretax income					
+ Owner's salary and payroll tax					
+ Owner's benefits					
+ Depreciation and amortization expense					
+ Interest expense					
+/– One-time expenses or revenues					
= Adjusted cash flow (ACF)					

Given the importance of ACF, accurate calculations are essential. Review the sections addressing ACF calculations (primarily Chapter Four in the book but also relevant sections of the CD-ROM, such as the "Use of Income Statement" of the "Accounting Primer") to ensure proper usage. If data are available on an interim basis (e.g., for the first six months of a year), annualizing the half-year ACF may provide useful insights into trends. At least three years should be reviewed, preferably five years.

2. After asking the owner to list the major strengths, weaknesses, opportunities, and threats for the subject company (SWOT analysis) and repeating question 19 in Section Two, conduct a preliminary industry search to complement your current Five-Page Tool results and generate an updated list of pluses and minuses:

"Pluses"	"Minuses"
_____	_____
_____	_____
_____	_____
_____	_____
_____	_____
_____	_____
_____	_____
_____	_____

This particular list should be started immediately during the evaluation process (Five-Page Tool) and updated as your analysis continues and your knowledge of the business and its industry increases. These pros and cons ultimately will determine the relevant multiple of cash flow for the first component of the ARM approach and the relationship between the subject company and the industry norm or average under the market comparable component (most rules of thumb are also based on a range of values depending on the pluses and minuses of the subject company).

3. At this juncture, a number of different analytical tools can be used to evaluate the subject company in light of the average performance of similar companies. In addition to trend analysis (how performance indicators change year to year), comparisons of the subject company performance with industry averages can be enlightening. At a minimum, select and use one of the following sources of financial information, categorized by SIC code for privately held companies:

Robert Morris Associates   [*www.rma.com*]
Their data is comprehensive in breadth and depth, covering hundreds of SIC codes with average income statements and balance sheets and financial ratio performance grouped into quartiles from best to worst.

Almanac of Business and Industrial Financial Ratios   [*www.valuationresources.com*]
This information is compiled from IRS data and broken down into thirteen asset sizes for more than 170 industry groups, differentiating between companies that earned a taxable income and those that did not.

Financial Studies of the Small Business   [*www.frafssb.com/*]
This publication focuses on businesses with less than $1 million in capitalization (debt plus equity) for more than seventy SIC codes.

Regardless of the source of comparative data, many useful evaluation techniques may be used to analyze the subject company, including the following:

a. *Perform trend and common size analysis:* This financial statement tool calls for evaluating changes in account balances or financial statement ratios from year to year and comparing account balances and ratios with industry averages over the past three to five years for

Gross revenues
Gross profit
Total operating expenses (general and administrative)
Earnings before interest and taxes (EBIT)
Earnings before interest, taxes, depreciation, and amortization (EBITDA)
ACF
Advertising, payroll, rent, T&E, telephone, and other expenses as a percentage of revenues
Return on assets (ACF divided by total assets)
Return on revenues (ACF divided by total revenues)
Revenues per employee
Revenues per dollar of assets
Average collection period
Average inventory turnover
Current ratio (current assets divided by current liabilities)
Average cash, accounts receivable, and accounts payable balance
Quick ratio (current assets less inventory divided by current liabilities)
Times interest earned ratio (ACF divided by interest expense or EBIT divided by interest expense)

Fixed charge coverage (ACF or EBITDA divided by interest expense
plus lease expense plus other fixed charges such as insurance, property
taxes, and owner's living expenses)

Dollar cost of new equipment and other fixed assets purchased each year

Average inventory level during different times of year

Product sales by category

Gross profit per product

Actual federal income tax paid per dollar of revenues

Any other industry-specific measure,* such as average tax return billing
for a CPA practice or average returns and allowances for retail business.

For a quick, user-friendly analysis of ten financial statement ratios generated automatically by a customized calculator, go to *www.dinkytown.
net/java/Ratios.html* (presented by KJE Computers of Minneapolis,
Minnesota). Numerous financial tools and calculators are presented free
of charge on this interesting Web site, including a cash forecasting model.
Another general yet informative look at financial statement analysis can
be found at *www.uoutperform.com/NewFolder/fundamentalanalysis.htm.*

b. *Use managerial tools and techniques:* Many other evaluation tools exist
that can aid in the analysis of the subject company and industry, ranging from simple to complex. Prentice Hall's *Vest Pocket CEO* by
Alexander Hiam contains a remarkable collection of management
techniques that address the following areas:

Financial decisions

Leadership skills

Manufacturing and operations

Marketing decisions

Organization and human resources

Product development and innovation

Sales management decisions

Strategic planning decisions

General decision-making tools

Some of the more commonly recognized tools covered here include:

Altman-Z Bankruptcy Predictor

ADL Product Life Cycle Matrix

---

*These indicators often are the most intriguing and enlightening of all when attempting to assess the subject company's
position relative to the norm.*

Pfizer's Sales Forecasting
General Electric Matrix-Based Strategic Planning
Orchard Matrix of Product Attractiveness
Heebner's Seven Laws of Forecasting

In addition to the dozens of useful tools in the *Vest Pocket CEO,* other options exist that do not take a great deal of effort to learn or apply, including the following, each of which contributes to the plus and minus analysis that drives the valuation process:

- Perform a walk-through of premises while taking notes in all areas
- SWOT (strengths, weaknesses, opportunities, threats) analysis
- Porter 5 Forces (threat of new entrants, threat of rivalry between competitors, threat of substitutes, bargaining power of suppliers, bargaining power of buyers)

Deciding which of these evaluation tools to use is a matter of personal preference and circumstances. At a minimum, trend analysis of the major financial indicators and comparison with industry averages is a must. The combination of trends and comparative performance measures will go a long way toward establishing the relative attractiveness (value) of the subject company.

c. *Industry or market research:* To the extent that review of the subject company and the subject industry are integral components of the valuation process, it is important to understand the broader, external forces that are at work in influencing the company's future financial performance. Both general economic conditions and the unique industry-specific factors should be analyzed and incorporated into the final analysis of the company (ultimately through derivation of the proper multiple to apply against cash flow or revenues). In addition to the sources listed in Chapter Five, consider the following Web sites when implementing market research in conjunction with business valuation:

Standard and Poor's Industry Surveys (*www.advisorinsight.com/ai/preview/ index.htm*)
MarketResearch (*www.MarketResearch.com*)
First Research Industry Profiles (*www.accountingweb.com/firstres/ index.html*)
U.S. Industrial Outlook (*www.ntis.gov/product/industry-trade-chapters.htm*)
Interactive Dow Jones (*www.wsj.com*)
FirstGov Search Engine (*www.firstgov.gov*)

An excellent one-stop guide to industry research can be found on a Web site affiliated with one of the top entrepreneurial MBA programs in the nation at *www.babson.edu/library/indcontents.htm*. It includes an incredible number of organized links for all industry-related facts and insights. Take a look and you will be pleasantly surprised.

4. Based on your analysis thus far, do you feel that the subject company is below average, average, or above average for this type and size of business? Why do you feel this way now?

5. Based on the average multiples of ACF taken from BIZCOMPS, VR Business Brokers, and IBA data for the following company sizes, where does the subject company fit based on your preliminary review of cash flow?

Amount of ACF	Range of Average ACF Multiple	Subject Company??
Less than $100,000	1 to 2 times ACF	
$100,000 to $249,999	1.5 to 2.5 times ACF	
$250,000 to $499,999	2 to 4 times ACF	
$500,000 to $999,999	3 to 5 times ACF	
$1 million to $3 million	4 to 10 times ACF	
More than $3 million	Price/earnings (P/E) ratios typically apply because most are public companies or comparable to public companies	

Remember that these are averages, meaning that several companies will sell for less or more than average. This question is meant to remind the valuator of the importance of cash flow size in determining the relevant multiples. The larger the company, the more likely alternative measures of cash flow are to be used (e.g., EBITDA, EBIT, or simply after-tax income or earnings as used in P/E ratios).

6. Return to the list of pluses and minuses started earlier on the "Key Valuation Factors" page of the Five-Page Tool. Using your newfound knowledge about the company and its industry, take the time to update the list. Be as specific as possible and remain as credible as possible. Use additional paper as needed to facilitate continuance.

7. Based on your analysis thus far, select the appropriate multiple and apply this figure to the company's ACF (the last year's results are most important, but an average of the past three years may be more conservative).

_____

_____

_____

Review the Rules of Thumb for Pertinence and Type

1. Before proceeding further, prepare a chart listing the company's gross revenues, ACF, and total assets over the past three years, referring to the Five-Page Tool results prepared earlier (five years is preferable):

_____

_____

_____

2. Ask your broker, attorney, and CPA and the seller whether they are aware of any particular rule of thumb that applies to the subject company.

_____

_____

_____

3. Review the list on the CD-ROM to see whether a rule of thumb is listed for the subject company. Other sources of rules of thumb are listed on the CD-ROM as well, notably the *2001 Business Reference Guide* (*www.businessbrokeragepress.com*). Typing in "business valuation rules of thumb" or "rules of thumb motel hotel," for example, as part of an Internet search may also be fruitful for some business types.

_____

_____

_____

4. If no particular rule of thumb exists for the subject company, use one of the generic rules of thumb, such as a rule of thumb that applies to all smaller retail businesses (1 to 1.5 times ACF plus inventory) or all middle-market manufacturing companies (4 to 6 times EBITDA).

_____

_____

_____

5. Describe the pertinent rule of thumb and note the subjective element of this particular rule and what factors might affect the final val-

uation result in terms of this subjective element (i.e., for a rule of thumb such as "one to two times ACF plus assets," the primary subjective element will be the choice between one and two times ACF and a secondary subjective element would be the value of the assets).

---

6. What key factors relating to the subject company tend to push the multiple involved either up or down (review the pluses and minuses worksheet)?

---

7. Based on a preponderance of the evidence, should the lower end or higher end of the rule of thumb formula be used for the subject company? List the key reasons in support of your decision.

---

8. Choose the most pertinent rule of thumb and apply the technique for the subject company based on your understanding of the business and industry.

---

9. Apply the "reality check" rule of thumb presented in the Asset or Cost Approach section of the CD-ROM. Follow each step as explained, being aware that the monthly payments in practice will include both principal and interest. How does this valuation result compare with the initial two results (multiple of cash flow and other rule of thumb)?

---

10. **Using the average of the two valuation results reached so far (multiple of ACF and rule of thumb) as the purchase price, evaluate the company's ability to service debt by assuming a down payment equal to 40 percent and seller financing (or bank financing) comprised of 7 to 9 percent interest and a payback period of three to ten years (bank financing typically is at a higher interest rate with a longer payback period, i.e., prime plus 2.5 percent and seven to ten years' payback). Calculate the monthly and annualized debt service and compare this with the company's ACF (after deducting a living wage for the new owner). If this ratio is not at least 1.25, banks probably will not fund. A ratio of at least 2 is desirable in terms of providing a cushion for the new owner.**

_____

_____

_____

Monitor the Market Comps to Ensure a Credible Estimate of Value

1. **What SIC code (or NAICS code) or codes does the subject company operate under?**

_____

_____

_____

2. **Is it possible that the subject company can be evaluated under more than one SIC code (e.g., a manufacturing company with a retail location or a restaurant that is a franchise)?**

_____

_____

_____

3. **Describe the subject company in terms of which market segment is most applicable (i.e., is the company most suited to be treated as a business brokerage company or a middle-market company)? Review the descriptions and lists in Chapter Two to support your answer. (*If the subject company is a middle-market company, continue with the next few questions; if not, skip to question 12.*)**

_____

_____

_____

4. If the subject company is a middle-market business, then the guide-line public company method and Pratt's Stats (or IBA Database or BIZCOMPS National Industrial Survey) may be the optimal combination of method and database. Does this situation apply to the subject company?

_____

_____

_____

5. If the subject company is a middle-market type business, what key features capture the essence of the operation in terms of finding similar companies for comparison (e.g., type of product or service line and SIC code, revenue and ACF or EBIT size, geographic markets served, trends in revenues and earnings, capital structure, or number of employees)?

_____

_____

_____

6. Use the SIC code to search Pratt's Stats, BIZCOMPS National Industrial Survey, Mergerstat, and Heller Financial Data for actual sales of middle-market companies or turn to one of several online sources of individual share price data such as Hoover's Online, Free EDGAR, Multex Investor, Institutional Brokers Estimate System (*www.ibes.com*), Thomson MarketEdge (*www.marketedge.com*) or others listed in Chapter Five to locate information on similar companies. Remember that one can use the comparable sales method for middle-market companies as long as the database matches the type and size of company under evaluation. Use of the guideline method depends on current share prices and P/E ratios that must be ultimately adjusted to match the size of company under evaluation (guideline method requires publicly traded share price data). List seven to twenty such transactions or P/E ratios here (use additional worksheets as necessary, carefully cross-referencing between the questionnaire and the supplemental analysis:

_____

_____

_____

7. If using the comparable sales method for middle-market companies, make sure that the comps are similar in regard to product line (SIC code), size of revenues, assets and cash flow, and geographic markets served. If using the guideline public company method, it is necessary to ensure similar accounting methods or adjust for differences and then factor in a size effect discount to their average P/E ratio. *Do not forget that the comparable sales method relies on ACF, whereas the guideline method relies on after-tax earnings for their corresponding P/E ratio*. The guideline method also entails adjustment of the subject company's income statement to reflect a normalized after-tax earnings figure (e.g., excessive owner's compensation should be added into after-tax earnings). Based on these above instructions, refine your list to those that remain most similar.

_____

_____

_____

8. If using the guideline method for the middle-market companies listed in question 6, list the resulting P/E ratios and take an arithmetic mean for the group. Next, adjust this arithmetic mean for the size effect.

_____

_____

_____

9. If using the guideline method, incorporate your overall analysis of the subject company relative to the norm by applying a discount or premium to the size-adjusted arithmetic mean derived above (i.e., if the subject company is superior to the size-adjusted norm, increase the multiple by the appropriate factor and apply to the subject company).

_____

_____

_____

10. If using the comparable sales method for the middle-market company, make sure your sample size is large enough to account for the various terms and conditions across all deals that tend to push a multiple up or down such that a credible average multiple of ACF can be

calculated. Don't forget that certain types of businesses (e.g., service or restaurant-related businesses) may rely heavily on the multiple of price to gross revenues rather than price to ACF. Calculate the average multiple for your group of comps.

_____

_____

_____

11. Based on your overall analysis of the subject company (pros and cons), determine its position relative to the average multiple and apply the adjusted multiple to the subject company's ACF or revenues.

_____

_____

_____

12. If the subject company is smaller (revenues under several million dollars and ACF under $1 million), the comparable sales method and one of the other three databases (BIZCOMPS, IBA, VR Business Brokers) would be the ideal combination. Does this situation apply to the subject company?

_____

_____

_____

13. If the subject company is smaller and the comparable sales method applies, what key features capture the essence of the operation in terms of finding similar companies for comparison (e.g., primarily type of product or service markets served, company size in revenues and ACF, and geographic markets served)?

_____

_____

_____

14. Based on your knowledge of the three databases applicable to the comparable sales method, does any one of the three appear to be more suitable at first glance (e.g., the IBA database has nearly 200 comps for accounting or tax practices; BIZCOMPS comp data ex-

clude inventory, making it more difficult to apply to inventory-rich businesses such as retail shops)? Which database should be searched initially?

———————————————————————————————

———————————————————————————————

———————————————————————————————

15. For the smaller privately held companies, BIZCOMPS and IBA data are available to the public. Pratt's Stats data is also available, but the typical transaction value is much higher than IBA or BIZCOMPS data. If time permits, call each organization and ask them how many comps they have for the specific type of company at hand (SIC code description preferable) and list the results here. If it is deemed that one particular database will be superior or if only one database is available, use this database to conduct your search and describe the results of this search.

———————————————————————————————

———————————————————————————————

———————————————————————————————

16. Review the list of comps provided for each SIC code to ensure that they are similar. For each of the comps found to be similar, list all relevant data. At a minimum, list the gross revenues, ACF, and deal price along with the multiples of price to gross revenues and ACF. Recall the slightly different cash flow measure contained in the IBA and the exclusion of inventory in the BIZCOMPS price and multiples (most BIZCOMPS transactions present the inventory figure, so it is often possible to add inventory back into the price to arrive at a more comparable measure of cash flow). Calculate the average price to revenue and price to cash flow multiples for comparison with the subject company.

———————————————————————————————

———————————————————————————————

———————————————————————————————

17. Based on your overall assessment of the subject company, determine whether it is below average, average, or above average relative to the norm calculated in question 16. Each valuation method contains

such a subjective adjustment, so it is prudent to be well prepared in defending your final judgment regardless of who the audience might be (e.g., buyer, seller, tax court, spouse, partner, bank, insurance company). It is important to appear credible by incorporating both pluses and minuses into your estimate of any multiple (or capitalization or discount rate, which are essentially the inverse of multiples; e.g., a multiple of 2 is equal to a cap rate of 50 percent, 3 is equal to 33 percent, 4 is equal to 25 percent). Write down your final multiple estimate and apply it to the subject company's revenues and ACF and state the key factors underlying your decision.

Section Five

Weight Your Findings and Prepare the Final Value Estimate

1. List each of the results from the ARM components and take a straight arithmetic mean.

---

2. Is there any reason why one of the three components should receive a higher weighting in your opinion? For example, is the rule of thumb well accepted among practitioners and industry professionals or participants? Are the market comps extremely similar and clean (i.e., was there a large sample size of legitimate comps with full information for each transaction)? If there is no accepted rule of thumb and the comps were of questionable quality, reliance on the multiple of cash flow or revenues may be most appropriate (e.g., restaurants sell for a multiple of revenues in the 30 to 60 percent range). Remember that occasionally rules of thumb may be based on a multiple of ACF, so the first and second component of the ARM approach may appear similar. The primary difference between the first and second component in this regard

is that the first component is based solely on a review of the subject company without any predisposition toward a certain range of multiples, as is the case with rules of thumb based on ACF. If a relative weighting is desirable, explain the rationale behind such an allocation and calculate the results here.

_____

_____

_____

3. Using common sense and a sanity check, which of the above two results from the ARM approach appears to be more credible and supportable? A sanity check is based on assuming a typical deal structure and calculating the corresponding debt service and leftover cash flow. For example, assuming a 35 percent cash down payment with the balance payable over five years at prime plus 1 percent (currently 9 percent), calculate the debt service on a monthly and annual basis. If the company's ACF is not at least 1.5 times the debt service, most banks would not make such a loan. A safe figure here is at least two times the debt service. Based on this analysis, which valuation result now appears more reasonable? Your choice here almost concludes the valuation analysis.

_____

_____

_____

4. Finally, remember that the valuation results obtained via the ARM approach are based on the typical financing terms associated with seller financing. *Accordingly, if one seeks an all-cash equivalent price, a discount to the valuation result is needed*. Recall that a review of the BIZCOMPS database by Mr. Toby Tatum (available through *www. BVResources.com*) showed that on average companies sold with seller financing sold for 28 percent more. Going in the other direction, businesses sold for all cash generated an approximately 22 percent lower purchase price (the difference results from the use of different base figures for calculating the percentage change). Taking an average of these two figures provides a credible estimate of the average discount for all-cash sales. Thus, business owners selling for all cash received 25 percent less than the price associated with seller financing. Apply the

25 percent discount to the final value estimate to arrive at the approximate all-cash price.

_____

_____

_____

Addendum 1: Minority Interests

As explained in Chapter Seven, situations may arise in which only a portion of
a going concern is relevant for valuation purposes. The primary valuation consideration relates to the so-called minority interest discount or discount for lack
of control, which means that a 10 percent interest is worth less than 10 percent
of the entity value.

**1. What is the relevant percentage ownership applicable to this as-
signment?**

_____

_____

_____

**2. List the ownership breakdown for the subject company in percent-
age terms.**

_____

_____

_____

**3. Consult the information presented in Chapter Seven for concep-
tual and procedural insights before completing this analysis.**

_____

_____

_____

Addendum 2: Franchises

If the subject company is a franchised operation, a unique set of additional queries
is needed to ensure a credible valuation outcome. In addition to reviewing the

franchise agreement and the Uniform Offering Circular carefully, contact the person responsible for processing and approving the franchise transfer; this person is a valuable information source.

In conjunction with the ARM Approach Questionnaire, the following questions should also be asked that relate to the transferability and general appeal of franchise operations.

1. What are the processes and restrictions regarding the transfer of the franchise agreement?
2. What is the cost of such a transfer?
3. What training is needed before and after the transition of ownership? Costs?
4. What is the remaining term of the agreement? Can it be extended?
5. What type of restrictive clauses are in effect that could limit future growth (e.g., product line restrictions, territorial restrictions, mandatory purchases)?
6. What is the nature of the ongoing support offered by the franchisor?
7. What is the royalty percentage and advertising percentage (if applicable)?
8. Who owns the land, building, and equipment?

Caveat

Note that these addendums are brief and should not be relied on as the sole analysis for these two scenarios. Note also that there is a complete chapter devoted to minority interest issues later in this book (Chapter Seven). If the subject company is a franchise, it is incumbent on the reader to search out additional information regarding the intricacies of evaluating and buying (or selling) a franchised business.

It is critical that the buyer recognize that there are numerous state and federal laws and regulations governing franchise and business opportunities. Technically speaking, a franchise differs from a business opportunity: The former typically involves a greater cost and more substantial relationship between the parties. For a user-friendly compilation of terms related to franchising, see the glossary on the Franchise Solutions Web site: *www.franchisesolutions.com/glossary.cfm*.

Examples of additional information include the following books and Web sites:

www.franchise-update.com

Comprehensive online access to magazines, articles, books, research reports, surveys, and other information dealing with hundreds of available franchise opportunities (established 1988).

Business Opportunities Handbook

Magazine-format publication that contains a wealth of information on more than 2,000 business opportunities and franchises available to the public. This publication lists businesses with investment requirements from $100 to $1 million and features success stories and analytical articles for people interested in purchasing a business opportunity. It is indexed alphabetically both by business category and by company name.

Franchise Opportunities Handbook [by Laverne Ludden, published by Park Avenue Publishing in conjunction with the U.S. Department of Commerce]

Contains information about the entire process of locating, evaluating, buying, and operating a franchised business.

www.franchise.com and www.franchisedirect.com

Other one-stop destinations for franchising information.

CHAPTER 4

Business Valuation Through the ARM Approach, Part I

Having covered the basics of classical business valuation and introduced the ARM approach and its related questionnaire and Five-Page Tool, we can now turn to the nuts and bolts of the valuation process. As we have seen, the ARM approach to business valuation is rooted in classical valuation procedures and techniques (collectively known as generally accepted valuation principles [GAVP]) and revolves around the ARM Approach Questionnaire and the Five-Page Tool. Having read through the questionnaire, you should find it easier to visualize how the valuation process can unfold.

The valuation process as it relates to the questionnaire calls for the following steps:

1. Describe the valuation environment (Section One).

2. Collect key information regarding the company and industry (Sections One and Two).

3. Analyze all information as gathered using the ARM Approach Questionnaire and Five-Page Tool (Sections Two and Three).

4. Estimate company value via each of the three ARM components (Section Four).

5. Weight these findings and present final value estimate (Section Five).

Naturally, there is some overlap between the steps and sections, but these are the primary sections for each step. This chapter begins the journey through the three major valuation components of the ARM approach, with the understanding that the information gathered throughout the valuation process will feed into the three components and their valuation estimates.

Practical Nature of the ARM Approach

Once again, the acronym ARM stands for

Adjusted cash flow

Rules of thumb

Market comparables

The premise of the ARM approach is that any company can be credibly valued through careful application of the valuation techniques related to each of these components. Although rooted in the three major approaches of classical business valuation (income, cost or asset, and market), the ARM approach has a definite practical orientation, as evidenced by the following operational guidelines:

Use multiples of cash flow rather than discount or capitalization rates.

Use rules of thumb.

Use private company sales data rather than public company sales data.

These procedures are optimally suited for valuing the typical privately held company because they reflect the valuation procedures commonly used in the buying and selling of such companies; that is, these techniques are used "in the trenches" by business brokers and entrepreneurs alike. They use such an approach not because it is simpler than other methods but because they are confident that it will lead to a credible and acceptable estimate of fair market value (FMV).

Adjusted Cash Flow

We begin with the first component of the ARM approach: adjusted cash flow (ACF). As noted throughout this book, it is no secret that a company's ability to generate cash flow for its owners is the primary determinant of business value. One must also be aware of the many variants of cash flow (e.g., ACF, earnings before interest and taxes [EBIT], net income, and net free cash flow) while recognizing its supreme importance in business valuation.

Specifically, the amount, timing, and probability of future cash flow is the most important assessment to make in valuing going concerns. Whether you are developing a multiple to apply against a derived cash flow measure or using a pool of recent market comparable sales results to develop an average cash flow multiple to apply against the subject company's derived cash flow, evaluating a company's ability to generate cash flow is critical for obtaining a credible, useful valuation result.

Modern financial theory as taught in universities around the world is based on the related concepts of net cash flow and the time value of money. In short, the value of any asset is equal to the present value of all future net cash inflows. In terms of business valuation, this means that the value of any business is equal to the present value of all future cash flows accruing to the owners. The greater the cash flow, the higher the value of the subject company. In a more subjective manner, the higher the "quality" of earnings, the greater the value.★

Naturally, if a business is not generating positive cash flow (or revenues, for that matter), then the valuator must turn to other options to obtain value estimates. For example, a business that is shut down probably will be viewed as an asset sale, meaning that the primary source of value is the tangible assets. In such situations, only minimal value attaches to the intangibles such as trade names and customer lists. Note that the term *asset sale* has another important, more common meaning. The same term is used to describe a type of deal structure (i.e., the sale of assets versus the sale of stock). Alternatively, a business with little or no tangible assets probably will be valued predominantly by evaluation of cash flow.

All Roads Lead to ACF†

Given the critical role of ACF, an introduction to its chief components is warranted. Proper calculation of ACF involves a careful inspection of the company's

---

★*The "quality" of earnings is a financial analysis term that refers to the "cleanliness" of a firm's profits or the extent by which a firm's profits (or cash flow in the realm of private-firm valuation) are realistically portrayed in the financial statements, i.e. reported results that are not misleading or do not tend to "overstate" or "understate" the true earnings capacity. For example, if 50% of a firm's profits (or cash flow) were generated by a one-time event (non-recurring, unusual in nature), the quality of these earnings would be suspect. Quality earnings may also refer to those that are generated by the core activities of the firm on a day to day basis and expected to continue into the future.*

†*Although the material presented in this chapter generally is sufficient for calculating ACF in the context of the ARM approach, additional insights and perspectives can be found on the CD-ROM. The novice valuator should read the entire book before approaching the material in the CD-ROM. More experienced readers may want to use the CD-ROM materials associated with each chapter as they progress through the book. Either way, the CD-ROM is as important as the book itself.*

income statement and various peripheral circumstances. For purposes of introduction, however, note that ACF is calculated as the sum of pretax income and
a series of addbacks including owner's compensation and benefits, depreciation
and amortization, interest expense, and any one-time, nonrecurring expenses
(or revenues). The basic formula is

$$
\begin{array}{rl}
 & \text{Pretax net income} \\
+ & \text{Owner's salary and payroll taxes} \\
+ & \text{Owner's perks} \\
+ & \text{Depreciation and amortization} \\
+ & \text{Interest expenses} \\
+/- & \underline{\text{One-time expenses and revenues}} \\
= & \text{ACF}
\end{array}
$$

In general, this figure represents the company's ability to generate cash-
equivalent benefits for a single owner of a business working full-time. Brokers
and entrepreneurs commonly apply derived multiples to this figure for purposes
of estimating business value. For purposes of perspective, note that the "average" multiple of ACF for the thousands of businesses sold through the VR
Business Brokers network has consistently hovered around 2.3 times, i.e., from
year to year, the average multiple has remained amazingly constant at or near
2.3 times ACF. It is also frequently used in rules of thumb and almost always
used in assessing market comp data. From the buyer's point of view, this figure
can also be interpreted as the amount of cash flow available for debt service, the
buyer's salary, and a return on the buyer's cash investment. Being comfortable
with properly calculating this number is critical for effective business valuation.

Before we analyze its specific components, a formal working definition for
ACF may be helpful: *ACF is the pretax, cash-equivalent benefits accruing to a single
owner working the business full-time.*

This interpretation spells out the boundaries or rules for the calculation and
provides a framework for evaluating and valuing companies. One of the most
important guidelines to follow when valuing companies is to remain consistent
in applying valuation techniques. The importance of consistently using the approach for calculating ACF outlined in this section is found in tradition and in
the way in which information is presented in market comp databases.

Not only do most business brokers and many business owners rely on this
approach, but most market comparable sales statistics are presented based on this
specific formulation of cash flow (e.g., VR Business Brokers, BIZCOMPS®).
Although different terms may be used to describe ACF (e.g., *seller's discretionary
cash* [SDC], *net,* or simply *cash flow*), they all describe the same collection of

components (pretax income plus addbacks). In addition, most SBA lenders utilize this same framework for evaluating the cash flow to debt service ratio involving business acquisition loans.

In other words, an important goal of business valuation is to compare apples with apples. Each specific method and each component within a method should be applied on a consistent basis, including the calculation of the all-important cash flow measure known as ACF.

Pretax Basis

As stated in our working definition, ACF consists of pretax, cash-equivalent benefits accruing to the owner of the subject business. Proper understanding of this framework calls for careful elaboration of its individual elements. The term *pretax* informs us that ACF is calculated before federal and state income taxes paid by the owner. Note that *pretax* does not refer to sales taxes on retail sales or other types of excise taxes. The meaning of *pretax* in this framework refers to income and payroll taxes applied to the owner. Thus, ACF is calculated from a base of pretax income (also called earnings before taxes [EBT]). In other words, to properly calculate the ACF for a business, the addbacks are added to a base of income before income taxes or payroll taxes incurred by the owner of the business.

It is standard practice among most business brokers to use a pretax measure of income as the base for ACF calculations. The logic is found in the fact that each business owner faces a unique tax picture. Depending on the owner's other sources of income and modes of ownership, a given pretax income would result in differing tax burdens from one owner to the next. One owner may have several years' worth of tax loss carryforwards; another may have substantial income from other sources such that the subject business income would be pushed into the highest tax bracket. One owner may be subject to the double taxation associated with C corporations; another may be a sole proprietorship using a Schedule C on an itemized personal tax return.

In short, given the diverse nature of tax situations faced by business owners, cash flow calculations based on the current owner's taxes probably would be irrelevant. On the other hand, certain other income approach valuation techniques (differing from the multiple of ACF method) call for application of an average or probable income tax burden (i.e., an after-tax cash flow measure is applicable). Notable among these other techniques is the discounted cash flow (DCF) technique, used primarily by professional appraisers with the time needed to generate this time-consuming valuation result and securities professionals involved in mergers and acquisitions (M&A).

In addition, the Small Business Administration (SBA) has begun to ask for or require business appraisals in support of the loan applications related to business acquisitions (see the CD-ROM section titled "SBA Business Valuation"). These appraisals are based in part on formulas that use an after-tax measure of cash flow (as per SBA recommended valuation techniques), such as the discounted future earnings method. Finally, it is essential that the business owner attempting to value a given company for acquisition be able to distinguish between calculating cash flow for valuation purposes (ACF on a pretax basis) and forecasting cash flow for operational purposes.

In other words, forecasting taxable income and the corresponding tax liability are an important part of business management. Ignoring or underestimating income tax liabilities is a common cause of business failure. Just because income taxes often are ignored for valuation purposes does not mean they can be ignored in running a business or even evaluating a business for purchase. Income taxes are a real cost of doing business.

Cash-Equivalent Basis

The phrase *cash-equivalent* can be important in specific valuation environments. The relevance of this term is found primarily in cases where the business owners give themselves, family members, friends, and even other companies free products or services. Although these cash-equivalent benefits are a type of perk, they differ from other perks in that there is no direct monetary implication; that is, the perk consists of products or services given away that otherwise could have been sold for money.

A relevant question here is how to value such giveaways. For example, should a piece of manufactured furniture given away to a parent be counted at cost or at retail value? An argument can be made either way. To value the gift at cost would represent the actual out-of-pocket expense incurred by the owner, whereas valuing the gift at market value would represent the foregone profit as well. In most cases, brokers and business owners conservatively value the gifts at cost. Regardless, the challenge is to properly assess this area in light of certain documentation problems. The owner may not account for such gifts directly in the income statement or tax return, so a certain amount of "fishing" is necessary. In a buyer-versus-seller framework, the actual amount credited to ACF for such gifts is subject to debate and negotiation. In many cases, the dollar value of such gifts is small and can reasonably be ignored.

Another case in which a cash-equivalent estimate may be necessary pertains to the owner's health care insurance package. If the owner is covered under a collective health insurance package with other employees, it is prudent to take a proportionate share of the actual dollar expense for such health care coverage. In some cases, however, the owner may have a health condition that necessitates more expensive coverage, and this costly coverage is grouped together with the health care insurance cost of the entire company. In other words, a proportionate share may not be a fair share in cash-equivalent terms. Fortunately, this situation is rare.

Single-Owner Basis

Next, note that the definition of ACF refers to a figure generated by a single owner working the business full-time. If two different businesses are operating under two different ownership configurations, the figure must be adjusted to facilitate comparisons. In other words, the concept of cash flow known as ACF and used by most professional business brokers always refers to a single owner working the business full-time.

This criterion has several implications for assessing a company's ACF. First, a single owner working full-time is just that; it is not a single owner working part-time or a husband-and-wife team working full-time. Adjustments must be made to bring the measure back to the full-time single-owner framework. For example, if there are two owners (e.g., partners, each with a 50 percent ownership interest and each working full-time), then one subtracts a reasonable replacement salary for one of the two owners from the ACF figure generated by both partners working together full-time.

In other words, the company's initial ACF calculation includes both owners' cash-equivalent, pretax benefits (salary, payroll tax, perks, bonuses, and other benefits typically included in ACF) followed by a subtraction of an amount equal to the probable cost of replacing one of the partners. Note that if a second owner can be replaced with a salary only (i.e., without paying the replacement manager the same benefits as the original partner), then only the salary should be deducted.

It may already be clear to you that such an adjustment is subjective to the extent that one must decide which owner to replace and what the appropriate replacement salary will be. A general guideline is for the buyer to subtract a replacement salary for the specific owner to be replaced with a new employee after purchase of the company. Once this decision has been made, the replacement salary level should be based on the hiring of a new employee to fulfill the precise function and provide the same services as the replaced owner. However, a common approach used by business brokers is to subtract a replacement salary for the owner who can be replaced at the lowest cost (i.e., replace the owner who would generate the smallest reduction in the company's presented ACF). Current compensation levels by industry and geographic location are available at many Internet sites, including *www.bls.gov*. Other sources provide similar services on a fee basis, for example, *www.salarysource.com*.

A second common type of adjustment related to the single-owner premise concerns family members. There are two general situations that necessitate such an adjustment. First, family members may be working substantial hours at the business without being compensated, particularly at family-run businesses such as restaurants, convenience stores, and car washes. In this case, as in the two-partner situation described earlier, a replacement salary must be subtracted from ACF to reflect the work effort and contribution made by these uncompensated family members.

Practically speaking, it may be difficult for a buyer to know for sure how many family members are involved and precisely how many hours they are working without proper compensation reflected in the books. For specific types of businesses, such as restaurants and convenience stores, it is prudent for the buyer to ask the seller how many employees are working at the business. Furthermore, it is prudent to ask this question more than once and to ask the owner whether all family members are being paid a fair market-based salary. The optimal approach may be to ask the seller to answer such questions in writing to solicit full disclosure. Although this approach may appear to be merely a due diligence tactic, it is important to realize that a buyer's due diligence can lead to a reduced purchase price, reflecting discoveries that affect the company's ACF and hence its FMV.

A similar adjustment can be made for family members who are underpaid for their services. For example, if a family member is acting as a full-time night manager and is being paid only minimum wage, a new owner probably would have to pay a new employee a substantially higher wage. Obtaining this information is easier said than done, but such an inquiry is justifiable if the buyer's goal is to pay FMV based on a correctly calculated ACF figure.

The third common adjustment related to the single-owner premise concerns family members who are being paid a salary and benefits without actually working at the business. In this case, the ACF should be increased by the amount paid to the phantom employee, including the cash-equivalent amount of any benefits accruing to this party. This practice is common in businesses in which the owner pays a son or daughter a handsome salary while the child is at college or pays his parents a salary after retirement. Most business owners volunteer this information to qualified buyers (after they have signed a confidentiality agreement) because of its favorable impact on the overall ACF generated by the company. The challenge for the buyer is to determine its validity by establishing that the family member is not working at the business.

It may also be the case that a family member is working at the business and is receiving compensation beyond the normal market level of compensation. In other words, certain family members may provide limited assistance while being paid a full-time salary. This assessment can be difficult, but an interpretation of the company's operations can generate material findings that aid the buyer in determining the company's true value.

Remember once again that the goal of such fact-finding analysis is to allow the buyer to use a framework that can be applied consistently from one business opportunity to the next. Without such consistency, the valuation results from company to company are misleading.

Full-Time Basis

The next major premise of the ACF definition is that the owner is working full-time. Again, if owners work less than full-time or on an absentee basis, the ACF figure, so important in estimating a company's worth, must be adjusted. For businesses with absentee owners, the most common adjustment is to add back the salary and benefits earned by and paid to the company's top manager (assuming that the manager is working full-time).

A second approach for handling the absentee owner situation is to apply a higher multiple to the company's ACF without adding back the manager's compensation package. The difficulty here lies in determining the appropriate increase in the selected multiple to be applied to ACF.

If the owner is working only part-time (in between full-time and absentee), the most common adjustment is to increase the cash flow by an amount representing the probable reduction in payroll expense associated with the new owner working full-time instead of part-time (i.e., if the new owner works full-time, it is possible that one of the current employees could be replaced or work fewer hours, thus decreasing payroll expense and increasing ACF).

ACF Component Analysis

The valuation case study in Chapter Eight contains an example of the process related to calculating ACF under situation-specific circumstances (as does the "Case Study Analysis" section on the CD-ROM). At this juncture, it is useful to provide examples of where to locate the necessary information to generate estimates of ACF. Given our working definition of this commonly used measure of cash flow (i.e., it represents the pretax cash-equivalent benefits accruing to a single owner working the business full-time), we turn now to a closer look at each of the ACF components.

Pretax Income

The starting point for ACF analysis is the company's pretax income. A measure of pretax income can be found on the company's income statement or tax return. For ACF calculations, the typical starting point is the company's income statement. Given the variety of presentation formats accountants use to prepare compiled statements, it is important to carefully review the individual line entries near the bottom of the income statement. Many different headings and subheadings and different ordering of entries make interpretation of pretax income challenging in certain cases. Make sure that your pretax income is in fact pretax. Occasionally one encounters federal and state income tax payments under the heading "Other Expenses." Such payments should be added back to arrive at a true pretax income. Comparison of the income statement results with the federal income tax return data can also aid in determining the actual pretax income of the company (see Schedule M-1 in corporate returns for complete insight into this calculation).

Accounting for Book Versus Tax Purposes

Being aware of the differences between accounting for book purposes as opposed to tax purposes is essential for a full understanding of measures related to cash flow. Book accounting almost always differs from tax accounting because of differences in the manner in which revenues and expenses are recognized. For example, it may be possible to use straight-line depreciation of fixed assets for book purposes and some sort of accelerated depreciation for tax purposes (or vice versa), which would lead to two different bottom lines based on different depreciation deductions.

In general, the goals of accounting for tax versus book purposes are conflicting: Most businesses would like to generate the maximum profit on the books (to impress a potential buyer, for example) while minimizing taxable income to reduce their tax obligations. In addition, it is common for companies to postpone recognition of substantial sales into the next tax year to reduce taxable income in the present year. For book purposes, the company may recognize the sale in the current year, thus conflicting with the reported revenues and profits on the tax return.

Business valuators should not be surprised if tax returns differ from financial statements. Attempting to learn why they differ is an important exercise in developing a full understanding of the company's ability to generate positive cash flow. Most federal income tax returns for corporations and partnerships contain a schedule that reconciles the difference between taxable income and book income (Schedule M-1). Review this section carefully if it is available.

The next decision to make regarding pretax income (after deciding to use the income statement rather than the tax return) concerns which specific measure of pretax income to use. Realizing that each accountant may choose to organize a company's income statement in a slightly different fashion, there may be one or two different measures of pretax income. In other words, there may be a distinction between pretax operating income and pretax income overall, with the latter accounting for items such as gain or loss on the sale of assets and possibly interest income or dividend income from investments.

In most cases, the pretax income overall is greater than pretax operating income because of interest income or "other" income. The decision as to which measure of pretax income to use should boil down to whether the extra income or expense (or gain or loss) included in the overall pretax income is expected to continue for the new owner. If this extra income or expense is not expected to accrue to the new owner, then the pretax operating income figure should be used.

Owner's Salary and Payroll Taxes

Once pretax income is determined, the addbacks can be analyzed and included in the ACF calculation. The first and most important addback is normally the owner's salary and payroll taxes. As discussed earlier, this figure should reflect the owner's compensation in the form of wages, salary, dividends, bonuses, and related payroll expenses such as unemployment, Social Security, Medicare, and Medicaid for a single owner working the business full-time. Note that for a sole proprietor there is no such addback because there is no salary paid to a sole proprietor (i.e., all profit flows to the owner as compensation). On the other hand, S-corporation entities must pay the owner–operator a "reasonable salary" to prevent the company from avoiding payroll taxes. Because limited-liability company (LLC) members must pay tax on all distributions, high salary levels are less common. Most corporations (S and C) and LLCs pay their active owners a salary and incur payroll expenses.

The operational challenge in determining the precise amount of salary and payroll tax to add back is to be able to locate the line item on the income statement that contains the owner's salary (may also be called "officer salary"). There may be a clearly defined line titled "owner's salary," or it may be buried in salaries and wages in general. It is important to determine the precise amount because it often constitutes a large portion of the company's overall ACF. Calculating the amount of payroll tax paid in relation to the owner can be difficult if all payroll taxes are lumped together (for all employees, including the owner), and the sliding scale or ceiling (maximum payment) of FICA payroll tax compounds the difficulty. It is best to ask the company's accountant to provide this information precisely to avoid potential understatements or overstatements of ACF.

Owner's Perks

The next addback is owner's perks, which can range from extremely important to practically nil, depending on the nature of the company and the aggressiveness of the owner in taking business deductions for discretionary or personal expenditures. Even though most perks are of a noncash nature (they are not received by the owner in the form of cash), they do represent benefits accruing to the owner that are paid for with cash. The decision as to whether a certain expense is considered an addback revolves around the nature of the expense: Is it of a personal or discretionary nature?

Personal expenses are expenditures that directly and exclusively benefit the owner, such as car payments for the owner's automobile. Discretionary expenditures are those that are not directly related to the company's day-to-day business; that is, they are not needed to generate the revenues and profits that the company has earned. An example of a discretionary expenditure would be travel by a gift shop owner to a destination that is known for similar gift shops. Although the owner may pick up a useful idea or two, it is unlikely that this trip was necessary to generate the company's current level of revenues and cash flow (as opposed to a trip to the industry's most important trade show where the bulk of purchasing for the upcoming Christmas season takes place). Of course, an expense may be both personal and discretionary, as this latter example illustrates. The travel was both personal and discretionary. Further examples of typical perks include the following:

Personal auto expenses (monthly payments, gas, and repairs)

Insurance (auto, health, life)

Miscellaneous credit card purchases

Excessive travel and entertainment

Second home construction, boat, or plane

Payments to babysitters or nannies

Giveaway of company products or services as gifts

Contributions to charitable organizations

Purchase of computer, security system, furniture, and other home office
expenses

Frequent flier mile benefits

Pension plan contributions

Bonus or incentive payments

When evaluating these perks, it is important to verify their existence as best
as possible. It is easy to make a claim about a certain expenditure when it is not
necessary to provide support (e.g., invoice, entry into general ledger), so the
valuator must use caution and common sense in adding such expenses into cash
flow. Recall that other addbacks or deductions may be necessary as they relate
to family members. For example, it may be common to include payments to
children who do not actively work or who are overpaid as perks. The categorization is not important, but proper calculation of the overall ACF figure is essential for proper valuation.

Depreciation and Amortization Expenses

In the typical evaluation of a company's ACF, it is the norm to add back the expenses related to depreciation and amortization. Depreciation is to tangible assets as amortization is to intangible assets. In regard to calculating cash flow, the
important point to consider is that both depreciation and amortization expenses
are noncash deductions against revenues; that is, they are not directly associated
with a period-specific cash outlay. In other words, depreciation and amortization expenses reduce operating income but are not a use of cash in the relevant
time period.

Some entrepreneurs question the addback of depreciation because they recognize that there was or may still be a cash outlay associated with paying for the
fixed asset. Despite this correct perception, it is standard valuation procedure to
add depreciation back into cash flow for purposes of establishing the company's
generation of ACF. To the extent that all relevant market comparable sales statistic databases (BIZCOMPS®, VR Business Brokers, Pratt's Stats) use cash flow
figures that include these addbacks, the valuator must also do so despite any perceived shortcomings (only the IBA database excludes depreciation and amortization expenses from its cash flow figure, defining their cash flow figure as
"annual earnings before owner's compensation expense, interest expense, and
income tax expense.").

On the other hand, the experienced entrepreneur recognizes that owners of asset-intensive companies such as manufacturing companies face annual expenditures necessary to maintain the productive capacity of the business or possibly augment its production capabilities. Such capital expenditures must come out of the company's future cash flows (if not borrowed), so it is prudent from a planning perspective to incorporate future cash outflows associated with capital expenditures into the company's business plan or cash flow forecast. Also note that the most sophisticated and academically correct valuation technique (discounted cash flow analysis) does account for capital expenditures in the cash flow analysis (as well as working capital infusions and corporate income taxes). The bottom line is that both depreciation and amortization are added back into cash flow in arriving at the company's ACF.

Regarding amortization expense, intangible assets such as software or patents may be relevant in evaluating cash flow. However, the most substantial impact of amortization expense is found when the subject company was acquired by the current owner as a sale of assets (as opposed to a sale of stock). In other words, if a company is purchased as an asset purchase, both buyer and seller must agree on an allocation of the purchase price to five separate IRS-stipulated classes. Such allocation affects both the seller's immediate tax obligation and the buyer's future tax obligations.

In the case of an asset sale, the difference between the FMV of the identifiable tangible assets (accounts receivable, inventory, furniture, fixtures, equipment, land, and buildings) and the purchase price is allocated to one or more intangible accounts (e.g., goodwill, trade name, covenant not to compete, customer list) that are subsequently amortized. This is another accounting issue that is handled differently for book purposes versus tax purposes. For tax purposes, all intangible assets must be amortized over fifteen years (no exceptions), whereas for book purposes they must be amortized over their useful lives (subject to the accountant's assumptions, ranging from as short as two years to as long as forty years). Miscellaneous startup costs may also be amortized, thus generating amortization expense.

Overall, the valuator typically must add back both depreciation and amortization expense to arrive at ACF. Noting that the valuation process is distinct from the operational process, savvy entrepreneurs will know to incorporate anticipated future expenditures related to capital goods such as furniture, fixtures, and equipment into their overall cash flow forecasting and analysis.

Another interesting topic related to amortization expense is goodwill. Many businesspeople think of goodwill in terms of a company's relationship with its customers; that is, a company with good service generates goodwill among its customers. Although this is an accurate interpretation of goodwill, there are several others. For example, under the so-called excess earnings method for estimating business value, a company is worth the sum of the FMV of its tangible assets and its goodwill. In this scenario, goodwill is calculated as the capitalized value of the company's "above-average" earnings or rate of return. In other words, the goodwill is a reflection of the fact that the subject company is earning a return greater than the norm for investments of similar risk. Thus, goodwill in this instance is the company's ability to earn above-normal profits. Of course, these above-normal profits may arise from exceptional service, but in general these are two distinct interpretations of goodwill.

The final interpretation of goodwill relates to a company's balance sheet. GAAP does not allow a company to estimate the value of its goodwill and then place this figure on the balance sheet. The historical cost principle makes such an entry impossible under GAAP. However, in the case of a business acquisition, goodwill can be placed on the postacquisition balance sheet, reflecting the excess of the purchase price paid over the FMV of the identifiable tangible assets. In practice, this excess may be allocated to other intangible assets besides goodwill (e.g., customer base, trade name).

One thing is sure, however. If the asset called goodwill shows up on a company's balance sheet, this means that the subject company was purchased by its current owner rather than started from scratch or the company has purchased another company in its history and entered a portion of the purchase price as goodwill on its balance sheet for future period amortization. In other words, if you encounter goodwill as an asset, you know that the current owner purchased the business from a prior owner or the company has purchased another company in the past via an asset acquisition. If nothing else, this should prompt you to discuss this transaction with the owner to gain information about its purchase price multiples. The CD-ROM contains a more thorough discussion of goodwill and intangible assets in general in two different sections ("Asset or Cost Approach to Business Valuation" and "Accounting Primer").

Interest Expense

As explained earlier, each company has a unique capital structure (remember that *capital* in this sense refers to financial capital, not physical capital such as equipment) as evidenced by its combination of debt (liabilities) and equity (investment in stock and retained earnings). Because of the unique nature of a given ownership's debt to equity relationship, it is standard valuation practice to add back all interest expense related to a company's debt (with the exception of interest expense directly related to the sale of product).

The general idea is to determine the overall amount of cash flow (cash-equivalent benefits) accruing to the owner from which an owner-specific amount of interest expense may be supported in addition to paying a reasonable salary to the owner and earning a positive return on the invested cash. In this regard, the interest expense paid by the subject company is available to a new owner to use as she sees fit (she may pay all cash for the business and incur no debt or may borrow 90 percent of the purchase price and incur substantially more interest expense).

On the income statement, interest expense may be separated from other operational expenses (on income statements that include segments called earnings before interest and taxes [EBIT]) or included with all other operational (i.e., general and administrative) expenses (typically in alphabetical order) under the title "Interest Expense." Another common location is under the heading "Other Income and Expense." It may even be found under "Cost of Goods Sold" or under the heading "Credit Card Expense."

As mentioned earlier, there may be more than one way to handle interest revenue or interest income. To the extent that interest expense is added back, interest income or revenue should be subtracted based on similar logic. The key question is whether the interest revenue will continue under the new ownership. If a similar situation eventually will arise for the incoming owner, then it makes sense to include the interest income (i.e., do not subtract it from ACF). Professional business appraisers must be much more strict in handling this issue. For the typical entrepreneur seeking to establish a credible yet loose estimate of FMV, however, simply being consistent in handling the issue is sufficient. If the buyer expects a similar operating scenario after the purchase is concluded, keeping the interest revenue as part of ACF is a plausible assumption to make in reaching the final ACF result.

One-Time Expenses or Revenues

Next to the decision as to what constitutes a fair perk, the handling of one-time expenses (possibly one-time revenues) is one of the most controversial elements of calculating ACF. Generally speaking, if an expense or a revenue is of a one-time nature, it should not be included in the company's ACF. In the world of GAAP, these items are called "extraordinary" gains or losses and are defined as having the following two characteristics:

Unusual in nature
Infrequent in occurrence

The term "unusual in nature" means that the event is highly abnormal and either unrelated to or only incidentally related to the ordinary and typical activities of the company given the environment in which the entity operates. The term "infrequent in occurrence" means that the event is highly unlikely to occur again in the foreseeable future, given the environment within which the company operates. What is extraordinary for one company may be ordinary for another; there is a subjective element involved in the final determination.

In the context of business valuation and business brokerage, inclusion of such expenses (or exclusion of revenues) is subject to debate and negotiation. In many instances, the buyer and seller of a business may agree that the subject company is worth a certain multiple of ACF (after assessing the unique characteristics and features of the company, the industry, and the economy in general) and then end up disagreeing on what the relevant or precise cash flow is because of items such as extraordinary expenses or revenues.

One example of a potential dispute might arise in the event of a flood. If the flood occurs along the Mississippi River in an area that is routinely flooded, such expenses should not be considered one-time expenses, whereas if this flood occurs in an area of the country where floods are extremely rare, the expenses may be considered one-time expenses and added back into the ACF calculation (similar to the impact of a blizzard in Arizona as opposed to northern Minnesota).

The following are further examples of such one-time expenses:

Repairs resulting from a customer driving a car through the front window of a retail company

Advertising flyers that were never delivered because of fraud or because the service provider filed for bankruptcy

Moving expenses for relocation of operations

Startup costs of second or new retail location

Embezzlement or theft of cash or major assets

In general, the expense must meet both criteria (i.e., unusual and infrequent) to be added back into ACF. Note that writing down accounts receivable year in and year out is not an extraordinary expense, but if one major customer accounting for 33 percent of total revenues files bankruptcy after ten years of steady sales, this may be an addback (provided that these lost revenues could be easily replaced by other customers, which typically would not be the case). Common sense and credibility should ultimately be the determining factor as to whether expenses such as these can be included in cash flow.

Another example concerns the gain or loss associated with the sale of company assets. Certain businesses routinely buy and sell assets as part of their normal operating procedures. For example, a company that continuously replaces equipment or trucks to maintain state-of-the-art capabilities will incur these gains and losses every year without fail. For such a company, these gains or losses are not extraordinary and should be included in the company's ACF results. Another company such as a small florist would not be buying and selling equipment regularly. Thus, if this company sold its truck for a substantial gain or a loss, these results should be taken out of the ACF calculation (i.e., pretax income should be adjusted accordingly).

On the revenue side, it is rare to see a business presented for sale at a price based on an ACF that includes a deduction of one-time revenues. Most sellers argue that there is always another customer that would make a similar purchase under similar conditions, thus precluding this type of subtraction from ACF. Examples of one-time sales include the following:

Dramatic sales increase resulting from a large one-time event such as retail sales for businesses located near the location of a Super Bowl or World Series

One-time contract of a magnitude equal to the entire amount of business conducted in the entire previous year

One-time, unique services provided by an attorney or accountant (e.g., an attorney helping a client file for bankruptcy or accounting services related to preparation of paperwork for terminating the operations of a company; in both cases, the relevant customer will no longer be around to generate revenues)

Unrelated Expenses and Revenues

This category is similar to personal expenses in that they are not directly related to the subject company and its generation of revenues and profits. It is not uncommon to see a business owner start a second business using the foundation of the first business to provide working capital and even employees. In such an event, it is helpful if the owner maintains a second set of books from the beginning. However, this does not always happen because of the associated costs (money and time).

Regardless of the circumstances, it is necessary to separate the revenues and expenses of the second company when evaluating the first company. If the second company is related to the first company or they could be sold together, there may be a rationale to keep their records in one set of statements. Even then, however, it is necessary to subtract the one-time startup expenses to generate the commonly accepted ACF measure.

Importance of the ACF Calculation

It should be clear now that there are numerous variations of cash flow measurements as used by business valuation professionals. In general, the term *cash flow* relates to some measure of net proceeds accruing to ownership, that is, a measure of spending power generated by the company for the owner. In practice, the actual measures of cash flow range from a bottom-line accounting measure such as net income (used in P/E ratios for publicly traded companies) to more inclusive measures such as EBIT or the complex measure known as net free cash flow (used in discounted cash flow analysis, also typically for larger or publicly traded companies). This latter measure takes into account items such as working capital investments, capital expenditures and income taxes, whereas EBIT, EBITDA, and ACF do not.

As discussed later in this chapter, alternative interpretations of the general concept of cash flow also exist, such as cash flow from operations as found on a statement of cash flows (GAAP-required financial statement) and cash flow as calculated in cash flow forecasting for effective business and financial management.

For the typical business owner, however, ACF is the most pertinent and useful measure. Regardless of the term used to describe this measure (e.g., "net," "seller's discretionary cash," "annualized cash flow," "recast earnings," or "adjusted cash flow"), the calculation behind the term generally remains the same. ACF (as used throughout this book) is calculated as follows:

$$
\begin{array}{rl}
& \text{Pretax net income} \\
+ & \text{Owner's salary and payroll taxes} \\
+ & \text{Owner's perks} \\
+ & \text{Depreciation and amortization} \\
+ & \text{Interest expenses} \\
+/- & \text{One-time expenses or revenues} \\
\hline
= & \text{ACF}
\end{array}
$$

ACF and Other Cash Flow Applications

In conclusion, ACF is the most commonly applied measure of cash used in valuing privately held companies. Most professional business brokers use this figure as an important component of their valuation analysis. The majority of small privately held businesses sell for one to three times ACF (*small* being defined generally as companies with revenues as high as approximately $3 million and ACF as high as approximately $300,000 per year), recognizing that the higher the cash flow, the higher the multiple.

Astute readers will notice that different revenue and cash flow amounts are presented to characterize different sizes or segments of businesses in regard to business valuation. This variation is intentional and is meant to illustrate that there are no absolutes in this area, and every business valuation must be based on its own unique facts and circumstances. There is an empirical relationship between the size of ACF and the average multiples. When the ACF lies between $250,000 and $500,000 or so, the relevant multiple range rises from one to three to two to four (between $500,000 and $1 million, the average multiple rises to approximately three to six times ACF, and so on).

Just as there are many different versions of cash flow, the term also has several different meanings and applications in the business world, including our current usage as a measure of benefits accruing to the owner of a business. Overall, cash flow can refer to each of the following four specific applications.

ACF for Business Valuation

As explained earlier, ACF is the sum of pretax income and various addbacks that represent the amount of pretax benefits accruing to an owner–operator. ACF is the primary determinant of business value for the typical privately held company.

Cash Flow and the Statement of Cash Flows

The statement of cash flows is a GAAP-required financial statement that breaks down changes in a company's cash balance over the course of a year into cash flows generated by (or used in) operations, investing activities, and financing activities. For example, the first part of this statement lists the cash flow generated by the company's day-to-day operations by documenting the switch from accrual basis accounting to cash basis accounting. Overall, this statement clarifies major sources and applications of cash between operating, investing, and financing activities.

For example, a specific statement of cash flows might show that the $200,000 increase in the company's cash balances over the course of the year was generated by the following overall changes:

Cash flow provided by (used in) operations	$300,000
Cash flow provided by (used in) investing activities	($200,000)
Cash flow provided by (used in) financing activities	$100,000

Each section would contain numerous details describing the major activities that transpired over the year. Cash flow provided by operations is calculated by transforming the company's accrual basis net income into a cash basis net inflow amount (e.g., an increase in accounts receivable during the year would be associated with a reduction in accrual basis net income because sales have been recorded for which no cash was received). In other words, net income includes sales for which no cash was received. Investing activities involve primarily the purchase and sale of long-term, fixed assets (e.g., capital expenditures). A negative number here shows that the company has invested in new fixed assets. Finally, the financing section clarifies changes associated with debt or equity issuances or retirements (e.g., money borrowed from a bank or repaid to a bank). An example of the finer points associated with this statement is found in the fact that interest expense is not a financing activity but an operating activity. Overall, this statement can answer questions such as the following:

If a company is profitable, why is it always carrying a low cash balance?

If a company is operating at a loss, how can it generate positive cash flows from operations?

Is the company making the necessary expenditures on capital goods to modernize and remain competitive?

Did the company maintain its operations by selling off assets?

How much cash was raised through the sale of stock or borrowed money?

Did the company reduce its overall debt burden during the period under consideration?

Although most privately held businesses do not prepare a statement of cash flows, companies with reviewed or audited statements or companies that rely on bank financing in the form of a line of credit often have their accountants prepare this illuminating statement.

Net Free Cash Flow and Discounted Cash Flow Analysis

Net free cash flow, as used in discounted cash flow analysis, is based on the time value of money. This measure is similar to ACF in that it represents cash flows accruing to the owners, but it is broader in scope in that it addresses changes in working capital infusions and capital expenditures and income taxes (thus it is an after-tax measure of cash flow). A business is worth the present value of all future net free cash flows accruing to equity holders (interest expense is not added back) over the life of the investment, including the terminal value of the company (value of business at the end of the holding period net of transaction costs and taxes upon hypothetical sale).

Discounted cash flow analysis is used by M&A valuation professionals as the primary valuation technique for evaluating publicly traded companies. It is gaining in popularity among valuators active in middle-market scenarios as well. Perhaps most telling of all is the increased acceptance of DCF analysis by the courts and the IRS. Even the SBA refers to this method generically in one of its standard operating procedures related to acquisition financing and business valuation. The credibility of the results generated by this method is a function of the many assumptions, estimates, and other subjective elements of the discounting process. Not only must *all* future cash flows be forecasted, but a discount rate must be developed to match the particulars of the subject company and industry.

Cash Flow in Cash Flow Forecasting and Budgeting

Cash flow forecasting calls for a detailed analysis of every cash inflow and outflow over the relevant future period of time (e.g., one year in the case of a business acquisition financing loan via SBA guarantee; see the CD-ROM section titled "SBA Business Valuation" for more information). Various levels of detail are possible when forecasting future cash flows, which in every case revolve around the important forecast for future sales revenue generation. Also referred to as budgeting, cash flow forecasting is essential for both managing a business properly via cash management and for helping prove to a bank that a loan will be repaid as part of a business acquisition or for other purposes such as expansion through advertising and new facilities or simply for working capital purposes.

Relationships Between Cash Flow Concepts

These various cash flow concepts are interrelated; for example, a formal cash flow forecast is the foundation of discounted cash flow analysis based on net free cash flow. The net free cash flow is calculated by adjusting the actual cash inflows and outflows in the manner prescribed by this valuation technique (e.g., projected capital expenditures are backed out of the forecasted cash flow generated by operations). This cash flow from operations is very similar to the upper portion of the statement of cash flows, providing another example of how these concepts and measures are linked in practice. For purposes of valuing businesses, however, the most important measure of cash flow is ACF.

Business Valuation

Understanding the many factors that drive the multiple applicable to the company's ACF up or down is a critical step in arriving at a credible and accurate estimate of FMV. Later chapters address these many factors in detail under an array of industry-specific conditions.

Restating the definition of this important measure once again, ACF is a measure of the pretax, cash-equivalent benefits accruing to a single owner working the business full-time.

Taking this concept full circle allows a second interpretation of the ACF figure as the approximate amount of pretax, cash-equivalent resources available to a new owner to service debt and pay taxes, pay the owner a reasonable salary, and earn a return on the owner's cash investment.

This interpretation often is expanded to include a component for replacing or maintaining the fixed assets (i.e., provide for necessary capital expenditures). Such an addition makes intuitive sense in that ACF calculations include an addback for depreciation expense (because of its noncash nature). Note that despite the logic supporting a reduction of ACF by required capital expenditures (i.e., they reduce the cash flow available to the owner), common practice and tradition dictate that such a reduction not be made. The logic behind this exclusion is similar to the tax situation whereby each owner undertakes a unique course of action after the closing (lease versus buy decisions, for example).

Overall, an owner's handling of business structure for tax purposes (C-corporation versus LLC), capital expenditures (labor versus machine, lease versus buy), and the company's capital structure (debt versus equity) is entirely personal and subject to the unique preferences of the particular owner. Once the ACF has been determined via this framework, the real work begins. It is necessary to evaluate the subject company and its operations from a historical, future-oriented, and comparative perspective to estimate the proper multiple to apply against the calculated ACF.

Financial statement analysis and industry research must be conducted to help gauge the company's value. Whether a multiple is determined or a discount or capitalization rate is developed, the fundamental relationship between risk and value will help form the value conclusion. The more stable and predictable and the less risky the future cash flows, the more they are worth. Conversely, the more unstable, unpredictable, and risky they are, the less they are worth.

Overall, an assessment must be made of the subject company and its cash flow–generated value in comparison with what the average business of this type and size would be worth. After the ACF is calculated, the applicable multiple must be applied to generate the first estimate of value under the ARM approach. Once this multiple-driven estimate of value is determined, the valuator can move on to the second component of the ARM approach related to rules of thumb. To review how the move is made from one component to the next in practice, return to the ARM Approach Questionnaire in Chapter Three.

The CD-ROM section titled "Asset or Cost Approach to Business Valuation" contains an overview of a commonly used yet theoretically dubious technique called the excess earnings method. Interestingly, this method is based on both a measure of cash flow and the value of tangible assets. This hybrid method was created by the IRS but is recommended for use by the IRS only when no other method is applicable (more details on the CD-ROM). In connection to the ARM approach, the excess earnings method could be considered a required technique for professional practices given its high prevalence in valuations for this type of business. The courts have grown accustomed to seeing and using this method in divorce proceedings in particular, so familiarity with this technique may be worthwhile.

We conclude this chapter with a look at one of several possible approaches for estimating the proper multiple to apply to the company's derived ACF figure. The Snowden technique is user-friendly and attempts to assess the pertinent valuation factors in a mathematical format that generates a proxy of value in the form of a cash flow multiple.

APPENDIX

Example of an Income Approach Valuation Method: The Snowden Technique

To conclude our coverage of cash flow and the income approach, an example is in order. In his book *The Complete Guide to Buying a Business* (AMACOM, 1994), Richard Snowden cites a dozen areas that should be considered when using an income approach method he calls capitalization of income valuation. He recommends giving each factor a rating of 0 to 5, with 5 being the most positive score. The average of these factors is referred to as the *capitalization rate* (technically a multiple, not a capitalization rate), which is multiplied by the buyer's discretionary cash (ACF?) to determine the market value of the business.

The factors Snowden uses are very similar to the factors listed in Chapter Five (and on the CD-ROM "Rules of Thumb" section) that relate to determining the relevant multiple for a given range of values suggested by various actual rules of thumb. The specific factors recommended by Snowden are as follows:

Owner's reason for selling

Length of time the company has been in business

Length of time the current owner has owned the business

Degree of risk

Profitability

Location

Growth history

Competition

Entry barriers

Future potential for the industry

Customer base

Technology

After deriving the cap rate (multiple), it is necessary to come up with a figure for buyer's discretionary cash which, according to Snowden, is 75 percent of the annual owner benefit (seller's discretionary cash for one year, calculated in the same manner as the process used to calculate ACF). One can only speculate why 75 percent of the owner benefit is used, but by reducing the owner benefit by 25 percent it can be argued that this measure becomes an after-tax measure of cash flow rather than a pretax measure. Alternatively, one could argue that this is simply a conservative move to account for the difficulties in passing ownership of a given company to new owners.

In any case, simply multiply the owner benefit figure by the capitalization rate (determined once again by adding up the 0 to 5 ratings for each category and then dividing by 12) to estimate FMV for the company. For example, if the twelve categories and their scores add up to 36 (as would be the case if each category received a value of 3), a multiple of 3 is derived (36/12 = 3). Note that a multiple of 3 is synonymous with a capitalization rate of 33 percent. Given that the buyer's discretionary cash is pretax, this cap rate is interpreted as being a pretax figure. It appears that an average rating of 3 implies an above-average rank (for a 0 to 5 scale, a 2.5 would be the mean or average rating), which means that a multiple of 3 is a slightly above-average multiple.

Based on market comp data from sources such as the IBA and VR Business

Brokers, this appears to be a good reflection of reality for businesses because the VR Business Brokers average multiple of cash flow has been consistently in the vicinity of 2.2 to 2.4 times ACF, and the IBA database has typically generated an average multiple of about 2.5 for businesses with ACF less than $500,000. It is critical to understand that this method does not work for all types and sizes of companies. Importantly, if the subject company generates an ACF of $1 million or more, this model tends to understate its value. The higher the cash flow, the higher the multiple.

As your business valuation skills grow, you may be able to adapt this model to larger businesses by increasing the derived multiple figure. For example, instead of a 0 to 5 scale, you might decide that a 3 to 7 scale is proper for businesses with $1 million to $2 million or more in ACF. Alternatively, you might multiply the derived multiple using the 0 to 5 scale by a premium factor to account for the larger size. You could locate a credible database such as BIZ-COMPS® or Pratt's Stats and verify the percentage increase in the average multiple for businesses with $1 million to $2 million in ACF as compared with businesses with $500,000 or less in ACF. If the difference turned out to be 25 percent, you could simply multiply the derived multiple by 1.25 to obtain a more accurate multiple. Don't forget the importance of being consistent in your valuation efforts (to compare apples with apples) and to support your derivations with facts.

Other methods besides the Snowden approach have been created for developing a multiple to apply to cash flow on a consistent basis from one business to the next. For example, Jeff Jones of Certified Business Appraisers in Houston, Texas, has developed a table with ten factors that are weighted from most important to least important and given a score of 0 to 3. The premise of his system is that a small business will not sell for more than 3 times ACF. Although this may be generally true for businesses with an ACF of less than $100,000 or so, the actual market comp data from various databases contradict this proposition. To the extent that the average multiple of cash flow within the VR Business Brokers database has hovered around 2.3 or 2.4, it should not be a surprise that some businesses would sell for more than 3 times ACF (because others sell for less than 1 times ACF). Jones brought the results down to a 1 to 3 scale by dividing the total points by the sum of the weighting factors (10 + 9 + 8 + 7 + 6 +5 +4 + 3 +2 + 1 = 55). For example, if the total points were 110, the final multiple would be 2 (110/55).

Note that this system easily could be adjusted to account for higher multiples by extending the scale for each question from between 1 and 3 to between 1 and 5, which would account for most privately held companies in existence today. For purposes of illustration, note that the category "historical profits" is ranked the most important (given a weight of 10), so a score of 3 here would be multiplied by 10 to contribute a total of 30 points to the overall system points. Under the original system, if each factor were assigned a 3, the total points would be 165, whereby 165 divided by 55 would generate the overall multiple of 3 corresponding to the value of 3 assigned to each factor.

A complete copy of this system is available through Tom West's *2001 Business Reference Guide* and the Business Brokerage Press (*www.businessbrokeragepress*). Jones is the co-editor of *The Handbook of Business Valuation* (John Wiley & Sons).

CHAPTER 5

Business Valuation Through the ARM Approach, Part II

We continue our application of the ARM approach by analyzing its second and third components: rules of thumb and market comparable sales data. Consider the following definitions:

Rules of thumb: market-driven formulas rooted in traditional valuation concepts such as revenues, cash flow, and assets that evolve over time

Market comparable sales data: collections of data including sale price, down payment, gross revenues, adjusted cash flow, and sale price multiples based on actual business sales

A slight expansion of our ARM acronym provides the following valuation foundation:

Adjust the cash flow and apply the multiple.

Review the pertinent rules of thumb.

Monitor and modify available market comparable sales statistics.

Having completed our review of the first and generally most important component of a company's adjusted cash flow (ACF), we seek to round off our valuation analysis via two additional practical valuation tools. Both rules of thumb and market data techniques share the following characteristics:

Use ACF as part of the valuation process

Are market-based, -derived, or -influenced

In other words, the remaining two components are distinct yet based in great part on the results derived from the first component and are fundamentally based on actual, historical sales results; that is, they are market-oriented.

Many rules of thumb contain a cash flow element, and one of two primary methods for using market comp data involves comparing the average ACF for a basket of similar company sales with the ACF of the subject company. Thus, it should be clear that proper and consistent calculation of ACF is a necessary condition for accurate business valuation. Not only is cash flow the primary reason for buying a business in the first place, but this measure is used in each of the three ARM components to one degree or another.

Similarly, both rules of thumb and market comp data are based primarily on the results of actual business sales that have taken place in the past. Rules of thumb typically evolve over time to match the general tendencies and outcomes of prior transactions for specific types and sizes of companies. This fact often is overlooked by those who choose to downplay their significance. By definition, market comp data are market-based, and careful use of such information can help to ensure that the final estimate of business value properly reflects recent market conditions for a particular type and size of business.

In Chapters Four and Five we introduce each of the three ARM approach components (ACF, rules of thumb, and market comparable data). Bear in mind that all the issues covered on the ARM Approach Questionnaire and Five-Page Tool ultimately are aimed at applying each of these three valuation methods to estimate the subject company's value for the task at hand (typically to estimate fair market value [FMV] on a going-concern basis for purposes of buying or selling a company).

Introduction to Rules of Thumb★

We turn now to a focused analysis of the second component of the ARM approach. Although there is no formal category called "rules of thumb" in classi-

---

★*The attached CD-ROM contains substantial information on rules of thumb (including more detailed coverage for specific industries such as Internet-based companies), ranging from a comprehensive list of rules of thumb by company type (in-*

cal valuation methods, most such rules are rooted in the traditional valuation concepts related to cash flow (income), assets (cost or asset), and historical values (market). Greater cash flow and more assets equal higher value. More stable and predictable cash flow equals higher multiples and higher value.

The most pertinent link between rules of thumb and classical valuation is the market approach to the extent that rules of thumb are grounded in actual sales for particular types of companies. It is the unfolding process whereby actual business sales are transformed into approximations of value that gives the many rules of thumb their relevance. Some rules are based on cash flow, and others are based on revenues or assets. Many are combination rules based on both cash flow and different categories of assets.

Almost every rule of thumb has grown out of the perpetual supply of actual market transactions. They evolve over time. For example, as the Internet has grown in magnitude and importance, the applicable rules of thumb for Internet service providers (ISPs) have changed (dollars per account have risen). When interest rates reached high double digits in the late 1980s, the rule of thumb multiple range for real estate brokerages sunk dramatically. As the high–flying, high-tech NASDAQ stock exchange lost more than half of its value during 2000, a wide variety of rules of thumb for related industries and companies fell substantially; for example, the price paid per customer in the telecommunication industry fell by nearly 50 percent in many cases (in this industry, certain rules of thumb are based on dollars per active customer).

Thus, there is a feedback process between market conditions and market multiples for many types of businesses that is captured through ever-changing rules of thumb. Furthermore, many rules of thumb have become self-fulfilling prophecies in that a business may sell at the value implied by a rule of thumb because the rule of thumb reflected historical sales. In every case, it is important to survey current market conditions and speak with as many market participants as possible to determine the proper rule and arrive at the appropriate estimate of value.

Overview of Rules of Thumb

Rules of thumb in their infinite variety are perhaps the most used and misused tools of business valuation. They cannot be dismissed out of hand, nor should they be used blindly without comparing the results of other methods.

cluding standard industrial classification [SIC] codes and pertinent Web sites for further research) and relevant commentary to the results of a national VR Business Brokers survey on business valuation and rules of thumb. The CD-ROM also contains thorough coverage of the asset or cost approach to business valuation. Because many rules are based in part on various assessments of asset values, the discussion of locating, evaluating, and valuing assets of all types is essential reading.

This broad category consists of formulas that are based on many factors, including ACF or some derivative thereof. Overall, rules of thumb can be classified as follows:

Multiple of revenues

Multiple of earnings (e.g., net income, ACF, earnings before interest, taxes, depreciation, and amortization [EBITDA])

Multiple of book value

Multiple of a measured unit (e.g., restaurant tables, hospital beds, subscribers)

Other

Because many investors and business owners focus on their return on investment from future cash flows, using a multiple of earnings or cash flow as a rule of thumb seems most appropriate. The other four categories do not directly assess the profitability of the business, presenting an obvious shortcoming. Even rules comprising multiple of earnings or cash flow, in and of themselves, do not directly provide sufficient information to assess the uniqueness of a given business. They do not directly provide a tool for evaluating factors such as management depth, customer relationships, industry trends, reputation, location, competition, capital structure, and other information unique to the subject industry and business. As is true for all valuation techniques, at some point the analysis depends on the unique perspective and judgment of the valuator. The ARM Approach Questionnaire and the Five-Page Tool are designed to help capture the relevant valuation factors for each technique.

There is a downside to the use of rules of thumb. I have often been approached by business owners saying something like, "I hear that businesses can be valued at three or four times income; is this true?" I quickly point out that it is difficult to generalize across all types and sizes of businesses and that such rules of thumb can be misleading. Unfortunately, no single rule of thumb applies to all businesses at all times. Great care must be taken to ensure that only applicable and useful rules of thumb are used in valuing a given business.

Another tool for ensuring proper use of rules of thumb is the review of market comp data for similar companies. For example, a particular type of business may have one rule of thumb that is cash flow–based and another one that is revenue-based. Which one is preferable? Besides determining which one is customarily used more often, it is possible to evaluate the statistical relationships between price and cash flow and price and gross revenues for a pool of market comp results. In short, the higher the correlation with price, the better the predictor is as a rule of thumb. For example, if there appears to be a tight relationship between sale price and gross revenues (they rise and fall together on a scattergram plot) and a very loose relationship between price and cash flow (there is no definite pattern), use of the rule of thumb based on gross revenues may be preferable. The IBA has conducted detailed analyses of such correlations, concluding that the price to gross revenue multiple is generally more reliable.

Example: Accounting and Tax Practices

On the other hand, certain rules of thumb for certain types of businesses are very important and *must* be incorporated into the valuation analysis. One of the best examples of this situation concerns accounting and tax practices. Because of widespread agreement among practitioners and practice owners, use of the rule of thumb based on gross revenues is mandatory when estimating fair market value for these companies. Specifically, it is widely agreed and understood that most accounting and tax practices are worth 90 to 120 percent of the anticipated gross revenues during the first year of new ownership (based in great part on the most recent year's gross revenue performance of the subject company).

This type of business illustrates vividly the need to understand the unique nature and environment surrounding each type and size of company. For example, the sale of accounting and tax practices is almost always based on the combination of a seller guarantee and an earnout, both of which are uncommon in most other business sales. The guarantee component means that the seller is guaranteeing that the buyer will earn a specified minimum amount of revenues during the first year (note that the guarantee is revenue-based, not ACF-based). If the actual realized revenues is less than the guaranteed amount, then the actual final price is reduced (typically dollar for dollar, but everything is negotiable) to reflect the lower revenue level. The earnout component is related in that the final price is determined by the actual amount of earned revenues; that is, the sale price could be higher than the contract price if the earned revenues exceed the expected level. In short, the ultimate price paid for these types of companies depends on the actual revenues earned during the first year of ownership.

This unique combination of a guarantee and an earnout is extremely rare for other types of businesses. In general, earnouts are much more common than seller guarantees. Buying a business is risky, and the success of a company is equally dependent on the efforts of the new owner and the historical foundation inherited upon purchase; it is unreasonable to expect the seller to guarantee the future success of the company once ownership has passed to the new operator. On the other hand, earnouts are fairly common when a business has tremendous potential beyond its current operating performance and the seller seeks compensation for this upside in earnings. The buyer typically is willing to pay the extra amount if the business performs at the higher level of revenues or profits, often creating a win–win scenario. Earnouts more effectively capture the true value of such a business as reflected by its cash flow generation over time; that is, they more efficiently link the purchase price with the company's ultimate value.

As is the case for almost every valuation technique, there is much subjectivity in the accounting and tax practice formula and rules of thumb. The difference between 90 and 110 percent can be several tens of thousands of dollars, so care must be taken in applying the proper multiple. Many factors affect this particular multiple for accounting and tax practices, including

Breakdown between tax and write-up (monthly) work

Average size of each tax and write-up client

Amount and quality of assets included in sale

Profitability or cash flow of subject company

Probability and amount of repeating revenues (minimal one-time revenues)

Many other factors, such as depth and breadth of transition period and geographic area (practices in large metro areas such as New York and Los Angeles sell for higher multiples)

Thus, the closer the balance between tax (seasonal) and write-up work (spread out over the year), the higher dollar value for each client, the better the assets, and higher the profitability, the higher the multiple. This same type of company-specific analysis ultimately is necessary for all rules of thumb (with the exception of a few often meaningless rules such as $X per bed in a motel or $X per lane in a bowling alley).

Example: The Restaurant Industry

Another example of an industry that relies heavily on rules of thumb is the restaurant industry (including all related types of businesses such as coffee shops, delis, and breakfast and lunch diners). Professionals and entrepreneurs active in this area agree that such businesses usually are worth 30 to 60 percent of gross revenues. For example, the *2000 Business Reference Guide* (often called the *Business Broker's Bible,* available at *www.businessbrokeragepress.com*) cites the following rules of thumb for this area:

Family restaurant	30 percent of gross sales
Niche restaurant	44 percent of gross sales
Fast food franchise	50 percent of gross sales
Bars	Up to 60 percent of gross sales

In fact, a check of market comparable statistics from two of the leading providers of such information (VR Business Brokers and BIZCOMPS) showed that over a recent multiyear period of time, restaurants in general sold for approximately 37 percent of gross revenues (median percentage) in both databases.

Rules of thumb can vary in scope and depth, depending on the particular rule. The *Business Reference Guide* lists several specific rules of thumb for the restaurant industry that are multi-tiered. For example, the following chart presented by the Boston Restaurant Group (Charles M. Perkins, president, available at *weperk@ix.netcom.com*) describes various revenue multipliers under different circumstances.

Boston Restaurant Group Revenue-Based Rules of Thumb

Rating Range	Description
15 percent	Short lease (less than five years and no options) New business (minimal or no profit history) All-cash sale (no seller financing offered) Marginal operation (breakeven cash flow at best)
25 percent	Average sales and profits Concept change needed All factors generally favorable Turnkey operation
35 percent	Excellent concept with replication potential Above-average sales and profits Excellent terms offered by seller

Many such businesses sell for multiples outside of these bounds and above or below the average, making the final application a function of fact-oriented but subjective decision making. It is always encouraging to see that average market comp statistics are compatible with and generally near the rule of thumb value estimates.

As verification of the dynamic process behind most rules of thumb, note that this particular chart contains multiples that were changed during the writing of this book to reflect less favorable overall valuation conditions (i.e., the multiples were revised downward to reflect current business conditions that had taken a turn for the worse). Specific factors cited for the downward revision were

Increased competition from large chains

Slowing economy in general

Large amounts of deferred maintenance

Staffing problems in recently vibrant economy

Spread of no-smoking ordinances

Americans with Disabilities Act raising costs of construction

Alcohol consumption patterns are trending downward

Bank financing increasingly difficult for restaurants

Thus, despite the 35 percent at the high end for restaurant rule of thumb applications (gross revenue multiple), Perkins generally advises clients that a multiple of 30 percent is the high end in today's market. He similarly advises that a multiple of three times gross cash flow is the high end of the value spectrum for independent restaurants (gross cash flow is similar to ACF).

Another important consideration is highlighted by the Boston Restaurant Group chart and worthy of repeated discussion. It is an empirical fact that terms and conditions (e.g., seller financing) in the purchase offer or contract can and typically do affect the transaction price. As discussed in Chapter Six, it is critical to understand the direct and sometimes overwhelming impact of terms on the final deal price (which ultimately becomes fair market value in market comp databases).

For example, it is widely understood that an all-cash offer is worthy of a cash discount from the asking price based on seller financing. Simply stated, the greater the cash down payment, the lower the purchase price. The interest rate, payback period, collateral and guarantees, potential employment contract between seller and new owner, and covenant not to compete all influence the final price (FMV).

Unfortunately, many businesses do not fit neatly into the categories outlined in the Boston Restaurant Group chart or any other similar categorization. Thus, the element of subjectivity once again takes center stage in attempting to estimate the company's FMV. Evaluation of all relevant factors is necessary to properly categorize a subject company using this and all rules of thumb. As just described in the case of restaurant multiples, the relevant factors change over time. For restaurants in general, however, important factors include the following:

Location and length and quality of lease

Condition of equipment

Historical trends in revenues, profits, and cash flow

Condition of books and records

Free-standing building or ability to buy the real property

General appearance

Time until remodeling is needed

Amount of competition in area

Levels of security and crime in the neighborhood

Parking availability

Hours of operation

Existence of noncompete agreement

Health inspection issues

Employee retention

Importance of owner to generating and retaining customers

Debt service

Perkins uses a short list of key factors for quickly sizing up the appeal of a given restaurant, as follows:

Sales	Potential for growth?
Cash flow	Is business profitable?
Condition of limited liability partnership (LLP)	Turnkey versus deferred maintenance?
Rent	Is it at industry or local average?
Terms of lease	Are there renewal options for long-term presence?

Other rules of thumb for restaurants that are used by various brokers or industry professionals include the following:

First-year revenues should be three times total investment.

Capitalize income using a cap rate of 35 to 40 percent.

The price is right if the cash flow after owner's salary of $40,000 can pay for the restaurant's total purchase in three to four years.

Two times net earnings (seller's discretionary cash or ACF as defined earlier) plus fair market value of assets (furniture, fixtures, and equipment [FF&E]).

$1,200 to $2,000 per seat.

Perkins of the Boston Restaurant Group cites the first of these rules as an increasingly common expectation among restaurant buyers in the northeastern United States. Another interesting insight from Perkins concerns the common practice among restaurants and other cash-based businesses of skimming. He notes that if a restaurant's cost of goods sold and payroll together exceed 70 percent of total revenues, there may be inaccurate reporting. Alternatively, if food costs exceed 50 percent of total revenues, a similar reporting problem may exist. Such occurrences in this industry are the primary cause of frequent visual audits, whereby a prospective buyer visits the restaurant at various times of day over a week or two to estimate head counts and average ticket values.

Are Rules of Thumb Optimal for Restaurants?

A final comment about restaurants and rules of thumb concerns the general appeal of such rules as compared with other valuation techniques (e.g., multiple of ACF or market-based analysis). A recent edition of Shannon Pratt's *Business Valuation Update*™ newsletter (1999) contained an article addressing the valuation of restaurants. Among other interesting findings, it was noted that both Pratt and Perkins (of the Boston Restaurant Group) agreed that the market approach is the best valuation technique for valuing smaller independent restaurants (using an average multiple of sales and earnings or cash flow for comparision with the subject business).

Although the article noted that the valuation of chain-related entities (including franchised locations) can be properly valued via rules of thumb based on gross revenues, it was agreed that the increasing availability of credible business sales data (BIZCOMPS, Pratt's Stats, VR Business Brokers) has dramatically boosted the appeal of the market approach for such businesses. In general, they recommend an approach similar to that presented later in this chapter (also similar to the Institute of Business Appraisers' [IBA's] direct market data method).

General Factors Affecting Rule of Thumb Results

As you have learned from the process of estimating a multiple of cash flow for a given business, many factors ultimately determine the final value estimate. As you review the rules of thumb found on the CD-ROM, you will note wide ranges within which each rule can be applied. The determining factors for each category and type of business are unique, but the following short list can be referred to as you try to make sense of the given range for all types of business opportunities. In addition to this condensed list, the ARM Approach Questionnaire is full of other company and industry-specific queries that can contribute to a more complete assessment for purposes of every valuation technique (including rules of thumb). The questionnaire will facilitate a well-rounded analysis of the subject company.

General Factors Affecting Rule of Thumb Multiples and Results

Location

Rent compared with market levels; options to renew

Years in business and years owned by current owner

Gross sales, ACF, and expense history and trends

General appearance of business

Lifestyle of owners (long hours? low stress?)

Recent sale prices of comparable businesses

Reputation, registered trade name or trademark, goodwill, proprietary products or processes

Amount of inventory, accounts receivable, or real estate included in sale

Reliability of business records and financial statements (computerized? bankable?)

Owner's function, special skills needed, and key employees

Percentage of sales from each of the top five and ten customers

Internet presence

Degree to which measures of liquidity, solvency, profitability, and activity (financial statement analysis) correspond to industry averages

Major regulatory, tax, or legal issues recently addressed or currently facing the business

Seller's willingness to sign employment agreement or covenant not to compete

Upside potential and downside risk

Barriers to entry that limit competition

Competitors recently entering or exiting the subject market

Degree to which the company has maximized its sales effort and reached its current capacity

Overall strengths and weaknesses of the subject company

ACF Multiples Versus Gross Revenue Multiples

Our coverage of rules of thumb thus far should make it clear that gross revenue multiples can play an important role in the valuation of many types of businesses, especially service businesses. All things considered, however, cash flow generated for the owner remains the focal point of valuation procedures for most types of businesses. The fact that publicly traded companies often are discussed in terms of price to earnings (P/E) ratios rather than revenue to earnings (R/E) ratios illustrates this preferential treatment. The importance of cash flow to business value generally is the same for small, privately held companies as well. Thus, the initial component of the ARM approach focuses exclusively on this important measure and value determinant.

Despite the higher ranking of cash flow compared to gross revenues, many businesses are valued in great part based on the price to gross revenue ratio. Not only accounting practices and restaurants, but also dry cleaners, landscapers, pest control operations, janitorial businesses, and practically every type of service business (especially account-based entities) should be valued in part based on gross revenues. Therefore, it is often the case that the most relevant rule of thumb for valuing many businesses consists of the price to gross revenue relationship.

Recall that assessment of market comp data is also based on evaluating the average price to cash flow and price to gross revenue multiples for a given type of company. Thus, gross revenues are important as a rule of thumb and as a contributing factor to the use of market comp data. In almost every case, for service businesses and other business types, it is probably worthwhile to use this relationship as part of the valuation process. This can be done either as a rule of thumb or in conjunction with the evaluation of market comp data. The use of gross revenue data is particularly helpful when financial statements are not reliable. Revenue data normally are easier to reconstruct (and more difficult to manipulate) than a complete income statement.

In addition, it is generally true that the more similar a group of companies are (i.e., similar cost structures and revenue patterns), the more likely the gross revenue multiples are to be similar in magnitude. This is also true when the relationship between profit as a percentage of sales (see *www.bizstats.com*) and business sale price is strong and consistent. If the average sale price for a particular type of business rises and falls consistently as the profit as a percentage of sales rises and falls, such industry data can be used to estimate a theoretically correct price to revenue multiple for a given company. At a minimum, use of a rule of thumb based on the price to gross revenue relationship serves as a check against other valuation results.

Finally, note that certain rules of thumb use gross revenues to estimate the goodwill or intangible asset value of particular types of businesses. For example, it is commonly accepted among valuators and entrepreneurs active in the new car dealership market that a dealership's goodwill value is equal to a percentage of sales somewhere between 1 and 6 percent (commonly between 3 and 5 percent). In other words, the value of a new car dealership is equal to the value of its inventory, other tangible assets, and goodwill as generated by the brand name, customer service, and other favorable perceptions resulting from the dealership's past performance.

General After–Tax Rules of Thumb

Before looking at the extensive list of specific rules of thumb contained on the CD-ROM, consider the following general after-tax, income-based averages that are bandied about by business brokers and mergers and acquisitions (M&A) specialists. Whereas after-tax multiples are more commonly used for larger businesses, almost all the rules of thumb or multiples used by business brokers for smaller companies are based on some figure similar to our ACF, most of which are pretax quantities.

Manufacturing companies:
> With proprietary or patented products: four to ten times net income (after corporate taxes)
> With nonproprietary products: three to eight times net income (after corporate taxes)

Retail stores: three to six times net income (after corporate taxes) plus inventory at cost plus accounts receivable if included in sale

Service businesses: four to seven times net income (after corporate taxes) or adjusted book value★

Wholesale or distribution companies: two to five times net income (after taxes) plus inventory at cost

Valuation Factors Affecting Larger Businesses

These rules of thumb are applicable only for "larger" small companies (sales more than $5 million and after-tax net incomes of $300,000 or more). The dif-

---

★*The adjusted book value method requires adjustments to be made for all assets to determine their true economic value. For example, fixed assets are appraised at their fair market value. Similar adjustments are made for other asset types and all other accounts (including liabilities) to reach an adjusted book value. See the "Asset or Cost Approach to Business Valuation" section of the CD-ROM for more insights.*

ference between after-tax net income and ACF can be significant for smaller companies. The following is another partial list of favorable characteristics that tend to increase the appropriate multiple for larger businesses in particular as defined earlier. These companies are of such a nature that there is at least a chance that they may emerge as a publicly traded company in the future.

Strong history of sales and earnings growth (pretax earnings)

Good reputation of company or brands

Strong research and development, quality control, and patent proliferation

Niche products with minimal competition

Strong employee, customer, and supplier base

Seller or key employees remaining active in business after sale

To summarize, rules of thumb are used often and therefore must be properly understood. In fact, knowing whether and when to use a rule of thumb for a particular type of company is one of the most important skills in business valuation. Their specific makeup and relevance vary over time, across the country, and from one type and size of business to the next. Even at a given time in a particular city, if you ask five different business brokers to value a business, you are likely to hear about several different rules representing a wide range of potential values. Despite this disparity, the fact that they are market driven helps provide a useful range of values against which the specifics of a given company can be evaluated.

Compiling Rules of Thumb

Review the formulas (the rules of thumb) on the CD-ROM and note how they change from one category of business to the next. Their application differs not only across categories but across the country and over time (depending on local conditions and customs). In general, valuation formulas for retail businesses rely heavily on inventory, and manufacturing business methods place a greater emphasis on total assets. Many service business rules of thumb rely on the number of accounts or sales per account. For example, the value of automotive repair businesses depends greatly on the number of bays, whereas accounting practice valuation is a function of the quantity of repetitive accounts (as opposed to one-time services). Travel agencies tend to be valued based on gross commissions and restaurants on gross sales receipts.

The rules of thumb listed on the attached CD-ROM were collected in an entirely unscientific fashion from various business brokers, CPAs, attorneys, and other sources across the country. Most of these rules were collected in a survey distributed to business brokers working for VR Business Brokers across the nation (approximately eighty offices serving all regions of the United States). Summary information compiled during this survey is presented at the end of the "Rules of Thumb" CD-ROM section.

In each case, the user must carefully consider and weigh the many factors that tend to increase or decrease the appropriate multiple. Discuss this process with your colleagues and advisers. The same factors are used in each of the three ARM components, so a great deal of the credibility of the valuation estimate depends on the quality of this list. Having read Chapter Three already, you are aware that this important list (pluses and minuses as described in the Five-Page Tool) should be updated throughout the analysis so that by the end of your work you have discovered all key factors and factored them into the final results.

In reading the industry-specific factors, you will quickly see that each specific type of business is associated with a combination of general and unique valuation factors. Complete the ARM Approach Questionnaire to be reminded of important valuation factors. Tapping into the knowledge and expertise of business owners, business brokers, accountants, attorneys, consultants, key employees, and even competitors is a normal part of the valuation process.

General SIC codes are provided for analytical purposes and to lead you to similar types of businesses. Remember that invaluable financial information can be found by SIC code number in publications from Robert Morris Associates, Dun & Bradstreet, the *Almanac of Business and Industry Ratios,* and other sources. Relevant trade association Web sites (and appropriately similar sites) are also presented to allow quick access to industry information. Note that typical averages for each category tend to be in the middle of the ranges presented on the CD-ROM.

Concluding Remarks About Rules of Thumb

If you are interested in locating a single publication that fully handles rules of thumb, I have three excellent recommendations. First, Glen Desmond's *The Handbook of Small Business Valuation Formulas and Rules of Thumb,* now in its third edition, is published by Valuation Press in Camden, Maine. This handbook is the original source of rules of thumb and related commentary and presents a credible framework for understanding and using rules of thumb for many different types of businesses.

Second, the *2001 Business Reference Guide,* written by Jim West and published by the Business Brokerage Press in Concord, Massachusetts, contains an ever-expanding collection of rules of thumb along with substantive insights into each category or type of business. There are now more than 300 rules of thumb collected from trade associations, industry experts, and specialists.

This book contains much more than rules of thumb and is often called the business broker's Bible. This is a must-have book for business brokers, other intermediaries, and anyone active in buying, valuing, and selling businesses. This publication is the leading source of rule of thumb information and will only improve with time as profiles are added each year that go well beyond simply presenting a particular rule of thumb and present a detailed analysis of the subject industry and environment.

Finally, the author of this book has written another book called *The Upstart Guide to Buying, Valuing, and Selling Your Business* (Dearborn Financial, 1998); it includes three chapters on business valuation in a user-friendly format (in addition to a comprehensive collection of contracts, contract clauses, worksheets, checklists, and other forms related to the buying and selling of small businesses).

In his book, Glen Desmond provides the following insight: "There is no single formula that will work for every business. Formula multipliers offer ease of calculation, but they also obscure details. This can be misleading. Net revenue multipliers are particularly troublesome because they are blind to the business's expenses and profit history. It is easy to see how two businesses in any given industry group might have the same annual net revenue, yet show very different cash flows. A proper valuation will go beyond formulas and include a full financial analysis whenever possible."

As noted near the beginning of this chapter, a common rule of thumb for accounting practices is 90 to 120 percent of the anticipated annual gross revenues. In most cases, the historical or last year's revenue level is used as the focal point for establishing the purchase price via this rule of thumb. I have witnessed a situation in which a small CPA company reported $200,000 in revenues including one large contract that was of a one-time nature and, to make things worse, was ultimately uncollectible. In this case, approximately 25 percent of the reported revenues were questionable, but the asking price was determined as a multiple of the full $200,000. An inexperienced buyer (even a trusting buyer who has confidence in their profession and the seller) may have agreed to a price that did not reflect the underlying economic reality when the company was valued based only on this rule of thumb. In this particular case, the company did not make a profit when this account was backed out of the income statement.

Most practitioners in the accounting and tax practice sales area believe strongly in this rule of thumb, often ignoring other valuation methods altogether. The popularity and acceptability of rules of thumb are evidenced by the substantial amount of data published on the subject. For example, Desmond first published his *Handbook* in 1987, with two subsequent editions over the next six years. Shannon Pratt, perhaps the nation's leading business valuation expert, cautions against overusing or relying exclusively on rules of thumb, but he presents a number of them in his two major publications addressing business valuation. Pratt's books are a major source of information for people seeking to become Certified Business Appraisers through the Institute of Business Appraisers.

The American Institute of Certified Public Accountants (AICPA) Consulting Services Practice Aid titled "Conducting a Valuation of a Closely Held Business" (#93–3) advises against exclusive use of these formulas but notes that "the valuer should not ignore what is being done in the industry. Frequently, an industry rule of thumb provides a representation of the perception that people have in the marketplace and should be one of the methods used in valuing the closely held business." State governments have even become involved with the use of rules of thumb via statute. The Florida State Legislature has put in the statutes that a business valuation performed by a CPA must conform to AICPA Practice Aid 93–3.

Final Caveats Regarding Rules of Thumb

The list of rules in this book is not all-inclusive, nor are the formulas to be used as a sole guide to establishing value.

They can be used to facilitate the determination of value in conjunction with other methods, such as discounted cash flow (DCF) analysis, market comparable statistics, and other approaches.

There is wide variation in multiples across industries, regions of the country, and time.

Do not exclusively rely on rules of thumb. Every business is different and must be realistically analyzed using a combination of methods such as those in the ARM approach.

Use of Market Comparable Sales Data

The final component of the ARM approach and the second section of this chapter deals with the use of historical business sale price data in estimating the value of a company of interest. After the valuator has adjusted the cash flow, applied the proper multiple, and reviewed the pertinence of rules of thumb and implemented them accordingly, the third step should be easy. Much of the analysis needed to apply the third component will have already been completed (e.g., calculating the company's ACF and gross revenue performance over recent years and assessing the major pluses and minuses of the subject company and industry). Completing the analysis related to market-generated sales statistics will balance and in a sense verify the results generated by the first two components.

As embodied in the ARM Approach Questionnaire, the results of the three-tiered valuation system can be improved or further verified via the reality check or payback method described in detail in the "Asset or Cost Approach to Business Valuation" section of the CD-ROM. This method could be classified as a type of rule of thumb, but its classification is not as important as its usefulness in assessing the credibility of the valuation result. Note that there will always be exceptions to the general usefulness of the payback method: Certain businesses will be worth a price that is not readily supported by its current cash flow. Startup businesses, businesses that have slowed down or shut down for health reasons, businesses that are asset-rich relative to cash flow, and so on may not be justifiable under the payback method but still represent valid and reasonable market values. Thus, the ARM approach could be extended to include the payback method as an optional but recommended component.

This section focuses on the use of market comparable sales data, which in strictly practical terms could be considered the most credible valuation approach of all. Given the typical goal of determining a company's FMV, there can be no better indicator of value than the prices at which similar companies have sold in the recent past. Only this approach allows one to estimate FMV based on direct review and application of other FMV results. On the other hand, many problems and challenges are associated with this seemingly straightforward component of the ARM approach and must be addressed to ensure useful results.

Overview of Market Approach Valuation Methods

Before delving into the specifics of market approach valuation methods, a quick overview of the different techniques within this approach is useful. In general, there are two distinct valuation methods based on historical data related to the sale of ownership interests: the comparable sales method and the guideline public companies method. In practice, several different titles are assigned to these techniques, so terminology can be problematic to the beginning valuator. In terms of the ARM approach, we will use primarily the comparable sales method. This method is emphasized because of its simplicity and pertinence to the typical small business.

Either of these methods can be appropriate depending on the type and size of the subject company. For the typical small business with an active owner-operator and an ACF of $1 million or less, the comparable sales method probably is most relevant. The guideline public companies method can also be useful but tends to be more applicable to "larger" small businesses, described earlier as middle-market companies. These middle-market companies are more likely to go public than their smaller counterparts. Most small businesses are unlikely to even consider going public, so the latter method will receive less coverage in this book. However, the larger a business becomes and the closer its characteristics match those of publicly traded companies (e.g., layers of management, audited financial statements, less reliance on the owner's efforts and skills), the more applicable the second technique becomes.

Comparable Sales Method

As the name implies, this method looks to the sales of comparable businesses for assessing the value of the subject company. Of course, each of the market-based methods relies on comparable businesses, but this method relies on the historical sale of whole privately owned companies as opposed to the sale of publicly traded fractional interests (individual shares at individual share prices) as used in the guideline method.

Note that the comparable sales method is effectively the same method recommended by the professional appraisers who oversee the IBA (the oldest business appraisal certification-granting organization in the world). The IBA has developed a comprehensive set of tutorials and sample applications that revolve around this method, which they call the direct market data method (DMDM). (For more information, go to *www.go-iba.com* and look for links to the DMDM content.) Membership in the IBA is worth the annual fee even if its only use is to learn the DMDM approach to business valuation. The annual fee also entitles the member to receive their periodical *IBA News* and complete access to their extensive market comp database.

Regardless of its name, this method calls for the location and compilation of key transaction-related data for a group of similar companies. In short, the average results from a group of similar companies are compared with and applied to the subject company. For example, a group of transactions related to franchised fast food businesses would be collected to estimate the FMV of a Dairy Queen operation. Preferably, only the sales of other Dairy Queens would be used, but this usually is not possible because of a lack of such specific data. Therefore, other fast food companies that have been recently sold could be used to represent the average fast food outlet for comparison to the subject company (perhaps trying to narrow the group down to hamburger-focused or ice cream-related fast food operations).

A common indicator of value in this method is the price to cash flow multiple. It may turn out that the entire group of fast food comps sold for an average of three times ACF. Care must be taken to ensure that the market sales data used here reflect similar companies of a similar size and in a similar geographic area (e.g., New York City or all major metro areas as opposed to the state of Oregon or all small towns). For example, if the basket of market statistics consists of substantially larger companies, the average multiple of cash flow will not apply to the smaller subject company.

This problem may be partially solved by reducing the market data average multiple to reflect a smaller company environment. The challenge is to determine exactly how much adjustment is needed to credibly compare the group average with the subject company. Later sections of this chapter will help shed light on such adjustments. Ideally, data on similar-sized companies (in terms of revenues, assets, or ACF) will be used to avoid this type of adjustment.

The next step (arguably the most important) calls for assessment of the subject company relative to the average multiple. This step is the most subjective element of this particular method, but the valuator must determine whether the subject company is above average, average, or below average and then quantify this determination into a derived multiple. If the subject company is perceived to be above average, the question becomes one of degree (i.e., how much above average the company is relative to the norm).

A careful consideration of all relevant factors is warranted here: the history and trend of cash flows, the quality of the lease and location, condition and value of equipment, and all other pluses and minuses of the subject company. There are no shortcuts for determining the exact multiple to be used, nor are there any rock-solid procedures for reaching this conclusion. As is the case for every valuation method and assignment, the judgment and experience of the valuator play a critical role in reaching the valuation conclusion. What is important, however, is that the valuator be consistent in applying the analysis across different businesses and be credible in the eyes of the recipient of the value estimate. Later sections of this chapter and lists of valuation factors presented in regard to rules of thumb will provide additional insights into the specifics of evaluating each particular company.

In addition, recall that the ARM approach is best applied in conjunction with the Five-Page Tool, which includes the preparation of a worksheet to track the various pluses and minuses of the company and industry as the valuation analysis unfolds. This worksheet should be constructed diligently throughout the valuation analysis and will prove very beneficial when attempting to derive the proper multiple for the first ARM component (ACF), the second ARM component (rule of thumb), and the third ARM component (comparison with the market average).

Note also that there is an infrequently used "public" variation of the comparable sales method. The first and most pertinent method for our purposes relies on the use of the various market comp databases that contain the sales results of smaller, privately held companies (e.g., BIZCOMPS). The second version relies on the sale of whole, publicly traded companies such as in the M&A arena. Thus, the most important version relies on the sale of whole privately held companies, and the second, less relevant version relies on the sale of whole, publicly traded companies.

The second version of the comparable sales method differs from the following guideline public companies method in that it uses takeover prices (controlling interest value) related to whole entities as opposed to individual share prices that reflect minority interests (lack-of-control value). Although the type of analysis applicable to this second version of the comparable sales method is relevant for purposes of evaluating minority interest discounts (as opposed to control premiums) as described in Chapter Seven, our focus in this chapter is on the first version, which is based on evaluation of whole company (privately held) transactions.

Guideline Public Companies Method

This market approach method seeks to find a privately held company's value primarily through comparisons with individual share price data of similar publicly traded companies. To a far lesser extent, transaction data from other similar privately held companies and past transactions of the subject company's own shares can be used in this method. Other names are used to describe this method, including the "public comparable method" and the "guideline method." In essence, this method seeks to estimate company value through assessments of what publicly traded shares from similar companies sell for (i.e., assessments of minority interest share prices for comparable companies). These minority interest share prices are used as a guideline for determining the subject company's FMV.

For clarification purposes, note that the important IRS Revenue Ruling 59–60 defines the value of such public company stock as "the market price of stocks of corporations engaged in the same or a similar line of business having their stocks actively traded in a free and open market, either on an exchange or over the counter."

The logic behind this method is that the performance and results of two companies operating in the same industry (regardless of size) will be affected by essentially the same market forces, so their revenues, profits, and cash flows should be closely correlated. In other words, the same environmental factors such as changing tastes and preferences among consumers, regulatory schemes, import barriers, prices of related goods, and general economic conditions will affect company operating results in a similar fashion, whether it is a publicly traded or privately held company. Despite substantial operational and tax differences between private and public companies (e.g., Occupational Safety and Health Administration [OSHA] regulations applying only to companies with more than fifteen employees, different tax rules), the same fundamental market forces are at work for either type of company. Thus, the same events that drive up the share price of a publicly traded company should tend to drive up the value of a similar company that is privately owned.

Can We Find Similar Businesses?

One of the strongest arguments against overreliance on the use of market comps is the difficulty of finding what can credibly be considered a similar business. Strictly speaking, no two businesses are exactly alike in the entire world, but reasonable and acceptable tools are available to the valuator that will lead to useful assessments of business value via comparisons with similar companies.

How Many Comps Are Necessary?

Before we address the process behind locating similar businesses, a compelling question concerns the appropriate number of comps to make such analysis worthwhile. Once again, there are no definite answers, but a few general insights should help. First, the more similar the comps are, the fewer are needed. Second, the more concentrated the multiples appear to be (e.g., price to cash flow multiples hovering closely around the mean), the fewer transactions are needed. All things considered, it is preferable to use a minimum of five high-quality transactions (more if the quality is questionable).

For certain companies, however, their unique nature may make them difficult to compare. It may be that there are only two or three truly similar companies, as was the case for the Hallmark card company referred to later in this chapter. Or the subject company may operate in two different industries or at two different levels, such as a dry cleaner that also operates as a uniform rental company and a tailor or embroiderer or a manufacturing company that operates retail outlets. Ideally, ten to twenty comps of a similar nature should be used to ensure optimal results.

Similarity Is the Key

The primary key to properly using market comp data to estimate a company's FMV is ensuring that similar companies form the basis for comparison. Much analysis has gone into the process needed to compile similar company data, but no single approach has emerged that can be said to cover all cases. In fact, the process necessary to determine what a similar company is depends in great part on the subject company's specific characteristics. The basic task, therefore, is to generate a list of the major or distinguishing features of the subject company to be used for comparison purposes.

However, many of these unique features are impossible to evaluate because of a lack of information in the market comp databases. For example, there is no database covering the sale of privately held companies that would describe the number of outlets, square footage of the primary location, number of patents on record, and experience of the management team. It is highly unlikely that you will even find common financial indicators such as the company's capital structure or degree of liquidity. It is true that such information is more readily available for publicly traded companies, but most privately held, small businesses are too dissimilar to their larger, public counterparts to allow meaningful comparisons. Despite the problems associated with this technique, there is a way to make the best of available market comp data, so we forge ahead.

Key Characteristics of Similar Businesses

As just noted, the more similar the comparable businesses are, the fewer comps are needed to ensure a credible outcome. Thus, there is a strong incentive to locate businesses that are as similar as possible to the subject company. The process involved with locating such companies often begins with the use of SIC or North American Industrial Classification System (NAICS) codes.

SIC Codes

The most obvious starting point for assembling a basket of market comp statistics is the type of business being valued. Thanks to the use of SIC and the increasingly used NAICS codes, general analysis of market comp data and industry research is much less daunting. Historically, SIC codes were the primary classification system. The numerous rules of thumb presented on the CD-ROM include the corresponding SIC codes. The prevalence of SIC codes is diminishing steadily, however, because of the decision by the U.S. government to switch over to the improved NAICS codes.

NAICS Codes

The new NAICS format features six-digit codes (as opposed to four digits for SIC codes) to account for more diversity and detail (more sectors and subsectors), with special attention given to new industries, service industries, and high-tech industries in recognition of the changing structure of the U.S. economy. The six-digit codes are broken down as follows:

XX	Industry sector (twenty broad sectors, up from ten SIC)
XXX	Industry subsector
XXXX	Industry group
XXXXX	Industry subgroup
XXXXXX	U.S., Canadian, or Mexican national–specific

The Web site at *www.naics.com* describes the history of these industry classification systems. This site contains both SIC and NAICS codes along with a handy cross-reference feature that makes comparisons user-friendly.

Use of Codes for Specific Purposes

Both codes are used in a number of publications relevant to business valuation and appraisals for a variety of reasons, including the following:

Common-size financial data: Robert Morris Associates (*www.rma.com*) presents common-size financial data by SIC code and by size (assets and sales) as compiled from participating bankers that rely on this data to evaluate their customers' financial performance. Information such as gross profit margins, current ratios, return on assets, inventory turnover, and total liabilities as a percentage of total capital are presented here for almost every type of business. This information is useful for general financial analysis and for determining what the average business looks like in a given industry to aid in collecting suitable market comp data. Similar information can be found in the *Almanac of Industry and Business Financial Ratios,* compiled by Leo Troy and available through Amazon.com or *www. valuationresources.com.*

General industry research: Hoover's Online (*www.hoovers.com*), the Department of Commerce (*www.doc.gov*), Polson Enterprises Industry Research Desk (*www.virtualpet.com/industry/howto/search.h#other*), and many other government and private sector industry research publications and Web sites use SIC and NAICS codes to categorize relevant data.

Market comp research: Last but not least, SIC and NAICS codes can be used to search for and analyze market comp data from a variety of sources including BIZCOMPS (*www.BIZCOMPS.com*), Pratt's Stats (*www. bvmarketdata.com*), and the IBA database (*www.go-iba.org*). For example, one can call the IBA and request market comp data for SIC code 2514 and receive a list of comps for metal household furniture manufacturers. Naturally, it may prove beneficial to widen the scope and request all market comps for the SIC codes beginning with 25, which will generate comps for all furniture and fixture manufacturers.

Most businesses can be readily classified into the primary types in the following list. Note that the NAICS code is more consistent and organized to the extent that there is less overlapping of types in a given range of numbers. For example, the 5000 series for SIC codes includes distribution, retail, and even eating places. Such dispersion of business types is not as problematic in the new system. SIC codes are grouped according to type of business using alphabetical designations A through J, including the following, which are the major sectors. The complete list can easily be found on the Internet.

Retail	G
Service	I
Manufacturing	D
Distribution and wholesale	F

SIC codes are then further classified according to a numerical system of four digits, ranging from general to specific as the digits increase; for example, the major groups for manufacturing range from 20 to 39, with subgroups arranged by type of industry, as follows:

Furniture and fixtures	25
Household furniture	251
Wood household furniture (except upholstered)	2511

Major SIC and NAICS Codes

Type	SIC Code	NAICS Code
Retail	5200 to 5999	44000 to 45999
Service	8999	56000 to 61999
Manufacturing	2000 to 3999	31000 to 33999
Distribution and wholesale	5000 to 5199	42000 to 42999

Classifying a company by SIC or NAICS code is a necessary step, but it is not sufficient for many reasons. For example, some businesses are combinations of two or more categories. A recent deal completed by the author was the sale of a manufacturing company with two retail locations. This situation is difficult to classify without making numerous adjustments or assumptions. In addition, size differences can also be critical in assembling a group of similar companies. As noted throughout this book, there is an empirical relationship between the magnitude of ACF and the relevant multiples: The greater the cash flow, the higher the multiple. Finally, geography can affect the similarity of companies. For example, it is widely known among practitioners that car washes in California sell for higher multiples than car washes in Arizona. In fact, this is generally true for all types of businesses when comparing California with Arizona.

Initial and Primary Similarity Requirements

To summarize thus far, initial considerations in assembling a basket of similar company market comps include the following:

Type of business
Size of business (revenues, assets, ACF, employees)
Geographic location of business

Other factors also should be considered to ensure similarity. Given the relative lack of data in the various market comp databases related to privately held transactions, this is easier said than done. The three major factors listed here may be the only information available in many situations and will form the crux of comparisons for the comparable sales method (as opposed to the guideline method).

IRS and the Courts' View of Similarity

The Internal Revenue Service, in its often-quoted R.R. 59–60 (spells out the important business valuation considerations for tax purposes), made the following observation about the use of market data:

Although the only restrictive requirement as to comparable corporations specified in the statute is that their line of business be the same or similar, it is obvious that consideration must be given to other relevant factors in order that the most valid comparison possible will be obtained.

In fact, the similarity of companies used in the market comp approach often is a primary area of concern for the tax courts and opposing valuators. An important benchmark case heard by a tax court in 1974 led to the listing of several important factors for assessing comparability, as follows:

Capital structure

Credit status

Depth of management

Personnel experience

Nature of competition

Maturity of business

This case, *Tallichet v. Commissioner,* often is cited in valuation disputes of a tax and nontax nature. Other landmark cases have carefully scrutinized the use of market comp data, leading to assessment of numerous distinct factors, including but not limited to the following:

Financial statement analysis (similarity of liquidity, solvency, activity, profitability ratios)

Nature of products and markets

Customer mix and geographic areas served

Number and size of retail outlets

Size of manufacturing facility and number of employees

Earnings, dividend-paying capacity, and other cash flow measures

Growth rates in revenues and earnings

Degree of financial leverage (debt to equity ratios)

Cyclical nature of revenues and earnings

Amount and frequency of share transactions

It is important to rely on the specifics of the subject company to determine which historical transactions are similar in nature. In other words, rather than relying on a list of features that could be compared, it is best to first describe the key features of the subject company and then go look for similar comps. In practice, there may not be any truly similar companies because of the unique nature of certain businesses.

It cannot be stressed enough that the type of detailed analysis implied by the factors listed earlier normally can occur only for publicly traded companies. Therefore, only the guideline public company method typically allows such in-depth comparisons. If the guideline method is used, a credible, reasonable, and thoroughly explained rationale must be presented in support of the particular companies selected for comparisons.

Tax courts generally welcome the guideline method, but they can and do find fault with the selected mix of companies. Common complaints run the spectrum from "too broad" to "not broad enough" in regard to the mix of companies used for comparison. In a well-known valuation case, *Northern Trust v. Commissioner*, the court welcomed the use of guideline companies but rejected both sides' selections as being incomparable in nature. The appraisers erred in relying on financial structure and performance rather than on markets served, to the chagrin of the court.

In another famous case involving Hallmark Cards, *Estate of Joyce C. Hall v. Commissioner*, the tax court ultimately insisted on the same type of analysis rejected in the *Northern Trust* case. All parties agreed that there was only one truly comparable company to the subject business (American Greetings) and that the use of only one company for comparisons was unacceptable. Accordingly, the court allowed a broader application in using companies that were similar in size, financial structure, market dominance, and brand name recognition, such as Coca-Cola, IBM, and Avon Products. In short, if companies that are the same are not available, similar companies may be used.

As is true for all valuation methods across the board, it is ultimately the judgment and experience of the valuator that determine which companies can or should be considered the same or similar. Depending on the size of the subject company, either the guideline or the comparable method is more useful. On occasion, both methods may be useful in estimating company value. At a minimum and regardless of which method is used, the three major characteristics (type, size, and location of business) should be covered.

Ensuring that these three factors are similar allows general comparisons if the sample size is large enough. Later sections in this chapter address the sample size issue in detail, but a larger sample size is preferable to a smaller sample size, and a minimum of five companies should be evaluated.

Comparing the Guideline and Comparable Methods

Although both the guideline method and the comparable sales method rely on the location and evaluation of similar companies, there is a significant difference between the two in regard to the amount and quality of available information. Before addressing these differences, it is worthwhile to return to one of the fundamental truths of business valuation that applies to every valuation method.

Fundamental Valuation Relationship Between Risk and Return

As is true for most valuation techniques, the fundamental concept underlying these market-based methods is the relationship between risk and return. For example, when the share price of a given company (or the average multiple of cash flow for a particular type of business) is driven down, the implications generally are twofold: Either the risk associated with future returns (cash flow generated for ownership) has increased or the anticipated future returns have decreased.

Regarding risk, it may be that a government agency has announced plans to increase regulation of a particular industry (e.g., the Food and Drug Administration decides that the sale of nutritional supplements is harming customers through misinformation and a lack of quality control and that a new regulatory body will be established to create strict guidelines on labeling and quality control). This will increase the risks facing these companies because they may be fined or even shut down if they violate the new regulations. Regarding anticipated future returns, a technological breakthrough might lead one type of business (industry) into declining sales while driving a second type of business (industry) to record sales levels (e.g., the advent of DVD technology has cut into the sales of VCRs and videotapes).

Overall, higher risk and lower expected returns translate into less value. This critical relationship applies to both privately held and publicly traded companies. One must be careful to distinguish between factors that are unique to a specific company and factors that affect an entire industry or group of businesses, but the irrefutable fact is that greater risk or uncertainty for any reason reduces the value of any business. In fact, many seasoned valuation professionals believe that the essence of business valuation is found in this relationship, holding that the value of any business is a function of the riskiness, quantity, and timing of future cash flows accruing to its owners.

In a nutshell, *the more stable, probable, and substantial the future cash flows are, the more they are worth.* This interpretation of business value can prove useful throughout the ARM approach to valuation and should be regarded as the foundation of business valuation for both private and public companies. Bearing this in mind will greatly improve your valuation expertise. Whether the higher risk is incorporated into a lower multiple or a higher discount or cap rate, the result is the same. Any factors that affect the amount and probability of future cash flows also affect the company's value via each of the ARM components:

Higher risk → Lower multiple of ACF

Higher risk → Lower range for rules of thumb

Higher risk → Lower value relative to average business

We now return to our comparison of the comparable and guideline methods.

Comparable Versus Guideline Comparison Continued

The guideline method relies on the use of publicly traded share price data and allows the user to evaluate such companies in great detail as a result of their public nature; their full disclosure–oriented financial statements and in-depth review by analysts allow outside parties to assess the unique financial and operational features of such companies.

On the other hand, the more pertinent version of the comparable sales method relies primarily on data available from a number of databases that typically contain only limited information about the transactions and the company details (e.g., BIZCOMPS). In its most common usage, the comparable sales method does not allow the valuator to compare the finer points of each company. Accordingly, a more general approach is needed, one that focuses on what information is available such as gross sales, ACF, and often asset values.

Privately Held Versus Publicly Traded Companies

Unless the subject company is large enough, use of the guideline method should be limited because of the substantial differences between small, active owner-operated businesses and publicly traded companies. The major differences include the following:

Privately Held	**Publicly Traded**
Shorter operating history	Proven track record
Compiled financial statements	Audited financial statements
Cash basis accounting	Accrual basis accounting
Seek to minimize taxable profits	Seek to maximize accounting profits
Active owner–operator	Layers of management accountable to board of directors
Sole proprietor, S-corporation, limited-liability company (LLC)	C-corporations (or other "passthrough" entities)
Typically asset sale	Almost always stock sale
Minimal information available	Substantial public records and analysis

If the subject company is large enough (another judgment call), the guideline method can work effectively. If not, use of the comparable sales method, which relies on transaction data from databases such as BIZCOMPS or Pratts Stats™, is preferable. The precise mechanics of each method are covered in the next section. The comparable method receives the bulk of the coverage because of its simplicity and relevance for the majority of privately owned companies (recall that this method is similar to the IBA's DMDM, as described in tutorials at *www.go-iba.com*).

Substantial support for the notion that the guideline method should be used only for larger, middle-market companies has been generated by a recent analysis of the BIZCOMPS business sales statistics by Toby Tatum in a publication called "Transaction Patterns: Obtaining Maximum Knowledge from the BIZCOMPS Database" (this interesting and useful publication is available through Business Valuation Resources at *www.BVResources.com*). Among other noteworthy findings, the Tatum study found that there was no empirical relationship between average multiples of cash flow or revenues for small, privately held businesses and the rise and fall of stock prices on major exchanges. In other words, a bull market does not pull up small company multiples in a material manner. Amazingly, such multiples have been flat for the past twelve years according to his study.

This finding is further supported by the fact that the average multiple of cash flow for all businesses in the VR Business Brokers database (now more than 40,000 sales) has been incredibly consistent over the years. Thus, the guideline method is not generally applicable to smaller businesses (e.g., sales less than approximately $3 to $5 million or ACF less than approximately $1 million; these figures are only approximations and should not be relied on as the final determination as to which method is preferable). For the majority of small businesses, the comparable sales method that uses one of the four market comp databases will prove superior in ease of use and quality of outcomes in estimating FMV for such privately held, active ownership going concerns.

Applying the Market Comparable Methods

We now turn to the nuts and bolts of the most relevant market-based valuation methods. The market comparable method relies on one or more databases that contain sales data for all types of companies, typically covering the past year or two. In general, more current data is preferable, but average multiples for various types of smaller businesses seem to be stable over time.

Validity of Market Comp Data Over Time

The VR Business Brokers database, which began in 1979 and tracks transactions covering all types of businesses, has generated a fairly consistent average of sale price to seller's discretionary cash over the past several years. VR's "seller's discretionary cash" (SDC, the title they give to cash flow) refers to the same measure as the ACF figure presented in this book. They are the same and are also equal to the BIZCOMPS and Pratt's Stats measure of cash flow called seller's discretionary cash flow (SDCF); only the IBA database uses a slightly different measure for cash flow (by excluding depreciation and amortization expense).

Over the past several years, the average small business sold through the VR network was purchased for 2.2 to 2.4 times ACF. In other words, the average price to cash flow ratio (mean price) has been remarkably consistent over time throughout the country. Because it is only an average, many businesses sold for more than 2.3 times ACF and many businesses sold for less than 2.3 times ACF. As a ballpark estimate for the average small business, a multiple of 2 to 2.5 times ACF seems to be a good starting point for assessing company value. Stated differently, the typical small business sells for around 2.3 times ACF (with the caveat that higher cash flows result in higher multiples).

Raymond Miles, director of the Institute of Business Appraisers, found the same relationship between average multiples over time in his analysis of the IBA Transaction Database called "Age Effects: Linear Regression of Price to Earnings Ratio on the Date of Sale for the Years 1982 Through 1991, and Linear Regression of Price to Gross Sales Ratio on the Date of Sale for the Same Years." He concluded, "The price to earnings ratio and the price to gross sales ratio of closely held businesses sold during the period 1982 through 1991 show essentially zero correlation with the date of sale."

This study is very important in that it establishes that transactions reflected in the IBA Transaction Database (and other databases, for that matter) that occur significantly earlier than a current valuation date can be used for valuation purposes. A possible explanation for this is found in the relationship between higher cash flow and higher multiples: As the economy grows and stock markets rise, small businesses also grow into higher production of cash flows that are rewarded with higher multiples. Thus, it is not the case that all multiples rise over time, as they do in a bull market. Rather, the company's higher cash flows over time lead to higher multiples.

Not surprisingly, this is not the case when publicly traded guideline businesses are used under the market approach to valuing closely held businesses. An article that appeared in *Barron's* in 1997 titled "The Long Stampede" indicated that the average P/E ratio for the Standard & Poor's 500 Stock Index increased from 7 in 1992 to 23 in 1997 (after rising further through the year 1999, these multiples decreased significantly in 2000 and 2001). In this case, most businesses received higher (or lower) multiples in general, regardless of cash flow levels (with the distinction being that the cash flow levels were on average several million dollars or more). This difference further highlights the substantial distinctions between smaller, privately held companies and larger, publicly traded companies.

Use of the average multiple of price to cash flow generated by averaging all types of business sales in a particular database (e.g., manufacturing and retail and service and distribution) is not the optimal approach for estimating the FMV of a specific company. Logically, the goal should be to collect the most recent sales statistics available for the particular type of company at hand.

Industry-Specific Trends in Average Market Comp Multiples

Given the finding that these multiples do not change over time, the time element does not appear to be as important. However, more recent comps are preferable. Despite the generalization concerning average multiples for all types of businesses taken as a whole, certain types of businesses enjoy rising average multiples over time, reflecting unique circumstances in the relevant industry (some will fall, but for different reasons). For example, privately owned video store multiples have fallen dramatically from their historically high levels because of the expansion of Blockbuster and other large chains, whereas ISPs and other Internet-based operations have enjoyed rising multiples reflecting the spread of Internet usage and consolidation in this industry. All other factors held equal, more current comps are a better gauge of current value.

Comparing the Major Market Comp Databases

BIZCOMPS, Pratt's Stats, and the IBA database allow searches for comparable transactions via SIC codes, whereas the VR database is organized by categories of business types (e.g., manufacturing, retail, service, wholesale). Overall, each database is uniquely operated and contains different pieces of the valuation puzzle. Because of the differences between databases, each one must be used on its own terms with its own unique pros and cons. For illustrative purposes, the following table presents the major features of the data contained in each of the four major market comp databases.

	BIZCOMPS	VR Business Brokers	IBA	Pratt's Stats
Type of business	Y	Y	Y	Y
SIC code	Y	N	Y	Y
Date of sale	Y	Y[a]	Y	Y
Days on market	Y	Y	N	N
Location	Y	Y	Y	Y
Asking price	Y	Y	N	N
Purchase price	Y[b]	Y	Y	Y
Asking down payment	N	Y	N	N
Actual down payment	Y	Y	Y	Y
Stock sale or asset sale	N	N	N	Y
Financing terms	Y	N	N	Y
Gross revenues	Y	Y	Y	Y
Adjusted cash flow	Y	Y	Y[c]	Y
Inventory	Y[d]	N	N	Y
Fixed assets	Y	N	N	Y
Price/adjusted cash flow	Y[b]	Y	Y[c]	Y
Price/gross revenues	Y[b]	Y	Y	Y
Rent/gross revenues	Y	N	N	Y
Financial statements	N	N	N	Y
Purchase price allocation	N	N	N	Y
Lease information	N	N	N	Y
Employment contract	N	N	N	Y
Other data	N	N	N	Y[e]
Multiple databases	Y[a]	Y[b]	N	Y[e]

Note: It is important to realize that each reported sale contains different amounts of information (i.e., not all reported sales include all of the data fields listed in this table).

[a]General time frame only (e.g., during 2001), for different categorizations (e.g., sales less than $100,000, sales more than $500,000, sales last year or last three years).

[b]BIZCOMPS sale price data excludes inventory (i.e., the amount of inventory included in the sale is backed out from the purchase price). Their data are grouped by region (e.g., Western states) and include a separate database for larger companies called the National Industrial Study that includes inventory in these sale price figures.

ᶜOnly the IBA database uses a cash flow measure different from our ACF because it may or may not exclude depreciation or amortization expense.

ᵈDespite backing inventory out of the sale price, they include inventory amounts in their database when they are available.

ᵉPratt's Stats contains by far the most data related to the reported transactions, as evidenced by this table. Other information addresses personal guarantees, balance of lease assumed, operating profit versus earnings before taxes (EBT) versus net income figures, number of employees, years in business, date of incorporation, eight separate multiples including price to net sales, earnings before interest and taxes (EBIT), and EBITDA. In addition, the same search apparatus will lead the user to BIZCOMPS, Mergerstat/Shannon Pratt's Control Premium Study, and the Public Company database.

Overview of Major Databases

As the preceding table illustrates, there are four major sources of comparable sales data concerning privately held companies available in the United States. Three of the four are available for direct purchase by the public, and the fourth source, VR Business Brokers, provides data in conjunction with its primary role as a business broker for buyers and sellers of small businesses. VR data are available for purchase on a case-by-case basis for those who are working with a VR broker. Each of the other three databases can be accessed in whole or on a company- or industry-specific basis either over the Internet or by phone or fax.

Before we study examples of how to use the comparable sales method, a brief review of each of the major market data sources is worthwhile. Blindly choosing a few comps and generating a simple average may be dangerously unproductive. As each database is unique, care must be exercised in using each one separately and in accordance with the specific features of the subject company.

BIZCOMPS

The BIZCOMPS study of small business sales was begun in 1990 by its author and founder, Jack Sanders. As of May 2001, the entire database consisted of more than 5,000 transactions from a wide variety of industries and across the nation. Its stated objective is to accumulate reliable comparable business sale information for entrepreneurs, investors, and advisors seeking to estimate the FMV of small businesses. The mean selling price in all BIZCOMPS databases is approximately $235,000 (median selling price equals $110,000). Only 15 percent of the database contains middle-market or what the authors call industrial companies, generating a mean selling price of $850,000.

In addition to the main business type categories (e.g., retail or manufacturing), several subcategories exist (e.g., manufacturing of electronics, manufacturing of injection molding). Different reports are produced for different geographic regions. One of the more useful features is the ratio of rent to total revenues. If available, inventory and furniture, fixtures, and equipment data are included as well as information on asking price and down payment. Importantly, revenue and cash flow information is presented, both in absolute terms and in multiple formats (e.g., price to cash flow). Finally, the transaction data include analysis of terms, specifically the amount of cash paid at closing as a down payment (e.g., approximately 25 percent of all businesses in a recent study were sold for all cash). There are twenty data fields in the BIZCOMPS database.

Note that a small percentage of the reported transactions are routinely eliminated because of their exceptionally high or negative multiples of cash flow and revenues. When applying the comparable sales method in general, it is often prudent to throw out the two or three highest and lowest multiples from each sample if the sample size is large enough. If there is a preponderance of multiples in the 2 to 4 range, throwing out a multiple of 10 or 0.2 is reasonable because these outliers will reduce the credibility of the results.

Each database is unique in its content and presentation of multiples. BIZCOMPS differs from other databases in that it excludes inventory from the reported sale prices and thus the reported multiples of cash flow and revenues (except for their National Industrial Study, which pertains to larger, middle-market companies). The logic behind eliminating inventory from the sale price is that this particular asset varies greatly across businesses and is subject to manipulation by the buyer and seller in such a way as to distort the true sale price. For example, some retail and manufacturing businesses may be sold with ample inventory, and others may be sold with little or no inventory as a result of the unique negotiations that occurred before closing.

Most businesses are presented with an asking price that includes $X of inventory, but it is quite common for the parties to adjust the purchase price by manipulating inventory. A buyer may not want to carry the particular amount of inventory included in the asking price because it is substantially higher than what is needed to run the business effectively. In other situations, the seller may continue to operate the business for several months pending close of escrow and intentionally avoid restocking to preserve scarce cash.

The fact that most purchase contracts include a clause that adjusts the final purchase price or the amount of seller financing based on the actual amount of inventory at hand the day before closing does not always prevent sellers from selling down the inventory and avoiding replenishment. Thus, the BIZCOMPS authors believe that excluding inventory from the sale price helps to avoid the distortions associated with this volatile asset. If it were possible to assume that every sale included the optimal or normal amount of inventory, this adjustment would not be necessary (according to the publisher of the data).

The BIZCOMPS survey data can be obtained online at *www.BIZCOMPS. com* or by phone at 858–457–0366. As described earlier, data can be obtained on a regional basis, for larger companies only (Industrial Survey) or for food service businesses only. Overall, the BIZCOMPS approach is straightforward and easy to use. Note that the BIZCOMPS data are also available through the Web site *www.bvmarketdata.com*^{sm} or *www.BVResources.com*^{sm}, which also houses the Tatum study of BIZCOMPS databases and an incredible amount of other business valuation information, including our next database (Pratt's Stats).

Pratt's Stats

This collection of market data is contained in the innovative and comprehensive Web site *www.BVResources.com*. The managing owner of this site, Shannon Pratt, is considered the leading business valuation expert in the world. The thoroughness of this site is intentional: It is intended to be a one-stop business valuation Web site for valuation professionals and entrepreneurs alike. The major sections and components of this site include the following:

www.BVLibrary.com^{sm}

Business Valuation Update (monthly newsletter)

Judges and Lawyers Business Valuation Update

Cost of capital survey

IRS statute materials

Full text of valuation court cases

Numerous papers, books, and other publications

www.BVMarketData.com^{sm}

Pratt's Stats^{tm}

BIZCOMPS

Mergerstat/Shannon Pratt's Control Premium Study

Public company database

The site also maintains an online store to facilitate purchases of all available information and products. Other useful features include a tip of the week, a court case of the week, and a business valuation term of the week.

Pratt's Stats is the most recent attempt to collect and disseminate useful sale price data for small businesses across the country. Created by Shannon Pratt, this database is uniquely thorough (up to seventy data fields, compared with twenty for BIZCOMPS) and growing rapidly. Within two or three years, this database may be the deepest and most reliable of all. The Web site *www.bvmarketdata.com* contains not only the Pratt's Stats data but also the BIZCOMPS data and other useful market-based valuation data applicable to publicly traded companies.

The Pratt's Stats data cover both "main street" businesses (described as being part of the business brokerage segment in Chapter Two) and larger M&A transactions (described as middle-market companies in Chapter Two and as industrial companies in BIZCOMPS). However, it should be stressed that the bulk of the transactions are middle-market: The mean selling price is approximately $16.5 million (compared with $235,000 for BIZCOMPS). Only 24 percent of the reported deals were for less than $1 million, and 17 percent sold for more than $30 million. More than 550 unique SIC codes are covered by this database, compared with approximately 380 for BIZCOMPS.

Because of the average deal size, it is not surprising that a substantial number of these transactions were stock sales as opposed to asset sales. For all stock sales, the "equity price" (effectively the sale price for the subject transaction) is presumed to include all operating assets and operating liabilities (current assets and liabilities). If long-term debts are assumed as part of the transaction, this is listed separately and combined with the equity price to arrive at the total deal price.

For all asset sales, the equity price includes only the operating assets (which may exclude cash and receivables), thus excluding operating liabilities. Asset sales in general are assumed to exclude the cash, receivables, and all debts, which is the case for BIZCOMPS, the VR database, or the IBA database (remember that only BIZCOMPS excludes inventory from its reported sale prices). Being able to distinguish between a stock sale and an asset sale is one of the major advantages of the Pratt's Stats database compared with the other three major sources. Another unique piece of information found in this source is the type of company being sold (e.g., S-corporation or LLC). Importantly, Pratt's Stats uses the same measure of cash flow (called discretionary earnings) as VR and BIZCOMPS (the IBA cash flow measure is slightly different, as described in detail later). In line with the comprehensive nature of this site, they also present multiples of EBIT and EBITDA to complement the traditional discretionary earnings measure. Overall, this source of comp data contains a deeper and broader array of information than the other sources of private transaction data. There is really no comparison because of the inclusion of such detailed information as number of employees, stock versus asset sale, personal guarantee and other financing features, complete balance sheet and income statement data, employment contract, and allocation of purchase price details. However, this database typically applies only to middle-market companies as opposed to the typical, smaller privately held companies that make up the bulk of all businesses in the country.

The market comp Web site *www.bvmarketdata.com* contains much more than Pratt's Stats. BIZCOMPS data are available as part of the same search based on a particular SIC code or company size and geographic location. The Mergerstat/Shannon Pratt Control Premium Study and a public company database round off this site to make it the leader in providing market comp data. On the search page of this site, one can enter the SIC or NAICS code, a range of revenues, applicable time period, a range of deal prices, and location information to begin the process. The response to such a query is an initial list of the number of comps available in each of the four distinct databases (Pratt's Stats, BIZCOMPS, Mergerstat/Shannon Pratt's Control Premium Study, and the public company database). The details are one click away for each database. The site is well supported with background information, major assumptions, and a useful list of frequently asked questions.

IBA

The next source of market data comes from the nation's oldest business valuation certification-granting organization. The Institute of Business Appraisers (IBA) was founded in 1978 and now enjoys a membership exceeding 3,000, several hundred of whom have earned the designation of Certified Business Appraiser (CBA). One of the major benefits of membership is their large collection of market comp data compiled over more than twenty years.

As of June 2001, the IBA Transaction Database contained information from nearly 15,000 transactions involving the sale and purchase of closely held businesses (making it the largest source of market comps available directly to the public). Most of these transactions related to small to midsize businesses. The IBA Transaction Database is prepared specifically for use with the DMDM, which was developed by the IBA to foster credible and consistent use of its market comp statistics. The IBA solicits information from individual business brokers, accountants, and other intermediaries involved in the actual sale and purchase of closely held businesses and from organizations of such people. Readers who choose to use the IBA market comp data are strongly encouraged to use the tutorials presented on the IBA Web site at no cost (*www.go-iba.com*).

These tutorials are clear and concise, allowing the reader to quickly grasp the essence of the DMDM. Despite the preference among valuators for using earnings or cash flow as the chosen indicator of company performance for using market comp data, the IBA states clearly that because of reporting problems (incomplete and inaccurate earnings information), use of a price to gross revenue multiple often may be preferable. The use of scattergrams for certain types of businesses helps to illustrate the closer correlation between gross revenues and sale price than between annual earnings and sale price. To a certain degree, the IBA thus encourages the use of price to gross revenue multiples as the preferable mode for implementing the market approach to business valuation.

Not surprisingly, a distinctive feature of this database relates to the measure of cash flow used for developing comparative multiples. The distinction is primarily one of terminology. The "annual earnings" figure that forms the crux of this database is quite similar to our familiar ACF figure. Specifically, the IBA defines annual earnings as "annual earnings before owner's compensation expense, interest expense, and income tax expense" and then cautions the reader that "this data category is not available for all transactions, and is of only marginal utility given the quality of small business financial statements." This comment is intended primarily as a warning to the valuator that different parties include different components in the "owner's compensation" category. For example, some include pension contributions, some do not; some include personal travel and entertainment, some do not; some include payroll taxes, some do not.

The IBA definition should be interpreted to mean that the relevant earnings figure (annual earnings) is equal to pretax income (or taxable income plus tax expense) plus owner's compensation and interest expense. Thus, the IBA's cash flow figure called annual earnings does not include depreciation and amortization. This means that their measure of cash flow is not directly comparable with BIZCOMPS, VR, or Pratt's Stats.

A separate figure is reported reflecting the owner's compensation, but their "annual earnings" measure has already backed out this amount to arrive at EBITC. Consider the following chart:

ACF	EBITC
Pretax income	Pretax income (net income plus tax expense)
Plus owner's compensation	Plus owner's compensation
Plus interest	Plus interest
Plus depreciation and amortization	

This table clarifies the ultimate distinction, which is that noncash charges such as depreciation and amortization are not included in the IBA cash flow figure. Some valuation professionals would argue that this is a more correct interpretation of earnings or cash flow because depreciated assets must be replaced over time. They believe that even though depreciation is a noncash expense, funds ultimately must be made available to replace FF&E as it wears out over time.

The IBA cash flow measure called "annual earnings" is the sum of EBIT and the owner's compensation. However, given the lack of depreciation and amortization expenses as addbacks, the IBA cash flow figure is not directly comparable with the other three database cash flow figures (ACF). More to the point, the IBA cash flow figure is smaller than the others, so IBA multiples are higher than the others to compensate for the lesser cash flow amount. In other words, the very same business will sell for a higher multiple to EBITC than to ACF because EBITC is a lower amount reflecting the lack of noncash expense addbacks. For example:

Sale Price	EBITC	ACF	Price/EBITC	Price/ACF
$100,000	$40,000	$50,000	2.5	2

The IBA multiples (price/EBITC) therefore are lower than the other multiples (price/ACF) because of the exclusion of depreciation and amortization in the IBA cash flow figure.

Despite the different cash flow measure, the IBA database is extensive and useful for many types of businesses because of the large number of comps it contains. Furthermore, because the essence of the market approach is to compare the subject company with a pool of similar businesses, as long as the same measures are used for both the market comps and the subject business, the results remain effective. The real caveat concerns the combining of data across databases (e.g., cash flow data from BIZCOMPS should never be lumped in with IBA data and vice versa).

More than 600 different SIC codes have at least five transactions, which is commonly considered a bare minimum for effective comparisons. Examples of SIC codes with more than 100 different comps are as follows:

Business Type	SIC Code	Number of Transactions
Restaurants	5812–15	2,705
Dental practices	8021	688
Commercial printers	2752	250
Accounting and tax practices	8721	186
Florists	5992	179
Service stations	5541	175
Beauty salons	7231	163
Gift shops	5947	156
Business services	7389	154
General auto repair	7538	136
Travel agencies	4724	127
Childcare services	8351	124
Auto home supply	5531	122
Miscellaneous retail	5999	116
Miscellaneous services	7299 and 8999	108 and 106

Seventy-four percent of the companies earned gross revenues less than $500,000 per year, and 16 percent earned gross revenues greater than $1 million. Each SIC code searched will generate a list of all related comps that contains data fields such as business type, SIC code, annual revenues and earnings, owner's compensation, sale price, P/E and P/R multiples, geographic location, and the month and year of sale. For more information on how to obtain and use the IBA database, visit their new Web site at *www.go-iba.com*. Online tutorials exist to clarify the use of their comps via what they call the direct market data method (DMDM), which is essentially the same as what we call the comparable sales method (as opposed to the guideline public company method). The tutorials are well organized and worth the time expended in reading them, especially for the nonprofessional valuator.

VR Business Brokers

VR Business Brokers is the nation's oldest and most successful business brokerage company in the entire country. Since 1979, the company has brokered thousands of deals across the continent from more than sixty-five individually owned and operated franchises. The VR database is one of the largest and probably the most diverse because of the geographic dispersion of offices and most accurate because of the mandatory reporting requirements that relate to the payment of franchise fees as a percentage of commissions paid (ultimately reflecting deal prices).

Their database is called BizStats and is grouped initially according to type of company, ranging from general (all manufacturing) to more specific (cocktail lounges, taverns, and bars). Specifically, alphabetic categories run from A to M, as follows:

Group	Description
A	Cocktail lounges/taverns/bars
B	Fast food (primarily take-out)
C	Restaurants
D	Miscellaneous food service
E	Cleaning operations
F	Markets
G	Liquor stores
H	Services
I	Retail
J	Inactive
K	Manufacturing
L	Distribution/wholesale
M	Land and commercial property

Transactions are further classified according to size (e.g., sale prices under $100,000 or over $500,000) and by time (e.g., calendar year or last three years). Averages for each of their data fields are available for each major category as well; for example, between March 1997 and March 2000, retail businesses sold for an average of 2.7 times seller's discretionary cash (exactly the same as our ACF figure) and generated approximately 82 percent of the asking prices after an average of 197 days on the market.

Overall, the size and accuracy of this database are its strengths. Its major weakness is that it is not readily available to the public. The company considers this database proprietary information that is used to differentiate the quality of their services from those of their competition. However, select data can be purchased through one of the VR agents or owners at a negotiated fee. For a list of VR offices across the country and other business brokerage–related information, visit their Web site at *www.vrbusinessbrokers.com* or contact the author at *www.scottgabehart.com*.

Examples of the Comparable Sales Method

Now that we are familiar with the different market comp databases relevant to this method, we can continue by walking through a hypothetical example. Remember that there are a few variants of the comparable sales method (as there are for most valuation methods), so we must choose between them at this point. We begin with a more complicated version based on merger and acquisition data relating to publicly traded entities to emphasize the relative appeal of the alternative version based on privately held company sales and the major market comp databases such as BIZCOMPS. After you realize the complexity and scope of the necessary adjustments applicable to the alternative version, the comparable sales method based on privately held company sales will appear increasingly attractive.

Comparable Sales Method Using Whole Public Company Transactions

One of the more challenging (and less commonly used) comparable sales method versions calls for using actual sales (mergers and acquisitions) of whole publicly traded companies (not privately held) for comparison with the subject company. The M&A market is dynamic and recently quite active, so similar companies that have been purchased in whole (taken over by another company, for example) by an acquiring company can be found for many industries. Using the ISP example again, there have been several acquisitions of whole ISP entities as the industry has tended toward consolidation.

Use of the company takeover or acquisition prices for comparison with a smaller, privately held counterpart is possible and may even be productive if the subject company is of a substantial size. If not, a direct comparison of the acquisition price multiples of the larger entities is not useful given the dramatic differences between the two market segments. If this variation of the comparable sales method is used under any circumstances, many adjustments must take place to ensure meaningful comparisons.

In this version, the income statements for each market comp should be adjusted to allow credible comparisons (e.g., all companies should generate earnings based on similar accounting policies such as last-in, first-out [LIFO] or first-in, first-out [FIFO] for inventory accounting). Depreciation methods should be adjusted to allow comparisons as well (e.g., restate all income statements to reflect straight-line depreciation). Any extraordinary gains or losses should be netted out of pretax and after-tax income.

The balance sheets should be analyzed to determine differences between a company with no debt and a company with substantial debt. There are significant differences between a company with no debt and a company with substantial debt. For example, a company with substantial debt may be more properly valued in regard to the market value of invested capital (MVIC) as opposed to the market value of the equity only. In modern financial theory, there are advantages for shareholders via the use of leverage or debt if the returns from the invested debt are greater than the cost of the debt itself. Overall, it is difficult to compare companies with dramatically different accounting procedures and financial statements.

Another common adjustment calls for downsizing the earnings multiples for the larger companies to a level consistent with the subject company. As discussed elsewhere, larger cash flows are associated with higher multiples, so it is not acceptable to compare a small, privately held company with $500,000 in cash flow with a publicly traded company with $20 million in earnings. If all comparable companies have earnings that are substantially higher, their average multiple should be adjusted downward. This is another judgment call that varies from one valuator to the next and complicates the valuation process from the entrepreneur's point of view.

Comparable Sales Method Using the Major Market Comp Databases

Because of the complexity of the whole public company version, we focus on a more straightforward approach that relies on market comp data obtained from one or more of the four databases described earlier in this chapter (thus avoiding the difficult and time-consuming adjustments needed to analyze publicly traded companies).

Our recommended approach is based on locating the maximum number of similar companies (at a minimum, the type, size, and location of business should be similar) and massaging the available data to generate average multiples of cash flows or revenues for comparisons with the subject company. Although this may seem like a simplistic approach, because of the tremendous variation between businesses and transactions that appear to be similar on the surface, such a general approach is appealing for many reasons.

We shall stick with the name "comparable sales method" for our recommended approach (recall that the IBA uses a similar approach in its DMDM). Use of this technique allows the valuator to apply market-based valuation results to the subject company without the difficulties of adjusting or micromanaging financial statements or downsizing average multiples, as was necessary in the first version outlined earlier. The ability to avoid these types of adjustments is a result of using a large, diverse sample of comps related to companies that are of a similar size in terms of revenues and cash flow and operate in the same industry.

Favorable Impact of Large Sample Size

As described in Chapter Six, several important terms and conditions can affect a final, negotiated deal price between buyer and seller. Some deals are stock sales, and some are asset sales. Some deals include a great deal of inventory, and some do not. Some are for all cash, and some are with seller financing. Some come with an employment contract for the seller, and some do not. Some are collateralized beyond the company's assets, and some contain only a personal guarantee, and so on. Overall, some sell for higher multiples, and some sell for lower multiples. Get the picture?

The logic behind this version of the comparable sales approach is based in part on the statistical properties of a large sample size. By maximizing the number of available comps, one can even out the odds of a deal possessing one feature versus another. In other words, if one selects a large sample size, the resulting average multiple is an average that pertains to all factors having been addressed. If the sample is large enough, it will be representative of all deals and of all the particular terms and conditions that permeate a particular type of business sale across time.

The Bell Curve and a Normal Distribution

Many valuators believe that the multiples of cash flow form a bell-shaped curve around the average multiple for the entire group of similar companies. A bell curve with a normal distribution would illustrate the fact that there is a strong central tendency (mean) around which lower and higher values exist in decreasing frequency as you move away from the mean. Loosely interpreted, this means that the majority of transaction prices hover around the average price in a manner such that the relative frequency of prices declines as the distance from the mean increases.

A publication titled "Introduction to the Direct Market Data Method," written by Ray Miles of the IBA, includes analysis that suggests that there is a bell curve, but it is skewed to the right because of a large number of small businesses that sell for higher prices than a normal distribution would predict. In other words, there is a tendency for small business prices to exceed the mean more often than they fall below the mean. Stated differently, the median value typically is greater than the mean (i.e., more than half of the prices are greater than the mean or average price).

Whether the transaction prices are a normal distribution or skewed to the right, the strength of this version of the comparable sales method is based on a large enough sample size. The many terms, conditions, and characteristics of particular deals and businesses average out over a large collection of market comp statistics, ultimately allowing the valuator to compare the subject company with the average or the norm in terms of cash flow and revenue multiples. In fact, it is the multiples of cash flow or revenues that reflect the particular pluses and minuses or pros and cons of a given business, with the average representing a typical set of terms, conditions, and characteristics.

For these reasons, our selected approach to using market comp data is premised on collecting the largest group of similar company market comps possible to reflect the diverse combinations of deal and company features that make up the universe of done deals. If our collection is large and diverse enough, we will have an average against which to compare our subject company in pursuit of our FMV estimate. It may be prudent to massage the collection by removing outliers, which are average multiples that are quite distant from the majority of multiples in the group. Statistically speaking, this might mean throwing out the scores that are three or more standard deviations away from the mean. Practically speaking, this might mean throwing out the top and bottom three or four scores from a sample size of thirty.

Once again, judgment and experience come into play because there is no absolute right or wrong way to implement any valuation method. Every valuation method contains at least one material subjective component that is a matter of judgment and opinion, to be backed up by a combination of fact and common sense. As you gain practice in using the market comp databases, you will begin to get a feel for what is acceptable and what is not.

For example, as you review a list of comps for a particular SIC code or business category, you may notice that only a few of those listed are similar to the subject company. Accordingly, you may decide to pick and choose among those listed for a particular SIC code to match the specific nature of the business under evaluation. Perhaps you are seeking to value an independent gift shop, so you choose the proper SIC code and notice that other types of businesses are listed as well, such as franchised gift shops or even a golf-related retail business. The goal is to find the most similar comps possible, so it may be necessary to refine your selection accordingly. On the other hand, if there are only a handful of comps for a particular SIC code, you may want to broaden the scope somewhat (e.g., by including the franchised gift shops in your group of comps).

Accounting Practices and Market Comp Data

Let's use a common type of business to put our method to the test. Let's assume that you own an accounting or tax practice (similar logic applies to all service businesses to a large extent, such as janitorial, landscaping, collection agency, and other account-oriented operations). To be thorough, turning to at least two of the market comp databases seems prudent. To make things easier, we could use two databases that use the same measure of cash flow and that are generally similar (e.g., Pratt's Stats and the VR database). BIZCOMPS uses the same measure of cash flow, but their prices do not include inventory, so they would not be directly comparable. It may be that time permits use of only one database, or it may be that a particular type of business is well covered in one or the other of the databases. As long as the sample size is large enough, this is acceptable. Ideally, the sample size will be large enough to account for all the unique features that were discussed in prior paragraphs.

Subject Company

Our subject company has been determined to have the following characteristics:

Well established (twelve years)

Diverse client base (seasonal tax versus consistent write-up or monthly work)

Revenues highly dependent on owner

High hourly billing rate (above average)

Lease rate is below market; long term options available

Two locations: one upscale, one in a strip mall

Key employee (CPA) handles upscale clients (will remain with new owner)

Seller will transition as "partner" (through the first tax season at a minimum)

Gross revenues of $290,000

Pretax earnings of $70,000

Owner's salary and perks of $40,000

ACF of $130,000

EBITC★ $120,000

We begin our analysis with the Pratt's Stats database. The relevant SIC code is 8721, so we can use this information along with the data in the preceding table to tailor our search. We go to the Web page *www.bvmarketdata.com* to begin the process. On the home page, we click the "Search" icon and then drag down to Pratt's Stats and click again. We are now on the advanced search page, where we will enter the appropriate SIC code (8721), among other entries. Pratt's Stats allows refined search capabilities to narrow the resulting list of market comps. Gross revenue, operating profit, net income, and total asset descriptions will narrow the search accordingly. In addition to these financial data, transaction data can be entered to further define the search (e.g., transaction prices between $100,000 and $500,000 can be selected to generate only deals that were completed within this range).

In this particular search, if we enter financial data restrictions that surround the subject company's performance (e.g., revenues less than $1 million, operating profit less than $200,000, net income less than $100,000, and total assets less than $100,000) and then execute the search, a new page will appear with the information about the comps that match our criteria. Unfortunately, these financial data generated one comp only. To make things worse, it was not even an accounting or tax practice (it was a billing and collection service).

We can try to broaden the scope by entering the SIC code as the only search criterion. The results of this broad search of the Pratt's Stats database were sufficient in size (fourteen transactions), but none of them were accounting or tax practices. They were also extremely large (average price greater than $14 million) compared with the subject company.

If we had carefully considered which database would be proper for a tax or accounting practice of this size, we would have realized that Pratt's Stats would not be a good source because of its average deal price of around $16 million. It

---

★Recall that the IBA database uses a different measure of cash flow that excludes noncash expenses (i.e., ACF is greater than EBITC by the amount of depreciation and amortization expense).

should be clear now that Pratt's Stats is more applicable to middle-market companies and the guideline public company valuation method. The other three databases contain smaller average prices, so we now turn to them for help.

Because BIZCOMPS data are also housed on the *www.bvmarketdata.com* Web page, we can return to the home page and select the "BIZCOMPS" icon. We move into BIZCOMPS because we are already using a Web site that contains these data, but if we remember that the IBA database had nearly 200 comps for accounting and tax practices, we may want to skip ahead to this tool.

We are now back on the initial search page that led us to Pratt's Stats, where the same choices exist in terms of search criteria. Let's begin with a general approach and try a search using only the SIC code. After scrolling up and down the SIC code list, it becomes apparent that BIZCOMPS does not contain any data related to this particular SIC code.

Therefore, we should move on to the remaining two databases, probably the IBA database. For the sake of thoroughness, however, I picked up the most recent hardcopy edition of the *2000 BIZCOMPS Western States* edition to double-check its coverage of SIC code 8721. To my surprise, its newest exhibit includes accounting and tax practices. Twenty-four such businesses are listed here, providing a useful sample size for our valuation analysis. The lesson here is that the more thorough one is in pursuing market comp data, the more likely the final valuation results are to be useful and credible. BIZCOMPS Exhibit #85 presents the following general valuation results for accounting and tax businesses:

Sale price to gross revenues	97 percent
Sale price to SDCF	(ACF):1.9

It is important not to lose sight of the big picture or the ARM approach in general. Under normal circumstances, by the time we are reviewing market comps, we have already completed the first two steps of the valuation process. We have calculated the ACF and determined the proper multiple to apply to our subject business. For the sake of simplicity, let's assume we arrived at a multiple of 2.5 times ACF for our subject practice, generating an estimate of company value equal to $325,000 (2.5 times $130,000). We would have also reviewed the pertinence and existence of rules of thumb, which in the case of our subject company turn out to be important. A widely used rule of thumb here is based on a multiple of gross revenues (e.g., 90 to 110 percent of annual gross revenues). Assume now that we determined that a multiple of 105 percent was proper, generating another estimate of FMV equal to $304,500 (1.05 times $290,000).

Thus, before evaluating market comps, we would have generated the following preliminary valuation results:

Multiple of ACF $325,000
Rule of thumb $304,500

Our review of the BIZCOMPS data for our subject company has provided us with mean multiples of 1.9 times ACF and 97 percent of gross revenues. Remembering that the BIZCOMPS transaction prices exclude inventory, we must exercise care before finalizing our conclusions. Given the relative unimportance of inventory for such businesses (rarely more than $3,000), this distinction appears to be irrelevant. The question now becomes one of comparing the subject company with the norm based on this database. A cursory review of the comp data shows that CPA companies sell on average for a significantly higher multiple of revenues, helping to make the case that our subject company is above average. In practice, a careful review of all factors related to the subject business should be undertaken, but for our current situation we shall assume that based on a review of all relevant considerations, the subject company is approximately 15 percent above the average. Thus, our subject company can be valued as follows:

Adjusted Multiples

ACF multiple: 1.9×1.15 = approximately 2.19
Gross Revenue Multiple: 97 percent $\times 1.15$ = approximately 112 percent

Subject Company Value Using Adjusted Multiples

$2.19 \times \$130,000 =$	$284,700
112 percent $\times \$290,000 =$	$324,800
Average of these two values:	$304,750

Using the BIZCOMPS database, we therefore estimate the FMV of our subject company at $304,750. In practice, the market comp portion of the ARM approach is subsequently evaluated in light of the first two portions (ACF and rules of thumb). Among other options, one prudent way to conclude the overall evaluation is to take an average of the three results, as follows:

ACF multiple result	$325,000
Rule of thumb result	$304,500
Market comp result	$304,750
ARM average	$311,417

Our finalized estimate of FMV for our subject company is $311,417, which turns out to be approximately 2.4 times ACF and 107 percent of gross revenues. Remember also that the result of the ARM approach is a price based on typical seller financing (e.g., 40 percent down at closing and the balance over three to five years at 8 to 10 percent interest). In terms of an accounting practice in particular, the sale will be made based on a seller guarantee, meaning that the actual final price will be adjusted pending the actual amount of gross revenues earned during the new owner's first year in operation.

The use of a straight average of the three ARM results is only one possibility. A better approach would be to weight each result based on the valuator's judgment as to the applicability and reliability of each result. For example, given that most accountants and business brokers involved in the sale of such practices rely chiefly on the multiple of gross revenues for establishing value, a higher weighting might be accorded to the second component (rule of thumb) or even the third component because of its partial use of gross revenue multipliers related to the market averages. Although we have had good success with the BIZ-COMPS data, we should take the time to review the IBA and VR database as they apply to accounting and tax practices.

Our earlier analysis of the IBA database showed that there are nearly 200 comps for tax and accounting practices, so this appears to be the optimal database. How do we obtain these comps? One way is via e-mail through their Web site at *www.go-iba.com*. After payment arrangements are made, it is only a matter of sending a request for comps for whatever SIC code you are analyzing. A brief memo asking for all comps related to the SIC code 8721 will result in a return e-mail that contains the comp data in a file (worksheet format) that facilitates the necessary analysis. IBA comps normally are listed in order of gross revenue size from largest to smallest. For accounting and tax practices, this is ideal because of the critical rule of thumb commonly used by accountants, business brokers, and valuation professionals alike that is based solely on gross revenues. Experience and various studies have confirmed the overwhelming importance of gross revenues in determining the value of such businesses (much more important than ACF, which typically controls business valuation results). Note that requests made for multiple SIC codes (e.g., 3560 through 3599) will generate a list that ranks the comps by size for each subsequent SIC code from the first to the last (rather than listing all comps in order of size).

Given the size of the collected comps for this type of business, we should be able to refine our search in a meaningful manner to ensure a credible, justifiable outcome.

The decisions made from here are a matter of judgment and opinion, but the general idea is to isolate the comps that are of a similar size. Because of the limited size of the BIZCOMPS database, we did not do any fine-tuning. We did not eliminate outliers, and we did not choose only the companies with similar revenues. However, this was not an oversight. A review of the comps showed that each one was for a practice that had revenues between $33,000 and $410,000. This seems to be an acceptable range overall given our desire to use the maximum number of comps to even out the particulars across all deals.

There are no hard and fast rules for refining the selected comps from databases such as the IBA or BIZCOMPS publications, but a practice with nearly $300,000 in gross revenues seems to be similar to other practices that generate between $200,000 and $500,000. Businesses that generate less than $200,000 are likely to be one-person entities (i.e., one practicing accountant with minimal administrative support). Such businesses with revenues over $500,000 are more diverse in their staffing (multiple accountants) and offered services (more specialization is likely). Thus, we collect the data related to the practices that generated between $200,000 and $500,000 for further analysis. Use of this revenue criterion reduces the collection to twenty-five transactions. One of these deals appears to be related to businesses that are not traditional accounting or tax practices, so it should be deleted from the group (billing services/medical, priced at $125,000).

Of the remaining twenty-four deals, only four appear to be well outside the concentration of multiples that fall between 75 and 125 percent of gross revenues, so they too are deleted (the top two and the bottom two multiples). Note that we could have completed the same step using the price to cash flow multiple, but once again the overriding importance of gross revenues for this type of business helps to clarify the proper choice. Most other businesses are valued primarily as a function of cash flow, with a few notable exceptions such as restaurants, travel agencies, and other service businesses.

The remaining twenty comps will serve as the foundation for our valuation analysis. Our goal is to produce an average multiple of gross revenues for the whole group to be used for comparison with our subject company. As described earlier, a large sample size allows the valuator to assume that the average multiple reflects an average deal. If the majority of deals are asset sales with an earnout included in the contract, this will be reflected in the average multiple. As it turns out, our refined sample size of twenty generated the following average multiples:

Price to gross revenues	120 percent
Price to ACF	2.73

Before analyzing these results in conjunction with the subject company, it is interesting to note that both average multiples are higher in the IBA database than in the BIZCOMPS database. Can you think of a good reason to explain this? If you guessed that the average size of the comp would lead to different averages, you are probably correct. Recall that the BIZCOMPS companies generated sales between $33,000 and $410,000. Both the lowest and the highest revenues in the BIZCOMPS database were less than the lowest and highest in the IBA selected database (revenues between $200,000 and $500,000). In fact, the average size in the IBA database was approximately 70 percent larger than in the BIZCOMPS sample ($275,000 versus $162,000). As noted throughout this book, a greater cash flow level is associated with a higher multiple of cash flow. It follows logically, then, that higher levels of cash flow tend to come from higher levels of revenues, so larger revenues should also be associated with higher multiples. Our present analysis certainly supports this proposition.

The next step in regard to the IBA data is to compare the subject company with what the average company has sold for on the open market, which turned out to be 120 percent of gross revenues and 2.73 times EBITC. The question boils down to whether the subject company is above or below average and, if so, to what degree. There are no fail-safe techniques to address this question; it is ultimately a matter of opinion. Any factors that affect business value could be reviewed in this process, as reiterated earlier. Each particular business has its own unique pluses and minuses (from both the individual company's and the industry's point of view) that collectively determine its status compared with the norm. In regard to accounting and tax practices, for example, each of the following characteristics pushes a subject company above the average:

Revenue base that is not extremely seasonal (balanced tax and accounting) or of a one-time nature

Large portion of revenues generated by staff rather than the owner

High hourly billing rates (high average monthly fees for financial statement preparation and high average tax return fees for individuals and businesses)

Below-market lease rate with short-term (not long-term) renewal options in favorable location

Experienced staff willing to remain employed with new owner

Software that is commonly used or actually used by purchaser

Seller willing to introduce new owner as partner and willing to remain active for more than one month (the longer, the higher the retention rate)

Newer computer system that is networked (more assets, higher multiple)

Reduced overhead from combining buyer's practice into one location and expansion of offered services (expertise) via acquired staff

In practice, each of these factors increases the deal price and hence business value. Note that the last factor actually applies to investment value as opposed to FMV, but such synergies do contribute to higher market prices that find their way into market comp databases. For example, industries that are subject to significant consolidation moves tend to generate higher multiples in reflection of the synergies that are spurring the consolidation in the first place. Water utilities, electrical contractors, ISPs, banks, and even accounting and tax practices to a certain extent are industries that are consolidating. On the other end of the spectrum, a lack of any of the value-forming factors will depress the company's value. Major detractors from value for tax or accounting practices include the following:

Minimal monthly or general accounting work to balance out the busy tax season

Owner responsible for all accounts and all revenues

Low billing rates (low monthly fees or low average tax return fees)

High percentage of nonrepeating revenues (e.g., bankruptcy, special consulting projects of a one-time nature, IRS representation)

Poor software programs or software that buyer is unfamiliar with (must reenter all data)

Substantial bad debt or slow payers (accounts receivable over ninety days)

Seller's staff capable of leaving business and taking customers

Prevalence of auditing work (high liability insurance rates)

Large percentage of revenues from only a few customers

Above-market rent with long-term lease (difficult to move if desired)

Overall, the preponderance of favorable or unfavorable features should dictate the applicable multiple for the subject company. In regard to our subject company, the pluses outweigh the minuses by a substantial degree, so we will be looking at a premium over the average multiple. Precisely how much is once again a matter of judgment and experience. There is no escaping this subjective aspect of this valuation method. Attempts have been made to turn this process into more of a science, but subjectivity always takes center stage. Processes such as the one presented at the end of Chapter Four (the Snowden technique) that attempt to develop a cap rate based on numerical responses to a variety of questions can help in terms of consistency, but opinion rules the day. Valuation is and will always be one part science and one part art.

When teaching students of business valuation, I often make the point that business valuation in a vacuum is meaningless. Valuation efforts and techniques take on meaning only in the real world. You can look at the process of developing the subject company's multiple via the norm as part of a battle with an opponent. You want to build the strongest case you can in support of your conclusion. If you feel the business is above average, state your case clearly and forcefully. Whether dealing with a buyer or seller or with a judge in divorce court, one must defend one's valuation results with confidence and measured zeal. Why is this business above or below average? List your reasons and be prepared to defend them by imagining a cross-examination.

Concerning our accounting or tax business, the valuator believes that a premium should apply primarily because of the following overriding factors:

We are valuing a CPA practice as opposed to a non-CPA practice

A second CPA is willing to sign an employment agreement

Seller is willing to introduce new owner as a partner to solidify transition

Billing rates and productivity are above average

Revenues are diversified among clients and around the year

Given the presence of a key employee who will remain with the new owner for at least one year, a great deal of the company's history and relationships can be more efficiently transferred to the new owner. As before, a 15 percent premium is believed to be proper, so increasing the average multiples each by 15 percent leads to the following adjusted multiples and estimated FMV:

Adjusted Multiples

ACF multiple	$2.73 \times 1.15 = 3.14$
Gross revenue multiple	120 percent $\times 1.15 = 138$ percent

Subject Company Value Using Adjusted Multiples

$3.14 \times \$130,000 = \$408,200$
138 percent $\times \$290,000 = \$400,200$
Average of the two values above equals $404,200

Using the same results for the first two components of the ARM approach, we can estimate the FMV of the subject company based on a straight average as follows:

ACF multiple result	$325,000
Rule of thumb result	$304,500
Market comp result	$404,200
ARM average	$344,567

Compared with the earlier overall result based on the BIZCOMPS data for the market-based component of the ARM approach, the IBA-based overall ARM approach estimate rises from $311,416 to $344,567. Although the IBA comps for accounting and tax practices generated an estimate approximately 33 percent higher than that of the BIZCOMPS data, when factored into the overall ARM approach the difference is only slightly more than 10 percent.

The decision as to which database to use ultimately is a matter of supported opinion. To the extent that the IBA comps appear to more reasonably mirror the subject company's size, it may be the preferred choice. On the other hand, my experience in selling accounting and tax practices tells me that a multiple of 138 percent of gross revenues probably is unattainable in the Phoenix, Arizona, market. The point is that geographic differences can also play an important role in determining business value. It is comforting to know that the IBA database comes with geographic information, so we could redo our valuation accordingly. Another possible step would be to include only CPA practices in our sample. There is no doubt that CPA practices generally sell for a higher multiple than non-CPA companies, so this may be a prudent step.

On the other hand, if we limit the analysis too much, we lose out on the power of sample size to average out all the particular features that permeate the sale of accounting and tax practices and influence the final deal price. Another possibility would be to simply average the results of the two market comp results or take the average of the two final ARM-generated results. Finally, taking a look at the VR Business Brokers database might be worthwhile if such information is readily available. Overall, the quality and quantity of information available and applicable to each separate technique should determine their relative weighting within the ARM approach.

Another interesting insight into valuation of accounting and tax practices via market comp databases involves the fact that most such businesses are sold via a seller guarantee (not to be confused with a buyer guarantee, which deals with the promissory note between buyer and seller). In other words, the reported deal price often differs from the actual, final price, which is subject to adjustment to reflect the actual retention rate and actual revenues earned during the first year of new ownership. The seller guarantees a certain level of revenues, below which the deal price will be adjusted (typically downward on a dollar-for-dollar basis). This situation is described as a combination earnout and seller guarantee. Although earnouts are fairly common, rest assured that seller guarantees are extremely rare for other types of businesses. However, most accounting and tax practice sales are based on a seller guarantee to one degree or another. Earnouts refer to the concept of tying the actual final sale price to some level of financial performance in the future (subsequent to closing and under the new owner's control), such as gross revenues, EBIT, or some industry-specific measure such as the number of dial-up accounts for an ISP or the number of closings for a real estate brokerage.

Concluding Remarks on the Comparable Sales Method

For more insights into how this version of the comparable sales method works, I highly recommend a careful review of the tutorials presented on the IBA's Web site (*www.go-iba.com*). They are clearly written, concise, and extremely educational for the beginning valuator. If you will be actively buying or selling businesses or will value a business several times in the next few years or so, I also recommend joining the IBA for access to the comps and their extensive library of learning tools. The tutorials are freely accessed over the Web, but comps are available only for a fee. Annual membership allows complete access to all available market comp data for a one-time fee of approximately $325 (includes a subscription to their newsletter as well).

The best overall advice possible given the myriad choices available to the valuator is to develop a consistent application for each component of the ARM approach. Contrary to what some professional appraisers would lead us to believe, there is a definite value to keeping the process as simple as possible. Following the ARM approach as presented in this book allows the valuator to generate consistent and credible estimates of FMV for all going concerns. Make sure you keep your audience in mind as you develop your valuation results because the ultimate value of business valuations is derived from some type of negotiation, whether it is to maximize the sale price for the seller (or minimize for the buyer) or to minimize the value for estate tax purposes. Visualize your audience, apply the ARM consistently, and keep it as simple as possible and you will improve your position relative to your counterpart.

As you gain experience and confidence in your valuation analysis, surprising and unexpected insights will arise. When working with valuation data and methods, you may find that a particular change here or a tweak there improves the results in terms of reliability or credibility. For example, the author stumbled on a creative way to use market comp data for companies that are asset-heavy and cash flow–poor. Such companies tend to be undervalued if a multiple of cash flow is the primary method for determining value. In these cases, the multiple of cash flow result often is less than the value of the hard assets alone.

A solution to this problem was found in part by using a creative approach related to market data. The solution called for evaluating as many market comps as possible related to the subject company (ideally fifteen or more). Value was estimated by calculating the average goodwill paid for such businesses as measured by the excess of the purchase price over the value of the identifiable tangible assets (FF&E plus inventory). In the case just described, it turned out that on average, buyers paid 42 cents for each dollar of the hard assets (i.e., the company was estimated to be worth 1.42 times the value of the hard assets). Granted, this particular innovation does not work in every situation, but it serves as an example of how creativity (if rational and credible) can aid the valuator in the heat of the battle.

Applying the Guideline Public Company Method

By now it should be clear that the guideline method applies generally to larger, publicly traded companies as opposed to smaller, privately held businesses. Therefore, limited attention is devoted to this method in this book. Useful outside sources will be presented along with pertinent details for those who seek to more fully understand and apply this version of the market data approach.

As discussed earlier, this method is based on comparison of the subject company with the share price data of similar companies that actively trade their stocks on the open market. Because of the numerous and diverse sources of company information available on the Internet and at major libraries regarding publicly traded companies, careful and detailed comparisons can be made with the subject company in most instances.

The goal once again is to locate and accumulate data related to price to cash flow, price to revenues, price to EBIT, or price to EBITDA multiples for publicly traded companies that are similar to the company under evaluation. As discussed earlier, after similar companies have been located, their financial statements must be adjusted to allow meaningful comparison of price to earnings or price to EBITDA multiples. In addition, the average multiple of the comparable publicly traded companies typically must be adjusted downward to account for the size effect. Advanced business valuation publications such as the CCH *Business Valuation Guide* or Shannon Pratt's *Valuing a Business* (4th edition) will cover all adjustments of all types in ample detail should the reader choose to learn more about this method and apply it to a subject company.

There are dozens if not hundreds of sources of corporate data that could be used when applying this valuation technique. Some of the more useful data sources for the guideline company method include the following:

Hoover's Online (*www.hoovers.com*)
FreeEDGAR (*www.freeedgar.com*)

Value Line Investment Survey

Standard & Poor's

Moody's Common Stocks

The list of Web sites at the end of Chapter One includes other company and industry research sources and tools that will help the valuator use the guideline public company method. In addition, the ARM Approach Questionnaire contains dozens of Web sites useful for a variety of purposes, including industry research from multiple perspectives.

Complete List of Possible Market–Based Valuation Techniques

All in all, there are five distinct market-based valuation techniques that could be used to value a privately held going concern. For reasons clarified earlier, the first technique listed here will be most suitable for the majority of privately held companies. The following information illustrates the essence of each of these five possible market-based valuation methods. For a description and discussion of the marketable, nonmarketable, minority interest, and controlling interest concepts, see Chapter Seven and its coverage of fractional interests. The summary description captures the type of interest and environment in which the valuation takes place.

Once again, the focal point for readers of this book is the first technique, which calls for accumulation of a large number of market comp statistics for comparison with the subject company. This method corresponds to the third component of the ARM approach and grounds the overall valuation result in the reality of the subject company's industry and operating environment.

Overall, the five possible market approach techniques are as follows:

Comparable sales of whole companies using four databases of privately held deals:

Information source: IBA, Pratt's, BIZCOMPS, VR, Done Deals

Summary description: nonmarketable, controlling interest, going concerns

Comparable sales of whole companies using publicly traded companies:

Information source: Mergerstat, Heller, Pratt's, Goodwill Registry, Done Deals

Summary description: marketable, controlling interest, going concerns

Comparable sales using prior sales of the company's own stock:
Information source: proprietary only
Summary description: nonmarketable, minority interest, going concerns
Guideline public company method using individual share prices (minority interest):
Information source: Hoover's, Value Line, FreeEDGAR
Summary description: marketable, minority interest, going concerns
Guideline public company method using company takeover prices (control premiums):
Information source: Business Valuations by Industry (I, II, III, IV)
Summary description: marketable, controlling interest, going concerns

Summary Caveats Regarding Market Data Methods

When the time comes to implement one or both of the market data methods, it is worthwhile to review the major caveats and tips to maximize the credibility and applicability of the derived results. Here is a list of such caveats and tips to be reviewed before beginning work in this area:

Find and use only similar businesses, comparing the relevant line of business, size, and geographic area at a minimum.

Find at least five and preferably fifteen comps for similar businesses. In general, the more the better to fill in the bell curve and a normal distribution.

Don't forget about the size effect when selecting comps (e.g., for a business with $1 million in revenues, find comps with revenues of $750,000 to $1.25 million and widen as necessary to find sufficient sample size).

Match your work to the applicable database (i.e., use Pratt's Stats for middle-market companies and BIZCOMPS or IBA for business brokerage level companies).

Remember the peculiarities from each source of market comps (e.g., BIZCOMPS excludes inventory from sale price and multiple data, IBA excludes amortization and depreciation from ACF, Pratt's Stats includes publicly traded data).

Other Sources of Market Comp Data

In addition to those listed elsewhere, consider the following sources of market comp data related to publicly traded companies (first two), privately held companies (third and fourth), and a hybrid source with both public and private company data (last one):

MERGERSTAT Review (*www.xls.com*)

Securities and Exchange Commission (SEC) Data (*www.freeedgar.com*)

Heller Financial Data (*www.hellerfin.com*)

The Goodwill Registry (*www.healthcaregroup.com*)

Done Deals Database (*www.donedeals.nvst.com*)

The Done Deals database lists hundreds of corporate transaction details for private and public mid-market companies sold for purchase prices between $1 million and $250 million, available on a fee basis.

Done Deals is the only comprehensive source of unique mid-market transaction data, with approximately 50 percent of deals less than $14 million and 50 percent more than $14 million, and approximately 66 percent of the selling companies are privately owned. In general terms, it may be considered in a similar vein as the Pratt's Stats database.

Mid-Market ($1–$100 million) M&A Done Deals:

Hundreds of completed transactions each quarter, with up to 1,000 deals reported on annually

Company contacts provided (name of the executive handling the deal, address, phone)

Price, terms, and financing sources

Seller financials, EBITDA, and ratios for every transaction

Key aggregate statistics and any price multiple graph for selected deals

Available online, CD-ROM, or in *The DoneDeals Complete Transaction Handbook*

Search and sorting functions to allow you to find just the deals you want

CHAPTER 6

Impact of Terms, Conditions, and Taxes for Valuing Businesses

Thus far we have learned about valuing businesses via traditional valuation methods within the context of the ARM approach. Chapters Four and Five introduced the finer points of adjusted cash flow, rules of thumb, and market comp data. As noted earlier, coverage of the asset or cost approach to business valuation (one of the three major classical valuation approaches) is presented in full on the attached CD-ROM. You may want to review this CD-ROM section at this juncture to survey all major areas of both traditional business valuation (income, cost or asset, market) and more importantly ARM-related valuation (adjusted cash flow, rules of thumb, market comparable data).

The ARM approach to business valuation ultimately revolves around the use of the ARM Approach Questionnaire and the Five-Page Tool, as presented in Chapter Three and applied in Chapter Eight. However, our analysis thus far has proceeded without a full discussion of the importance of terms and conditions in regard to the final deal price that emerges from buyer–seller negotiations. Because many readers of this book are interested in valuation primarily as it relates to the buy-and-sell process—that is, to assess the fair market value (FMV) of a business as purchaser or seller—careful consideration of the role played by the many related contractual details and the negotiating process is warranted.

The general assumption made by most valuation professionals is that the estimated FMV of a company resulting from the standard valuation process is based on typical seller financing arrangements (e.g., 30 to 40 percent cash down payment with the balance paid monthly for three to five years at 8 to 10 percent interest). Note that this is contrary to standard real estate valuation practice, which commonly generates value results that reflect an all-cash price because of the predominance of 100 percent bank financing in such deals. The main point of this chapter is that a variety of negotiated terms and conditions affect the final deal price.

Important Terms and Conditions That Affect Price

We begin our analysis by reviewing a list of many of the major terms and conditions that can affect a deal price. They include the following:

Amount of cash down payment

Level and type of interest rate

Length of payback period

Presence or strength of personal guarantee or corporate guarantee

Type, amount, and liquidity of collateral

Duration and scope of covenant not to compete

Allocation of purchase price under asset sale

Terms and conditions of employment contract

Length and depth of training or transition period

Dollar value of inventory and other valuable assets

Assumption of debt

The presence (or lack thereof) and the exact nature of each of these terms and conditions found in a given purchase contract affect the final, mutually agreeable price. In practice, there is normally a give-and-take process between buyer and seller that culminates in the final purchase price and terms and conditions. It is not uncommon for an original offer to be countered back and forth several times. In some cases, this give-and-take process can last right up until close of escrow (even during closing on occasion). Although a great deal of this process occurs through discussions between the buyer, seller, and their respective brokers and advisers, here are a few simple examples of this process as contained in actual counteroffers between the parties:

> *Example One:* Seller agrees to a reduced cash down payment in exchange for an increase in total price (both in the amount of $25,000); for example, the down payment is reduced from $150,000 to $125,000 and purchase price is increased from $275,000 to $300,000.

> *Example Two:* Buyer accepts seller's higher price of $200,000 but seller financing will be at 8 percent interest with a five-year payback period (instead of 9 percent and four years).

> *Example Three:* In exchange for accepting buyer's proposed allocation of purchase price, buyer and seller agree to increase the purchase price and cash down payment by $25,000 each.

Note that the verbiage contained in many such counteroffers may not be as direct as this, but the practical results are the same. In practice, such exchanges may occur verbally before they are written down. Buyer and seller will give and take while going back and forth until the final deal price and structure are completed. It is safe to say that if buyer and seller are not willing to compromise to a significant degree, then there will be no deal at all.

It is rare for a take-it-or-leave-it attitude to prevail. Only in rare circumstances in which the seller has almost no choice but to sell immediately and to the current buyer or the buyer has much to gain by purchasing the business (e.g., potential synergism or a uniquely appealing patent or trade name) will a true hard-line approach work. Hard-line negotiating works great in books or on paper, but most deals that make it to closing were negotiated out of respect for the other side and a strong mutual interest in completing the deal.

A common feature of almost all deals that make it to the end is a professional and friendly rapport between the parties. The importance of a productive working relationship built on mutual respect and trust cannot be overemphasized. As an active business broker, I have witnessed some amazing concessions made by sellers to buyers who were liked and respected by the seller. What was a deal breaker in one deal becomes no big deal in another when the two sides are getting along nicely. If the parties are enjoying each other's company, a deal is much more probable.

In terms of concrete examples, I have seen a seller change unexpectedly from insisting on full-price, all-cash from one buyer to accepting 50 percent down on a total price reduced by $75,000 (both events occurred within the same week). In short, a positive working relationship between buyer and seller can not only improve the chances of reaching the closing but can also improve the quality of the deal for both parties and minimize the chances of any legal problems occurring after close of escrow.

Terms, Conditions, and Market Comp Data

Each of the items listed earlier can have a material impact on the final price. Remember that it is this price that becomes tomorrow's market comp. This brings up an interesting question regarding the use of such market data. Sources of market comp data present some or all of the following pieces of information:

Price

Cash down payment

Annual revenues

Annualized cash flow (e.g., adjusted cash flow [ACF])

Inventory value

Total fixed asset value

Interest rate on seller financing

Payback period

The major sources of market comp data relating to privately held companies do not contain all these bits of information, let alone other useful information such as collateral, type of guarantee, or covenant not to compete. The lack of this information should be a cause of concern on the part of any valuator. For example, it is not uncommon to see a dramatically reduced purchase price in exchange for a substantial employment or consulting contract for the seller. This major factor typically is overlooked in the data used as market comparable sales statistics.

Chapter Five provides an overview of the specific data presented in each of the major sources of market comp data: BIZCOMPS, VR Business Brokers (VRBB), Institute of Business Appraisers (IBA), and Pratt's Stats. Every deal is different and is made up of a unique mix of attributes that can make the use of market comp data problematic.

Because of this great variety of underlying terms and conditions, market comp data should be used in such a way as to minimize the impact of this inequality across transactions. Specifically, market comp data should be used only as a general overall indicator of what a particular type of business will sell for on average. In other words, instead of selecting three to five of the most similar comps and trying to create an average multiple of cash flow or revenues on such a limited number of transactions, the valuation results will tend to be more credible if a large number of slightly less similar comps are taken as a group and averaged in terms of the two common multiples (cash flow and revenues).

By taking a large number of transactions, the valuator is more likely to obtain a true average given the wide variety of underlying terms and conditions involved with each sale. In other words, use of a large number of transactions tends to balance out the unique features of each deal. Of a large number of deals, some will be stock sales and most will be asset sales, some will have employment contracts and most will not, some will have high asset values and some will not.

After a larger number of transactions are located, the price to cash flow and price to gross revenue average multiples can be obtained. One can then say with some confidence that on average a given type of business sells for X times cash flow and Y times gross revenues. From there, one must determine whether the subject company is average or above or below average and by how much. Chapter Five contains a more comprehensive review of the use of market comp data in business valuation, including various lists of relevant factors that should be evaluated in selecting similar companies. Chapter Five also contains various lists of factors that should be evaluated in regard to the determination as to what makes a given company average or above or below average.

Asset Sale Versus Stock Sale

Another major factor that affects the deal price is the type of sale that is taking place. There is typically a major difference between the price paid for an asset purchase and a stock purchase. The difference in price reflects what is actually purchased and its impact on future cash flows. In general, buyers pay less for and sellers accept less for the sale of stock than for the sale of assets. A buyer typically pays less because of the risk associated with the purchase of stock. A buyer of company stock typically assumes all liabilities, known and unknown. Even if the stock sale is based on the seller delivering the business free and clear of all debts, the buyer is assuming any unknown liabilities related to the business.

Furthermore, even if the seller indemnifies (holds harmless) the buyer from any claims that might arise out of the preclosing (prior ownership) era, legally speaking the distinction is not clear; that is, the new owner of the company's stock may still be liable in whole or in part. For example, consider a playground equipment manufacturer and retailer that is sold via a stock sale to a new owner.

One year later a class action lawsuit is filed against the manufacturer of the playground equipment because of a faulty bolt. The class action lawsuit will be directed primarily toward the current owner. It is true that the new owner would be brought into the lawsuit even if the owner had purchased assets. However, there is a legal distinction between the two situations that places greater risk on the owner of the stock as opposed to the assets. Either way, the prior owner may be brought into the legal battle eventually, but this will not diminish the problem for the new owner. At a minimum, hefty legal fees probably will pile up whether it is the new owner's fault or not. Importantly, however, the legal exposure for the buyer of stock is greater than that of the buyer of assets. In short, higher risk means lower value.

It is important to realize that the lower price for the stock purchase is a *ceteris paribus* situation. *Ceteris paribus* is the Latin term for "all other things equal," commonly used by professional economists. If the buyer of stock is also inheriting a substantial amount of working capital, then the price should reflect this. In other words, if the buyer of stock is purchasing the business as it stands as of closing and the current assets are two to three times greater than the current liabilities, then this would drive the purchase price higher. Similarly, if the new owner is inheriting a substantial amount of long-term debt, this would tend to reduce the price. The main point is that because of the greater risk of buying a company's stock rather than assets, the purchase price reflects this risk in the form of a lower value.

Not only does the extra risk for the buyer drive the price downward, but the seller's ability to pay a lower tax bill also leads to a lower purchase price. Generally speaking, the sale of stock is treated primarily as a capital gain, whereas the sale of assets generates a substantial gain (typically) that is taxed in large part as ordinary income. Ordinary income tax rates can be as much as twice as high as the current capital gains tax rate. Most sellers realize this and agree to a lower price because of the tax savings.

For the sake of clarity and understanding, review the following major differences between an asset sale and a stock sale.

Asset Sale

Seller keeps cash and receivables but delivers company free of any debt.

Seller keeps corporate entity to later dissolve or use for new endeavor.

Seller pays combination of capital gains tax and ordinary income tax.

Buyer and seller agree to allocation of purchase price between IRS asset categories.

Buyer may redepreciate fixed assets based on allocation.

Buyer avoids assuming both known and unknown liabilities.

If price is greater than identifiable, tangible assets, the excess is allocated to one or more intangible assets (written off over fifteen years for tax purposes and up to forty-two years for book purposes).

Stock Sale

Seller pays primarily capital gains tax rather than higher ordinary income tax rate.

Seller endorses stock certificates over to new owner.

Buyer assumes all assets and liabilities unless specifically excluded.

Buyer takes on risk associated with unknown liabilities.

Buyer inherits tax depreciation schedules as they are (for better or mostly worse).

Buyer may inherit tax loss carryforwards to shield future income.

There is no allocation of purchase price or goodwill related to transaction.

Important Role of Taxation for Business Valuation

Besides the liability issues, no other issue affects future cash flows and hence business value more than taxation. To the extent that the ultimate source of business value is the amount of spendable income that goes into the owner's pockets, after-tax cash flows are the true bottom line for the entrepreneur. Beginning with the moment you decide to buy or start a business, you must address important tax issues. Sooner or later, you will be required to answer many significant tax questions, including the following:

Should I incorporate the business?

If incorporated, should I select S-corporation status?

How can I best withdraw cash without double taxation?

Should I consider a fiscal year end for my company?

Should I use a limited partnership or limited-liability company organization?

What recordkeeping should I have in general (e.g., for travel and entertainment expenses, to meet IRS requirements)?

What is the most beneficial depreciation schedule to use?

How can I get a deduction for my car?

Should I have a contractual agreement in place to dispose of the company if I become disabled or die?

Is there any way to shift income or expenses from one year to the next?

Is there any way to shift income or expenses between myself and my company?

Should I set up a 401(k) or a Simplified Employee Pension (SEP) retirement plan?

Are my salary and my spouse's salary reasonable for this size and type of operation?

Should I put my spouse on the payroll to take advantage of additional IRA deductions?

Would setting up an employee stock ownership plan (ESOP) be of benefit now or in the future?

Each of these questions will affect future cash flows and business value. Perhaps the most important initial decision to be made for either a startup or acquisition is the chosen form of business organization. General business organizational format choices include the following:

Sole proprietorship (SP)

Limited partnership (LP)

General partnership (GP)

Limited-liability company (LLC)

S-corporation (S-corp)

C-corporation (C-corp)

For SPs, LPs, GPs, or LLCs, the business itself does not pay income taxes. The sole proprietor, partners, or members include the profits or losses of the business in their personal tax returns. Profits for a C-corporation are taxed both to the corporation and to the shareholders when the profits are distributed as dividends. The ever-changing laws and increasing complexities make the assistance of CPAs and tax attorneys indispensable. For a good review of basic federal tax issues concerning business ownership, call the IRS and request a copy of their *Tax Guide for Small Businesses* (Publication 334). This guide covers income, excise, and employment taxes for proprietors, partners, and corporations. By calling 1–800–829–1040, you can try to speak with a representative or request tax forms. You can also visit their Web site at *www.irs.ustreas.gov*. (This Web site is quite useful, allowing subject searches.) You can also obtain tax forms by call-ing 1–800–TAX–FORM.

Tax implications relating specifically to the purchase or sale of a business are significant and must be considered as a major part of the sales and valuation process. In fact, the ideal time to begin planning for sale is the time of startup or acquisition. In our current context this relates primarily to choosing the op-timal business organization and exploring the basic choices related to taxation at the time of future sale. The tax effects of a business sale depend partly on whether the selling entity is an SP, S-corp, or C-corp. Additionally, there are material tax implications resulting from the mode of acquisition. Although 90 percent of all business brokerage and middle-market business acquisitions are exchanges of cash for assets, there are many options that are increasingly used as the financial size and acumen of the players increases. The following is a list of pertinent tax questions for a buyer to review with the assistance of legal coun-sel or accounting professionals:

What impact will my chosen business organization form have on present and future taxes?

What are the unique tax motivations of the seller?

Is an asset sale or stock sale preferable or possible?

Should the purchase be financed with cash, stock, or debt?

How will profits be distributed to the owners?

For starters, consider the following basic structures to be evaluated at the time of purchase or sale:

Sole Proprietor

1. Sell (buy) assets
   a. for cash   b. for note   c. for stock   d. combination of a, b, and c

Corporations

1. Sell (buy) assets
   a. for cash   b. for notes   c. for stock   d. combination of a, b, and c

2. Sell (buy) stock
   a. for cash   b. for notes   c. for stock   d. combination of a, b, and c

Whether you are an SP or a C-corp, selling the assets or the stock, you can manage taxes to a certain extent. Not only can you manage them, but you should accurately assess current tax liabilities as a seller at closing and future tax liabilities as a buyer after closing before agreeing on price and terms. Considering that more than 50 percent of the money received from the sale can go to different taxing bodies (federal and state), the time and money spent investigating and planning tax minimization are clearly worthwhile. Deals often disintegrate once a seller finally realizes exactly how stiff the tax bill will be.

Asset Sale Scenario

Let's begin with the simplest and by far the most common of scenarios. You are a sole proprietorship or corporation selling the assets of your business. Important tax characteristics of an asset sale include the following:

Buyer may redepreciate all fixed assets from current fair market value as per allocation of purchase price agreement on IRS Form 8594.

Seller pays taxes on the difference between purchase price received and the tax basis of the assets being sold (combination of ordinary income and capital gains).

Seller may face double taxation, once on the sale of assets and second on the liquidation distribution to shareholders (for C-corporations only).

The allocation of the purchase price, which must be mutually agreed on between buyer and seller, determines the extent of capital gains and ordinary income taxes to be paid. Generally, fixed assets are subject to capital gains taxes (currently a maximum of 20 percent) and inventory is subject to ordinary income taxes (which depend on your overall tax situation and the tax bracket you climb into as a result of the sale). So, all other things held equal, there appears to be a benefit to allocation toward fixed assets versus inventory for the seller. However, if these fixed assets are already fully depreciated on the books, their tax basis is low and the amount of gain is high. In addition, a depreciation recapture liability may arise for the seller if certain assets were depreciated on an accelerated basis for tax purposes (such recapture is taxed as ordinary income). If the allocation were to inventory, the amount of income would still be positive but smaller (assuming the allocation amount was slightly more than the original cost), even though the tax rate might be higher. Any consideration received upon sale that is greater than the value of the identifiable tangible assets will be allocated to one or more intangible asset categories such as goodwill, covenant not to compete, and trade name. Most intangible assets are associated with capital gains, with the exception of the covenant not to compete. For optimal results, both buyer and seller should consult their accountants.

A second issue for the sole proprietor or corporation selling assets (and stock, for that matter) is the timing of the gain or income. If the assets are sold for 100 percent cash at closing, the entire gain or income is taxable in the year of the transaction. Practically, this means that the taxable income resulting from the sale will be pushed into higher and higher tax brackets, again depending on your overall tax situation and the amount of this income. The capital gains portion is currently taxed at a rate of 20 percent, whether you receive all proceeds in the first year or over several years. It might be beneficial to spread the buyer's payments over a few years (i.e., offer to sell on terms; the IRS calls this the installment basis).

Congress passed a tax bill in 1999 that made it more difficult to spread out the income; for companies that maintained their taxes on an accrual basis, the entire tax bill was due upon sale whether there was seller financing or not. Reason has prevailed, however, and this change was reversed because of the great backlash from entrepreneurs and related professionals in 2000. Once again there is a tax benefit to selling with financing terms in that tax is paid only on the portion of the sale price received in any given year.

It should be clear that all of these decisions are complicated, interdependent, and dynamic. Tax rules are constantly changing. Several proposed probusiness tax changes may or may not come to fruition, including reduced tax rates overall (ordinary income and capital gains) and increased deductions for health insurance payments. It is critical to rely on a seasoned tax professional to minimize taxes. For example, many business owners are unaware that as part of the Revenue Reconciliation Act of 1993, entrepreneurs who started or purchased a corporate-type business and held the stock for at least five years could receive favorable tax treatment upon sale in the form of a capital gains tax rate reduced in half (other conditions apply, of course, so consult your tax professional).

Stock Sale Scenario

The second, generally more complicated scenario is the sale of stock as an S- or C-corporation. Noting that most businesses that incorporate are S-corporations (passthrough taxation and fewer than seventy-five shareholders), we focus on this type of corporation. The precise calculation of taxable gain in this scenario is discussed later in this section. Many basic concepts referred to in the context of an asset sale apply, such as stretching the receipts over a number of years. One major difference is that instead of tax basis in assets, the tax basis of the stock is the relevant concept.

Important tax characteristics of a stock sale include the following:

Buyer inherits existing depreciation schedule rather than redepreciating from current market values as per allocation of purchase price agreement.

Seller can avoid double taxation by selling stock only (instead of tax on sale of assets and then tax on money received by shareholders).

Buyer inherits potentially valuable tax attributes such as net operating loss carryforwards and unused investment tax credits.

Stock sales generally are associated with more complex transactions and more sophisticated parties. Typically, only an experienced, well-established company is willing to take on the risks of a stock purchase. A large number of stock sales are initiated by companies that have publicly traded stock to begin with because of the several favorable tax deferral schemes that work only in a stock-for-stock transaction.

In conclusion, the very same business will sell for two different prices under two different scenarios. The sale of stock typically is associated with a lower sale price than the sale of assets. The choice of sale mechanism affects the final deal price. As deal prices become market comp data, this fact should not be overlooked by valuation professionals and entrepreneurs.

Allocation of Purchase Price

The precise nature of the tax related to the sale of a business is primarily a function of whether it is processed as an asset sale or stock sale. Under an asset sale, the type of business organization involved and how the purchase price is allocated determine the specific tax details. For either side to minimize tax obligations related to the purchase or sale of a company, current advice and feedback should be obtained from a tax expert.

However, you cannot always expect a straight, 100 percent accurate answer. Even the IRS officials who answer tax questions through their 1-800 number are not consistent in their responses to fairly basic tax questions, nor can you rely on their answers in tax disputes. You cannot even assume that an experienced tax professional will know all of the relevant and correct maneuverings and posturings. Accordingly, it is incumbent upon you to be aware of the major concepts, tradeoffs, and choices to be made regarding the tax implications of the purchase or sale of a business. A second opinion on major tax issues is generally desirable, given the often nebulous nature of taxes.

Here are some thoughts to consider. First, don't forget that the buyer and seller must agree to the same purchase price allocation, and it should be completed before closing. Second, relying on experts in this area is wise, it is important to understand these procedures yourself and be prepared to offer a compromise if need be. At a minimum, however, you should consult an expert about any recent changes to applicable laws or the development of new material case law or court rulings.

Allocation Procedures for Tangible Assets

It will be beneficial to walk through the steps of such an allocation under various circumstances. Before reading further here, it may be prudent to review the contents of the IRS form used to account for the allocation of purchase price (IRS Form 8594, available online at many tax-related Web sites). A good place to begin our discussion is inventory, for which a value probably has been agreed to as part of the purchase contract (to be adjusted up or down near closing). If adjustments are made, the allocation is to be adjusted accordingly. Different buyers proceed in various ways from here. Some are interested in obtaining a minimal allocation to inventory and a maximum allocation to fixed assets, in search of future tax deductions (depreciation) and a taxable gain on the sale of the business figured as a capital gain (which is less than ordinary income in most cases). On the other hand, certain buyers look for a maximum allocation to inventory, in search of immediate, first-year write-offs against taxable income. The downside is that if the overallocation is extreme, the IRS might disallow the entire allocation and reallocate as it sees fit. Second, this will certainly increase the seller's immediate tax burden to the extent that the taxation of ordinary income is higher than capital gains taxes (remember that long-term capital gains currently are taxed at a maximum of 20 percent).

Next we move on to plant and equipment, or furniture, fixtures, and equipment (FF&E). Motivations typically are straightforward in this area. The buyer typically wants a large allocation for greater depreciation amounts each year in the future. Given that total deductions in the future will be the same irrespective of the allocation, the question is one of timing. Because of the time value of money, most business owners would like to pay less tax early rather than more tax early. By choosing a higher allocation to equipment, the owner can write it off over three to five years, whereas a higher allocation to goodwill or another intangible asset will take fifteen years to write off. One mitigating factor to the higher allocation to fixed assets is the fact the buyer (in many states) pays a personal property tax based to varying degrees on the allocated value of these assets.

The seller, on the other hand, ideally looks for a value close to the book value for tax purposes (depreciated tax basis), which is original cost minus accumulated depreciation and adjusted for special accelerated deductions or investment tax credits. A special concern here for the seller is the depreciation recapture, which leads to taxation at ordinary income and payments due immediately (even under installment-type sales). The depreciation recapture provisions were enacted to prevent taxpayers from trading a depreciation deduction one year for a "Code Section 1231" gain in later years (Code Section 1231 property includes depreciable business property and business real property, whereby gains are taxed at the preferable "capital gains" tax rate). If the allocation to fixed assets is greater than the seller's depreciated tax basis, the excess (up to the original cost) is taxable as depreciation recapture. If, by agreement, the allocation to these fixed assets is greater than the original cost, the excess would be a clear-cut capital gain. A worst-case situation for the seller would be a generous allocation to fixed assets that were fully depreciated, coupled with a minimal down payment toward the purchase of the business (perhaps only enough to cover the broker's commission). This could be a deal breaker if the seller doesn't have sufficient cash to meet the associated depreciation recapture tax. Most sellers are hesitant to pay money out of their pockets to facilitate the sale of their businesses.

Another common category relevant for this type of allocation is leasehold improvements, which in many ways resemble intangible assets because the owner cannot take them when she leaves. Therefore, they are normally treated as a capital (fixed) asset for tax purposes, which means they are also subject to depreciation recapture taxes. The buyer can depreciate the leasehold improvements in accordance with IRS policies for tax purposes and in accordance with generally accepted accounting principles (GAAP) for book purposes.

Allocation Procedures for Intangible Assets

Thus far, we have discussed allocations to tangible assets only: inventory, equipment, and leasehold improvements. If the purchase price exceeds these allocated amounts and the cash and accounts receivable remain the property of the seller, the balance must be allocated to one or more intangible assets (Class IV or V on Form 8594). If there is a noncompete agreement, as normally there is, a fair amount should be allocated here. The noncompete agreement (also called a covenant not to compete) is treated differently than other intangible assets in that it is associated with ordinary income taxation. It doesn't generally matter how the excess of the purchase price over the identifiable tangible assets is allocated among intangibles given that they are all amortized over fifteen years (except for the covenant not to compete). Consult your tax attorney or CPA as to what might be deemed reasonable for the noncompete agreement specifically and the overall allocation generally.

A slightly different situation exists for employment contracts or consulting agreements. Employment contracts are a useful mechanism for keeping the seller active in the business, ideally to the benefit of the new owner. The primary problem for the seller is that these agreements lead to ordinary income as opposed to capital gains, probably increasing the tax bill. Furthermore, the dreaded self-employment tax (approximately 15 percent) must be paid on any such earnings. However, such agreements can be helpful for the seller in spreading out the total compensation over several tax years and thus reducing the effective tax rate by way of a lower average tax rate (lower brackets for initial income in each tax year). The buyer, on the other hand, enjoys a full write-off each year for such payments to the seller, benefiting the buyer's overall tax situation.

Familiarization clauses (training agreements) also are common and generate a quick deduction for the buyer if they are handled separately from the allocation of purchase price. Once again, the seller is liable for the added ordinary income tax burden and the self-employment tax. When the seller is forced to pay this extra tax as part of the deal, it will certainly appear less attractive. Most commonly, the training agreement is included as part of the sale price (not paid for separately, as in the case of an employment contract) and allocated a minor amount (if any at all).

Finally, everyone is familiar with the mother of all intangible assets, goodwill. Whether the allocation is made to goodwill specifically or customer lists, trade name, trade secrets, telephone number, or any other such intangible assets, the tax implication is the same: It is amortized over fifteen years. As a final note, remember that if the final amount of consideration paid to the seller changes after the original allocation (because of earnout provisions or an unpaid carryback note), an amendment must be filed.

Tax Planning Tools for Optimizing Business Value

In addition to the important choices of business organization and asset versus stock sales, there are important choices to be made regarding taxable versus nontaxable deal structures. Most sales of privately held businesses are taxable events such as cash for assets or cash for stock. An obvious major disadvantage here is this immediate tax obligation. For larger acquisitions made by larger organizations, however, choices are available (beyond the often unattainable requirements of a leveraged employee stock ownership plan [LESOP] or a charitable remainder trust [CRT]), which can significantly reduce, eliminate, or postpone the relevant tax liability (thus enhancing business value).

To the extent that this book is a valuation book, not a deal-making book, a major implication of each of these tax-saving scenarios is that they are associated with mandatory business appraisals. Although such appraisals must be performed by independent third-party professionals, the business owner can ethically and productively contribute to the valuation process by presenting relevant facts and insights that might otherwise be overlooked. As stated earlier, entrepreneurs can benefit greatly from understanding the valuation process and proactively participating with professional appraisers when the need arises.

Before considering some of the other options, let's take a quick look at LESOPs and CRTs in the context of long-range business planning.

ESOPs, LESOPs, CRTs, and Tax Planning

Exit planning, estate tax planning, succession planning, tax planning, and business valuation are areas of expertise that tend to overlap. Entrepreneurs seeking to maximize the after-tax returns on their investments and time should become familiar with the basics of these areas and search out the best available professional help. Thanks to the efforts of crafty legislators and effective lobbyists, several legal tax deferral and tax minimization strategies are available. There are also many schemes that are of questionable legal stature, such as concocting an ownership trail that winds through a series of domestic and foreign trusts and domestic and foreign corporations simply to avoid paying federal taxes. The potential audit risks of such foreign trust schemes are overwhelming, as evidenced by recent IRS activity.

Several appealing options exist that can help reduce your tax burden. They will not work for every corporation (they might be too small or lack sufficient payroll), and they may not give you all the cash you want right up front (payments from the buyer and taxes are deferred), but they will reduce or delay the total amount of taxes paid and thereby increase the amount and present value of money received by the seller (thus enhancing business value). Two of these legitimate options are the ESOP and CRT.

An ESOP is a qualified retirement plan (under the ERISA Act of 1973) that purchases and owns common stock of the sponsoring employer. Until recently only available for C corporations, the process involved in creating this plan is very similar to that of a normal profit sharing or pension plan. However, its implementation depends on 100 percent participation of all eligible employees. The ESOP is funded by the employer (business) with tax deductible contributions. When the ESOP has grown to a sufficient size, the stock of the owner can be sold either in a lump sum or with periodic payments.

This process can provide additional benefits, if certain conditions are met, when the ESOP is leveraged (LESOP). This occurs when the ESOP actually borrows money from the bank, with the loan secured by the stock and assets of the company, to possibly buy out the owner in a lump sum transaction. Contributions to the ESOP made by the corporation thereafter are used to pay off the loan. The primary advantage here is that the loan is paid off with pretax dollars (contributions are tax deductible). In addition, recent legislation allows S corporations to utilize LESOPs funded through tax savings (the company operates income tax-free upon implementation of the SESOP).

The primary general benefit to the owners selling their stock is that the proceeds received may be rolled over on a tax deferred basis (C corporations only). If the proceeds are reinvested in eligible securities, such as domestic corporate securities, the tax on the gain is paid only when these new securities are sold or dividends or interest payments are received. Deferring this gain can be a tremendous advantage because most owners who reach this stage have owned their stock for a long time and have a very low basis (high gain).

Consideration of the following benefits will prompt most owners of large C corporations to at least consider this option:

Owner gains substantial tax deferrals.

Employee morale is improved.

The plan can facilitate a management (leveraged) buyout.

Dividends paid to participants (employees) are tax deductible.

Fifty percent of interest payments to LESOP lender are tax free.

Unfortunately, many of these sizable benefits are not available to all corporations. As implied earlier, one of the major obstacles has been removed through recent legislation and IRS rulings that collectively allow S-corporations to use this attractive tax and management tool. Recent experience of the author has illustrated the incredible power of such a tool. One of the author's business listings was a general contractor with approximately sixty employees and gross billings of around $7 million. Despite being modestly profitable, sale of the company had proven difficult, prompting the author to introduce the principal to an expert in ESOP design and implementation. Note the significance of the following benefits resulting from the S-corporation ESOP:

Owner quickly sells company but retains control of business through ESOP as trustee.

Owner receives full purchase price (subject to independent appraisal results).

Owner and spouse maintain salary and continue contributing to Social Security tax fund.

Owner participates in ESOP (effectively double-dipping on approximately 15 percent of business).

Business (S-corporation) operates tax free into the future.

Business also pays no unrelated business income tax (e.g., could buy and sell a building without capital gains tax).

Owner can withdraw retained earnings tax free (approximately $500,000).

If desired, owner can borrow funds to accelerate receipt of purchase price.

Owner may prepay related note to accelerate receipt of purchase price.

Owner may terminate ESOP at own discretion.

Needless to say, this attractive option was acted upon quickly (this owner actually gave the ESOP professional several other leads, many of which also executed the ESOP strategy). (For information on this appealing strategy, contact Evan L. Rhodes of ABRC, Inc. in Scottsdale, Arizona, at 480-556-9928 or abrc@cox.net; there are other offices in Nashville, Tennessee, and Denver, Colorado.)

The S-corporation ESOP and ESOPs in general do not work for every company for a number of reasons. Regarding the S-corporation option, consider the following potential obstacles:

Payroll amounts must be fairly large (approximately $400,000) to allow purchase of company or service of debt.

The option requires cooperation of employees, management, and owners, which can be quite cumbersome.

The costs of establishing and maintaining ESOPs can be quite high (actuaries, accountants, owners).

There is a maximum of seventy-five shareholders (ESOP counts as only one shareholder), which may be problematic in later years as shareholders vest and leave the company.

- Certain fringe benefits are taxable to shareholders with 2 percent or more ownership.

- Companies using last-in, first-out (LIFO) accounting are subject to LIFO recapture tax.

- State-level unrelated income taxes may apply (check with tax consultant).

- S-corporations are not eligible for Section 1042 rollover, as are C-corporations.

- Only one class of stock is allowed.

- Sale of assets is subject to a built-in gains (BIG) tax for ten years after conversion from C-corporation status.

It should be clear that one of the major considerations in evaluating the attractiveness of an ESOP is the appraised value of the subject company. The greater the value, the more appeal to the ownership group. One of the themes of this book involves encouraging business owners to empower themselves with the knowledge necessary to understand the business valuation process and participate in such a way as to improve their welfare. In this case, by understanding the key valuation factors and processes, a business owner may decide to devote a year or so to improving the business specifically in regard to enhanced business value before establishing an ESOP. Knowledge is indeed power.

A second option for large corporations is the CRT. This is an irrevocable trust created primarily to benefit a nonprofit or charitable organization. In return for transferring certain ownership interests in the company to the trust, the organization of the trust retains designated income interests. After the passing of a predetermined period of years, all the assets (stock) pass to the trust. If the CRT sells the contributed stock, it is sold on a tax-free basis (an important benefit for all nonprofit organizations). Basically, the creator of the CRT is guaranteed a stream of income for several years to come, and the nonprofit organizations benefit from being able to sell the stock or assets tax-free. The originator also receives a large tax deduction associated with the creation of the CRT. Again, seek expert assistance in tax planning for the sale of a business. Although the general principles, concepts, and options are fairly easy to understand, the devil is in the details.

Tax-Free (Deferred) Reorganizations

As a general rule, sellers must consider the sale of their business (stock or assets) as taxable and carefully incorporate the estimated tax bill into their decision making. In other words, taxes normally are an unavoidable cost of selling a going concern. As explained earlier, the positive difference between the consideration received and the adjusted basis of the stock or assets is a taxable gain. Because of the large dollar amount of the tax liability involved, it is often a prime factor influencing the final price, terms, and overall deal structure.

Tax-free or tax-deferred (these terms are used interchangeably in this analysis) deals typically revolve around the concept of an exchange in which the buyer exchanges stock for the assets or stock for stock. The key conceptual consideration by the IRS in allowing tax minimization or deferral upon the sale is the fact that the seller will remain directly involved in the business through equity ownership. Existing tax laws also allow partial taxation if the purchase is effected through a combination exchange of stock and receipt of cash. The tax-deferred portion of the gain would be based on the amount of stock ownership. The logic behind tax-free exchanges is that the seller has not effectively sold the business. It is much more of a combination (merger) than an outright sale.

The precise criteria to be met to qualify for tax-free status are quite involved, and professional guidance (CPA or tax attorney) is needed. Sections 351 and 368 of the IRS tax code are the most pertinent, but as always, regulations, rulings, interpretations, tax rules, and particular circumstances are constantly evolving. Additionally, available options can become further complicated by the existence of estate inheritance taxes. For example, shareholders of older companies with dramatically appreciated shares prefer the tax-free exchange because of a tax law allowing a tax-free step-up of basis to market value at the time of death. As a result, shares could be passed on to surviving family members without an associated income tax. Tax-free exchanges, in general, are preferred by the seller but may be unfavorable to the buyer because, for example, an increased basis in depreciable assets is not available (i.e., the fixed assets cannot be redepreciated). On the other hand, the ability to purchase the subject company at a reduced price typically more than offsets this depreciation shortcoming.

Such exchanges are commonly called reorganizations or mergers. Although the term *tax-free* often is used in these situations, most experienced businesspeople would agree that *tax-deferred* is a more accurate description of these transactions. In general, the seller can defer taxes if shares of the acquiring company are received and a continuous equity interest in the merged entity is maintained. The only instance that I am aware of in which *tax-free* seems more accurate is when a seller dies and passes the shares on to the appropriate heirs at a current, FMV basis as part of an estate settlement. Clearly, tax deferred is not as favorable as tax free but is far preferable to immediate payment of taxes (because of the time value of money). Pretax proceeds can be preserved through an equity interest in the surviving entity, which can appreciate in value without tax obligations until the shares are disposed of.

What is the incentive for the buyer to participate in one of these tax-free exchanges? The main reasons are as follows:

Businesses can be acquired without use of scarce cash (although ownership and earnings per share usually are diluted).

One can obtain a better price by reducing the tax pressure on the seller.

An important but fairly obscure accounting concept is most relevant to the stock-for-stock, tax-free transactions. If certain conditions are met (twelve criteria per the Accounting Principles Board's APB #16), the purchase of a business can be accounted for as a pooling of interests that allows the buyer to assume the historic basis in the seller's stock or assets and avoid the creation and amortization of goodwill. What this boils down to is that the buyer can pay a great deal more for a business than the book value (BV) of its assets without being burdened with goodwill amortization in future periods, which will reduce reported net income (remember that publicly traded companies seek the highest possible reported net income for book purposes, which is contrary to the typical business owner's goal of minimizing book [taxable] income). Due to recent regulatory changes, the "pooling of interests" method of accounting is subject to greater scrutiny. As a result, current tax and accounting advice regarding this topic is mandatory.

Overall, these tax-free (deferred) deals can be categorized as follows:

Type A reorganizations (statutory combination or merger)

Type B reorganization (stock for stock)

Type C reorganization (stock for assets)

Type A Reorganization

In this scenario, one company joins with another, creating a new entity that is a continuation of the previous two (statutory combination), or one company absorbs another completely (statutory merger). Once again, precise requirements are not always clear-cut, and experienced help is necessary to properly execute any of these reorganizations. To qualify for tax-free status, a minimum of 50 percent of the purchase price must be received in the form of the acquiring company's stock. For the portion of the acquisition paid for with cash, an immediate tax liability is incurred. There is generally more flexibility in a Type A than there is for Type B or C because consideration may take the form of voting, nonvoting, common, or preferred stock. Also, there is no specific requirement that substantially all of the assets be acquired, as there is for a Type C reorganization. Generally, the tax attributes of the transferring corporation's assets flow to the new entity. However, there may be restrictions as to future use of net operating losses.

Type B Reorganization

In this situation, the buyer acquires the seller's stock in exchange for its voting stock. A Type B reorganization requires that the stock consideration be voting shares only, with no exceptions. It can be preferred or common, but only voting shares are eligible. Also, the acquiring company cannot transfer cash, bonds, warrants, options, or other property or assume any liabilities of the selling stockholders.

Type C Reorganization

This reorganization format is much more flexible than the stock-for-stock option. Major considerations are the requirement that substantially all of the property (assets) of the acquired company be obtained in exchange for its voting stock. Generally speaking, this means 90 percent of the FMV of gross assets. A restricted amount of consideration (17 to 20 percent) may be paid in the form of other assets besides voting stock.

In practice, companies should seek a favorable ruling ahead of time from the IRS that a planned acquisition will qualify as a tax-free exchange. As described earlier, the IRS justifies such tax-free status based on the concept of continuity of interest. The new ruling would eliminate the required holding period, which is currently as long as two years, and focus on the percentage of the merger that was financed with stock.

Under current rules, shareholders who don't follow the IRS holding period guidelines can create serious tax problems for themselves and other shareholders. Generally, if a shareholder sells more than half of this acquired stock, the capital gains obligation is due immediately. Unfortunately, when such early sales occur, the IRS can force the other shareholders to pay the capital gains tax as well. Other complications arise, creating headaches for all parties, including even the IRS, which has proposed this change primarily in a quest for simplicity and a more optimal use of its own scarce resources (auditors).

There are obviously situations in which tax-free (deferred) transactions are desirable and worth exploring. Recall that these situations are rare (Type A, B, or C reorganizations or LESOPs and CRTs) for most businesses. Where larger, corporate buyers are involved, their importance increases. In any case, if your objective in selling is to obtain immediate cash, these options serve little purpose. There are significant restrictions on when the acquired stock can be sold. A common restriction is that the acquired stock (from buyer to seller) cannot be sold for at least two years. To provide immediate income for the seller, however, a type of preferred stock is used. Preferred stock often includes a preferred dividend that must be paid whether common shareholders are paid dividends or not. This type of stock is called a fixed income security because of its regular dividend payments.

Regardless of your personal experience and level of sophistication, you will need assistance with all of these choices. Make sure that your attorney, CPA, and consultants have the appropriate experience, or you will be wasting your time and money and possibly making a monumental mistake.

Detailed Analysis of Various Terms and Conditions

Now that we have identified the major terms, conditions, and deal structures that can affect a deal price (and ultimately market comp data and business value), let's take a closer look at a few of the more important items.

Cash Down Payment

Of all the factors that can affect price, this is the most direct, observable, and thus quantifiable of all. It is common knowledge among business brokers and entrepreneurs that there will be a cash discount for an all-cash offer. Buyers of businesses routinely expect a substantial discount if they offer all or nearly all cash payment at close of escrow. Typical discounts for all cash range from 10 to 33 percent, depending on the unique circumstances of each situation. The more motivated the seller is to sell, the greater the cash discount that will be acceptable. The more anxious the seller is to obtain the money for some other purpose, the greater the cash discount might be. The longer the business has been on the market, the greater the cash discount could be. The smaller the cash discount, the more likely the seller will be to accept it. It is possible to calculate a justifiable cash discount by using modern financial theory. In practice, however, the offered and accepted cash discounts are a function of the give and take of the two parties involved.

The various market comp databases provide insights into the cash discount phenomenon. For example, a recent BIZCOMPS study showed that businesses that sold for all cash generated an average price to cash flow multiple of 1.9, compared with a ratio of 2.1 for those that were sold with seller financing (businesses sold with terms generated approximately 11 percent higher sale prices). Another interesting statistic shows that businesses sold with terms sold for 85 percent of the asking price, whereas those sold for all cash generated sale prices equal to 81 percent of the asking price. Stated differently, businesses that sold for all cash were discounted more than businesses sold with terms when compared with the asking prices (between 4 and 16 percent, depending on region). This relationship can be interpreted to imply that businesses marketed for an all-cash price create concern on the part of buyers to such an extent that it affects the selling price. The concern is that the seller does not have enough confidence in the business to provide financing. Of course, sellers argue that the real concern is that the buyer will not pay the entire price because of the buyer's potential incompetence.

A more detailed study of recent BIZCOMPS data by Toby Tatum, author of "Transaction Patterns: Obtaining Maximum Knowledge from the BIZCOMPS Database" (available through Business Valuation Resources at *www.BVResources.com* or through the IBA at *www.go-iba.com*), led to confirmation and refinement of the cash discount factor. Tatum's analysis is exceptionally clear, useful, and well worth its cost. Business brokers, in particular, will find the information extremely beneficial. Using the entire database, he found the following mean and median multiples of cash flow in various financing situations:

	Mean	Median
More than 70 percent seller financing	2.31	2.03
Some seller financing	2.15	1.84
All cash	1.84	1.60

Recall that the BIZCOMPS studies include primarily smaller businesses (a small percentage of middle-market type sales) and that these multiples exclude inventory from the sale price multiples (if inventory were included, the multiples would be higher). Their cash flow figure, called seller's discretionary cash flow (SDCF), is synonymous with the ACF figures used throughout this book.

Not only is the use of an all-cash discount commonly known and understood, it is empirically justified by the time value of money. As explained in detail on the CD-ROM, it is a fundamental concept of modern financial theory that a dollar today is worth more than a dollar in the future for three primary reasons:

Inflation

Opportunity cost

Risk

Inflation

All modern industrialized economies (with the exception of Japan today) have experienced inflation to one degree or another every year since the end of the Great Depression. Accordingly, $100 today will be worth less over time because of the erosion of purchasing power (i.e., inflation). An inflation rate of 3 percent per year (current rate of U.S. inflation per the Consumer Price Index) over a ten-year period means that a dollar today will be worth at least 30 percent more than it will be worth ten years later.

In general, note that inflation can result in a wealth transfer from creditors to debtors (lenders to borrowers). In other words, as inflation accelerates, the borrower is repaying the fixed amount of debt with dollars that are increasingly worth less. Inflation is more relevant for long-term financing (e.g., ten or more years). Most business acquisition financing is ten years or less, although real estate financing can extend out to thirty years. Inflation is the primary reason why lenders may prefer to offer variable interest rate financing. This preference is the result of the general relationship between inflation and interest rates. In general, as inflation accelerates, interest rates rise to reflect the depreciating value of money. This relationship is empirically strong, practically a one-for-one basis. By offering variable interest rates, the banks (creditors) protect themselves from rising inflation.

However, most seller financing is based on a fixed rate of interest, so creditor beware. If the payback period is only one to three years, inflation is not a major concern. But if the financing is five to ten years, then the impact can be substantial. For example, if the seller offers fixed-rate financing for a seven-year period and inflation accelerates from 3 to 12 percent (as it did in the late 1970s and early 1980s), the buyer will receive a windfall profit because of repayment with dollars that are increasingly less valuable. If inflation persisted at 10 percent per year for five years, the dollars used for repayment during the fifth year would be worth only half as much as originally intended or hoped for by the seller.

Although inflation is associated with rising consumer goods prices, it is also true that the costs of running a business probably are likely rising, balancing the impact of inflation on the company's income statement. In other words, inflation will allow the company to charge higher prices to consumers, but the company eventually will be forced to pay higher wages and higher raw material costs as well. In general, however, inflation causes prices for consumer goods to rise quicker than wages and raw materials to the benefit of the producer. Thus, the higher revenues (higher profits) can be used to pay off the fixed-rate financing on a reduced "real cost" basis.

The primary point is that the borrower's company is not harmed as much by inflation as the lender. The borrower (buyer) uses inflated dollars to pay back the fixed rate financing to his benefit. The lender (seller) is receiving dollars that are worth less than originally hoped for when the deal was struck. Therefore, in seller financing, sellers protect themselves from unanticipated inflation by insisting on variable rate financing that rises and falls with a major interest rate such as the prime rate. This rate reflects the "price" major commercial banks charge their "best" customers to borrow money and is listed daily in the *Wall Street Journal* and on most business-related Web sites such as *www.Bloomberg.com*. Many business loans are priced in accordance with the prime rate (which tends to rise and fall with the tendencies of Federal Reserve policy), e.g., participating SBA lenders must charge between "prime plus 2.25 percent to prime plus 2.75 percent" on their government guaranteed "change of ownership" or business acquisition loans.

Opportunity Cost

Opportunity cost is a basic economic concept that refers generally to the idea that every choice we make has an implicit cost. In general, opportunity cost is the cost of the highest valued alternative forgone as a result of a particular choice. For example, the opportunity cost of a full-time employee who decides to purchase a business and operate it on a full-time basis would be the forgone salary of being an employee. Opportunity cost has many applications in economics and finance, but the key point in the current context is that by having a dollar today, one can invest the dollar and watch it grow over time. Stated succinctly, a dollar today is worth more than a dollar in the future because you have the dollar today and you can use it or invest it over time and watch it grow. If you must wait for one year or several years to receive the dollar, you cannot enjoy the benefits of ownership during this period of time.

Risk

This is the most important element related to the time value of money as it relates to business valuation and the purchase and sale of a privately held business. The essence of this feature is summed up nicely with the old adage "a bird in the hand is worth two in the bush." This simple statement captures the essential reason why most sellers prefer to receive as much cash as possible at the close of escrow (even if this means a higher overall tax burden). Once the closing occurs, there is no absolute guarantee that the seller will receive the balance of the money owed to her no matter how secure the seller financing might seem. There is always a risk that the seller will not be paid the balance owed.

From the seller's (creditor's) point of view, the more unlikely (risky) the future repayment might be, the more cash down at closing is required. If the seller has less than full faith in the buyer (borrower), the seller may insist on a high down payment in addition to other risk-minimizing terms and conditions. For example, the seller will almost always insist on a personal guarantee from the buyer (and spouse in community property states) and a full, first-place pledge of all company assets as collateral (unless a bank is involved, causing the seller to take second place).

If the seller is truly concerned, additional steps beyond a higher down payment, personal guarantee, and company asset pledge may be pursued. The seller may ask for specific collateral in the form of marketable securities (e.g., stocks, bonds, Treasury bills) or insert special clauses in the purchase contract or promissory note. For example, a so-called evergreen clause could be inserted that requires the new owner to maintain inventory levels at or above a certain minimum amount or risk immediate default on the promissory note. A "cross-default" clause would also be possible, declaring that if the new owner defaults on the property lease, a simultaneous default shall occur on the promissory note and vice versa.

In conclusion, the impact of inflation on money received in the future from the buyer, the lost opportunities of not having all cash as of closing, and the risk of nonpayment or less than full repayment by the buyer (borrower) almost always leads to a situation in which the seller will accept a lower price in exchange for a higher cash down payment at closing. Discounts of 10 percent to 40 percent occur in practice when sellers seek maximum cash at closing. As explained in the CD-ROM section covering valuation for SBA purposes, one of the primary benefits for the buyer of obtaining bank financing is the substantial discount that comes with providing the seller with as much as 90 percent of the deal price in cash at close of escrow.

Additional Seller Financing Terms

In addition to the amount of the cash down payment at closing, the terms and conditions related to seller financing can affect the final deal price. All other things equal, the following relationships hold:

Higher interest rate, lower deal price

Shorter payback period, lower deal price

Stronger guarantee, lower deal price

More collateral, lower deal price

The first two relationships are most commonly directly related to negotiations for the final deal price. The give-and-take process described earlier applies to the various tradeoffs between buyer and seller. For example, the seller may agree to a lower deal price if the buyer (borrower) agrees to pay a higher interest rate and to repay the loan in a shorter period of time. As a practical matter, issues of guarantees and collateral normally do not surface in full force until after the original purchase contract has been negotiated and accepted by both parties. The reason is that most standard purchase contracts used by brokers and even attorneys do not fully address guarantee and collateral issues. As due diligence progresses and closing nears, the parties begin to prepare the promissory note, which naturally leads to a fuller discussion of these issues.

Most sellers will not agree to any price unless the promissory note is personally guaranteed by the buyer (borrower). In community property states such as Arizona, a spousal guarantee is not legally binding unless both spouses sign the guarantee. Sly buyers will try to get away with offering only a "corporate" or "company" guarantee, but sellers who have legal representation or a skilled broker will reject such an offer immediately. In fact, the seller may respond by requesting both a personal and corporate guarantee.

Collateral issues tend to drag on to the very end because of the general resistance of buyers to offer any more collateral than the business assets they are acquiring. Buyers will argue that the loan is fully collateralized by the business assets (which may have an extremely low FMV or liquidation value [LV]) and personally guaranteed, thus eliminating the need for additional collateral.

Sellers will argue that the tangible business assets are minimal because of the primary importance of goodwill or "blue sky" (i.e., earning power) and that in the event of default, their value is questionable if the company has lost key customers and employees or has shut down operations. They will also argue that personal guarantees are imperfect because personal assets can be transferred to other parties or hidden from the seller. In the end, it is uncommon to find the buyer willing to offer additional specific collateral such as marketable securities or real estate. In the end, as is the case for negotiations in general, the relative bargaining power of each party at a particular point in the process will determine which side achieves its objectives.

Covenant Not to Compete

The significance of a noncompete agreement can range from immaterial to substantial, depending on the type of business and the seller's future plans, intentions, and background. For example, if the seller is clearly of retirement age or is suffering from a verifiable illness that affects his ability to work, then the significance normally would be quite low. However, most buyers will analyze this aspect of a deal carefully to minimize the risk associated with the seller remaining active in the subject industry.

In general, the more important the owner is to the success of a business, the more worried a buyer should be about the nature of the covenant not to compete. If a business is based primarily on the relationship between the owner and key customers and the particular product line or service is easily replicated, buyers should be legitimately concerned about crafting a thorough and strong covenant not to compete. For example, accounting and tax practice revenues typically are the result of years of contact between the seller and the customer base. It would not be very difficult for the seller of an accounting or tax practice to set up a new office across the street and send a letter or make phone calls to the entire customer base informing them that he has moved across the street (without mentioning that the practice has been sold). This would be devastating to the buyer of such a practice. For this reason, noncompete clauses related to the buying and selling of these practices are prepared carefully, reviewed by legal counsel, and on occasion supplemented by a separate document that is attached to the main body of the purchase contract.

The relationship between such covenants and business value should be clear. If the seller is not prevented from reentering the same industry and contacting the customer base, the buyer is at a great risk of losing his entire investment. As noted throughout business valuation literature, the bottom line of business valuation is the quantity and quality of future earnings or cash flow that accrues to the owner. In other words, the greater the amount and the lower the risk, the higher the value. The riskiness of the future cash flows or earnings has a direct bearing on their value. Without a covenant not to compete, the riskiness of the future cash flows is enormous and their value is correspondingly minimal. Less risk means more value. The covenant protects the integrity of the future cash flows and thus their value.

Employment Contract and Training Period

Although employment contracts and training and transition periods are distinct concepts, they are often intertwined in practice. In general, employment contracts are fairly rare, but the sale of almost every business includes a standard training period as part of the purchase price. Employment contracts are commonly one year in length, with options for extending provided to both parties. For example, if the seller has been responsible for working directly with the company's customers, the seller may sign a commission agreement against future sales to maintain the integrity of the company under its new ownership. If the seller has been deeply involved in production matters, on the other hand, the agreement may call for her assistance in this area. Typical training periods vary from business to business and deal to deal, but somewhere between two and twelve weeks of full-time assistance covers the majority of situations. The larger and more complicated a company is, the more important and "valuable" the training, or "transition," period becomes.

Depending on the nature of the business and the buyer's background, training periods may amount to no more than a familiarization effort consisting of simply pointing out where various documents are located. Buyers who are purchasing a type of business they have owned before may desire only to be introduced personally to key employees, customers, and suppliers. First-time business owners may insist on a lengthy training period as part of the deal (or there will be no deal). Experience has shown that most training efforts end up being substantially less than what was originally agreed on for a variety of reasons. Many buyers want the assistance of the seller in areas that require their unique knowledge, but generally they are anxious to run the ship in accordance with their personal tastes and preferences. Most sellers, on the other hand, are anxious to fulfill their training requirements and move on to their next endeavor.

As it relates to business value or deal prices, any training period that exceeds the norm may lead to a separate employment or consulting agreement if not simply a higher deal price. Note that employment or consulting agreements can take two substantive forms in terms of deal structure:

Employment contract separate from and in addition to the deal price

Employment contract as part of the deal price and structure

In other words, using an employment or consulting contract primarily for tax purposes entails including this contract and its compensation as part of the deal price. The expectations in this case generally are quite low because it is primarily a tax maneuver. The danger is that the buyer and seller may agree to cosmetically alter the structure for tax purposes (consulting fees are tax deductible in full for the buyer in the year they are paid), but in this process a document emerges that could legally bind the seller to many hours of work.

This problem is the result of trying to ensure that the consulting agreement appears to be legitimate for tax purposes and not just a hollow document created to minimize taxable income for the new owner. The point is that even if the "gentleman's agreement" is that the seller will not be called on to work the hours called for in the consulting contract, if problems arise in the relationship between buyer and seller, the buyer could place the seller in a dangerous position of not being paid the associated compensation.

FMV of Inventory and Other Assets

The concept of *ceteris paribus* plays a substantial role in the world of science. It certainly applies to business valuation as well. For example, to say that manufacturing companies sell for higher multiples than service companies requires use of the *ceteris paribus* assumption, i.e., all other things being equal, their multiples are higher. Overall, this relationship is true, but numerous service companies sell for higher multiples than manufacturing companies because of the unique circumstances of each business. For example, a franchised, well-established, profitable, and asset-rich service business will sell for a higher multiple than a start-up, nonprofitable, asset poor manufacturing company.

Empirically speaking, the reason that manufacturing companies sell for higher multiples than service companies (*ceteris paribus*) is the higher level of tangible, fixed assets used by manufacturing companies of all types. All other things held equal, manufacturing companies will own a higher FMV of tangible assets than a service company, so each dollar of cash flow will be worth more, for a direct and an indirect reason.

The direct reason is that tangible assets have value; that is, they can be sold for cash. The indirect reason concerns the concept known as barriers to entry. Barriers to entry are defined as any advantage that an existing company has over potential entrants into the industry. The cost of purchasing the necessary plant and equipment (or FF&E) to run a manufacturing business is a barrier to entry for would-be competitors. Because the cost of entering a manufacturing industry typically is higher than entering a service business, entry is deterred to one extent or another, buffering the future cash flows of the existing manufacturing company relative to the future cash flows of an industry in which entry is less expensive.

For these reasons and others, market comp data tend to verify this relationship in the real world. For example, note the following average multiples found in the latest VR Business Brokers database for business sales between March 1997 and March 2000:

Price to Cash Flow

Service businesses	1.01
Manufacturing businesses	3.49

Note that other business sales databases generally confirm this relationship, although perhaps not as decisively as the VR data. For example, a recent BIZ-COMPS report showed the following relationships:

Price to Cash Flow

Service businesses	2.3
Manufacturing businesses	2.0

For precise understanding of the various market comp database sources available for use in valuation matters, review the relevant pages in Chapter Five. Regarding the relationship between asset values and company value, it is also safe to say that as a company grows and matures, possibly going public, the strength of correlation tends to diminish. To the extent that publicly traded companies are valued first and foremost by assessments of past, current, and most importantly future earnings and cash flow, the relative importance of asset values declines.

Several rules of thumb are based on asset values as well, so the greater the FMV of the tangible assets, the higher the estimated value of the company. For example, a general rule of thumb for small retail businesses (among other variations) is "1 to 1.5 times ACF plus assets"

Other variations include the use of a multiple of cash flow plus an asset value equal only to inventory (excludes FF&E), but the essence remains the same. The greater the asset value, the higher the estimated value of the subject company.

In conclusion, it stands to reason that when comparing two businesses with equal cash flow and an equal operating history, the company with higher-valued tangible assets (e.g., inventory, tools and equipment, land, and buildings) will sell for higher multiples. All other things held equal, greater asset values are associated with higher deal prices and ultimately higher business value. For more insights into asset valuations, review the CD-ROM "Asset or Cost Approach to Business Valuation" section and the "Accounting Primer" segment covering intangible assets.

Allocation of Purchase Price

Just as a stock sale and asset sale result in different tax outcomes, so will different allocations of the purchase price as required by IRS for asset sales. As noted earlier, the purchase price must be allocated among several IRS-stipulated asset categories. This allocation results in a combination of ordinary income taxation and capital gains taxation (assuming the business is sold for a price greater than the existing basis in the various assets, which typically is the case).

Because the allocation of purchase price need not be part of the purchase contract, it is often a subject of discussion late in the sale process. Because of the often conflicting interest of the parties, for a given allocation to be acceptable to one side, a concession may be required from the other side. Such concessions may not involve a change in purchase price but some other material change such as the seller including another asset, such as a computer, or the buyer agreeing to forfeit one of the deposits originally intended to become the buyer's property. Although these examples seem trivial, it is precisely this type of give and take that characterizes most deals.

Assumption of Debt

Another potentially substantial adjustment to the recorded deal price involves the assumption of various types and amounts of debt. The choice between an asset sale and a "stock sale" plays an important role in determining whether and how much debt might be involved in a particular deal. Recall that the typical conditions of an asset sale call for the seller to retain all liquid assets such as cash, checking accounts, receivables, marketable securities, and deposits and to deliver the business free and clear of all debt. The purchase price under an asset sale is adjusted accordingly.

To the extent that almost every possible combination of assets and liabilities might be taken on by the new owner (everything is negotiable), even under an asset sale the buyer might assume a certain liability or two. For example, part of the deal might include the buyer assuming all notes payable related to equipment. Assumption of such a liability increases the "real price" paid by the buyer. Alternatively, the final deal price may be reduced by the amount of the assumed debt. Depending on circumstances, either scenario and interpretation is possible.

The main point is that for the typical business purchase (asset sale), any assumption of debt must be factored into the deal price. The actual, final "real" price must account for any such assumptions. As you might imagine, the presence of debt assumptions in an asset purchase can make the use of market comp data troublesome unless enough detail is available to properly assess the situation. Only one of the major four databases that track the sale of privately held businesses contains such information (Pratt's Stats™, in which businesses carry an average deal price of around $17 million).

In a stock sale, on the other hand, it is expected that the buyer will inherit and assume all liabilities (unless specifically excluded). The stock sale price is based on inheriting the balance sheet as it stands as of close of escrow, and any adjustments thereto result in a change in the "real" price paid by the buyer.

In terms of attempting to value a company using the ARM approach, one of the first steps taken involves a description of the interest that is being valued. Naturally, the valuation of stock differs from the valuation of assets, with one of the notable differences being the manner in which debts are handled. It is important to make sure that debt assumptions are evaluated in conjunction with the overall business valuation.

Sources of Tax Information

In most cases in which the federal government or the courts are involved, it is prudent to hire a professional business appraiser. From estate taxes to divorce settlements, it often takes a team of professionals to optimally present your case (attorney, CPA, Certified Business Appraiser). When thousands or even hundreds of thousands of dollars are on the line, paying the cost associated with professional assistance is necessary and beneficial. As repeated throughout this book, however, proactive involvement by the entrepreneur will maximize the chances for prevailing. You should not be expected to become an expert in business valuation for divorce purposes, but only you will know the finer points of your situation and business. Understanding the relationship between the facts at hand and the valuation process can only benefit your cause. Thus, becoming familiar with tax and legal issues related to business valuation may be necessary if such disputes become a reality. The more you know, the more you can help your team in the heat of the valuation battle. The following publications are recommended:

Business Acquisitions: Tax and Legal Guide, by Frank L. Brunetti and Stanley J. Yellen (Panel Publishing)

Dictionary of Tax Terms, by Larry Crumbley, Jack Friedman, and Susan B. Anders (Barron's Business Guides)

Federal Tax Valuation Digest: Business Enterprises and Business Interests, by John A. Bishop and Idelle A. Howitt (Warren, Gorham, and Lamont)

Tax Aspects of Acquisitions and Mergers, by Philip Cooke (Kluwer Law International)

Taxable and Tax-Free Corporate Mergers, Acquisitions, and LBOs, by Samuel C. Thompson (West Publishing Company)

Important IRS Rulings (Revenue Rulings) and Court Cases

For your convenience, a short list of major revenue rulings and court cases, each containing the appropriate citation and a brief description, is included here. One of the most complete and insightful books ever written about business valuation and the courts (all types of courts) is called *Valuing Your Privately Held Business* (written by Irving L. Blackman and published by McGraw-Hill, revised edition, 1992). For example, the book contains an impressive list of reasons why the courts have historically rejected comparable companies for use in the market approach to valuation (forty-three in all) and the complete text of major IRS Revenue Rulings and precedent-setting cases. The second chapter of the book, "The Legal Approach to Business Valuation," seems to capture the essence of this practical and unique book.

Revenue Rulings (R.R.) of the Internal Revenue Service

A.R.M. 34, C.B. 2, 31 (1920) and R.R. #65–92

R.R. 59–60, 1959–1 C.B. 237: Most important IRS ruling, modified subsequently by R.R. 65–193, R.R. 77–287, R.R. 80–213, and R.R. 83–120

R.R. 65–192, 1965–2 C.B. 259: Opens usage of 59–60 to income tax purposes and restricts use of formula per ARM 34

R.R. 65–193, 1965–2 C.B. 370

R.R. 68–609, 1968–2 C.B. 327: Clarifies usage of ARM 34 formula and requires use of R.R. 59–60 for all types of business interests (not only corporations)

R.R. 77–287, 1977–2 C.B. 319: Addresses discount applied to "restricted" shares in a closely held business

R.R. 78–367, 1978–2 C.B. 249: Involves the gift tax and effects of merger announcements on value of privately held stock

R.R. 79–7, 1979–1 C.B. 294: Addresses minority interest transfers as they affect estate taxes

R.R. 81–253, 1981–2 C.B. 187: Addresses transfer of entire business through multiple minority interests; disallowed minority discount under these circumstances

R.R. 83–119 1983–2 C.B. 57: Deals with recapitalization involving preferred stock and taxable dividends

R.R. 83–120, 1983–2 C.B. 170: Contains guidelines for the valuation of stock (common and preferred) issued under a recapitalization

Court Cases

Central Trust Co. v. U.S., 305 F.2d 393 (Ct. Cs. 1962): This is a thorough, often-cited case containing a broad range of analysis and descriptive insights.

Estate of Woodbury G. Andrews v. Commissioner, 79 TC 938 (1982): Deals with minority discounts and the court's efforts in reaching a middle-of-the road valuation.

Righter v. U.S., 439 F.2d 1204 (Ct. Cl. 1971): This case highlights the problems of finding comparable comparables.

Albert C. Luce, 84–1 USTC 13, 549: Highlights the applicability of the book value method.

Estate of Mark S. Gallo, TC Memo 1985–363, 50 TCM 470: An interesting dispute between appraisers, with the court stepping in to bridge the gap. (Yes, this is the Gallo wine family.)

Estate of Murphy, 60 TCM 645 (1990): The tax court refused to grant a minority discount for a gift made shortly before death (eighteen days).

Estate of Mildred Herschede Jung, 58 TCM 1127 (1990): Dealt with sale of company assets two years after decedent's death. Court agreed that this information is relevant and discoverable regarding settlement of estate.

Estate of Clara S. Reeder Winkler, 57 TCM 373 (1989): Here the court ruled that a 10 percent voting block carrying the power of swing vote is not eligible for a minority discount.

Estate of Riden Rodriguez, 56 TCM 1033 (1989): The tax court held that the value of the company's stock was significantly reduced as a result of decedent's expertise in business. Therefore, this expertise reduced the stock's marketability.

Estate of Dean A. Chenoweth, 88 TC 1577 (1987): The tax court agreed that a 51 percent interest passed to the surviving spouse was subject to a control premium concerning the marital deduction.

Victor I. Minahan, 88 TC 492 (1987): As a result of numerous tax court rulings negating the family attribution argument, the plaintiff was awarded attorney's fees.

Estate of Davis Jephson, 87 TC 297 (1986): According to the tax court, the stock value of a 100 percent–owned investment company is net asset value plus liquidation costs.

The Northern Trust Company, 87 TC 349 (1986): The discounted cash flow method was accepted by the tax court after it rejected the use of comparables. Also, a 25 percent minority discount and a 20 percent marketability discount were used by the tax court.

Estate of Curry, 83-USTC 13, 518 (7th Circuit): When the decedent maintains a controlling interest, both voting and nonvoting stock have equal per share value.

CHAPTER 7

Fractional Interests and Discounts

Minority and Marketability Discounts

Most small business transactions involve the purchase and sale of privately held, whole companies of a going-concern nature (i.e., 100 percent of all the operating assets or 100 percent of the company's outstanding shares). At the other extreme, the stock markets revolve primarily around the buying and selling of individual shares or fractional interests that only rarely exceed an interest of 1 percent or more of the fair market value (FMV) of the company's outstanding stock. These two valuation environments (privately held versus publicly traded) clearly are different in many ways, as discussed in Chapters Two and Five.

In addition, the valuation process related to such whole, privately held companies differs substantially from the valuation of partial or fractional ownership interests in the very same companies. In a nutshell, the sum of the parts does not equal the whole when it comes to valuing small, privately held businesses; fractional interests typically are worth less than a pro rata share of the control value for the entire company. This premise provides the foundation for the present chapter.

The buying and selling of minority interests in privately held companies is fairly common in the business world and is associated with unique valuation considerations and processes that are clarified throughout this chapter. In general, the ARM approach is geared toward the valuation of small, privately held businesses as a whole, whereas the present chapter deals with the exception involving only a partial or minority interest in such companies.

The importance of this chapter is heightened by the fact that the considerations and processes associated with minority interests are among the most litigated events in the business valuation environment. Not only are minority interest situations highly litigated, but the courts' interpretations and applications of theory are dynamic and constantly evolving. For example, the IRS historically downplayed the role of discounts in business valuation to maximize revenue collections. However, the courts have forced their hand and led the IRS to accept discounts as high as 65 percent (marketability discount only). In addition, the IRS and the courts are undergoing another dramatic shift in the way in which marketability discounts are estimated. It is now true that citing of case history regarding marketability discounts requires real-time access to court cases that involve the quantitative marketability discount model (QMDM), described later in this chapter.

The coverage in this chapter tends toward the general rather than the specific because of the high probability that involvement in these areas will necessitate outside professional assistance. However, you will emerge from this chapter with a solid working knowledge of the key concepts involved. This knowledge will help you obtain a higher-quality analysis from the chosen professional by highlighting pertinent facts and situations that may have a material impact on the final results.

In short, this chapter addresses the implications of the following two questions:

> Is the subject interest being valued a controlling interest or a minority interest?
>
> Is the subject interest easily transferred in a liquid market?

In practice, these two questions normally are considered separately and in the order listed here. On the other hand, there may be a substantive relationship between the two. For example, it appears to be true that a controlling interest in a company is more easily marketed than a noncontrolling, minority interest. In addition, be aware that the answers to these two questions commonly lead to discounts against the overall company value that are multiplicative (not additive) in nature, thereby softening the impact of both discounts.

Minority Interest Discount and Control Premium Overview

The concept of minority interest is fairly straightforward, with a few clarifications needed for complete understanding. The New York Stock Exchange (NYSE), American Stock Exchange (AMEX), and NASDAQ are all organized exchanges that facilitate the buying and selling of company securities (primarily equity securities such as common stock). Most transactions on these exchanges involve minority interests, even if the dollar value of such events seems staggering to the average person. One can invest billions of dollars without reaching a majority level of ownership. Thus, only in the case of an aggressive takeover attempt (whether friendly or hostile) is a majority interest ever obtained by any single investor.

The buying and selling of small, privately held companies, on the other hand, are not facilitated by organized exchanges. These deals occur in the business brokerage and middle-market arenas, wherein companies may be listed for sale and buyers search for the right company at the right price through various channels such as classified ads, professional intermediaries, and, increasingly, the Internet. In most of these transactions, the entire company is purchased. Thus, these deals involve not only majority interests but typically 100 percent interests.

In both publicly traded and privately held environments, exceptions to the norm occur. In the public realm, takeover attempts are made to procure majority or controlling interests (based on the accumulation of more and more minority interests). In the private realm, it may be that only a fractional or minority interest of a company is available for sale and purchased. Given our primary interest in small, privately held businesses, our focus is on the latter scenario dealing with fractional interests.

For a number of reasons, a small business owner may want to sell and a knowledgeable, motivated buyer may want to purchase only a fractional stake in the subject company. For example, a growing business may need additional capital that cannot be obtained in the form of a bank loan. In such cases, the owner may want to procure the needed funds through a partial sale of the company's outstanding shares. The owner receives the needed cash, and the investor (who may be a family member, friend, key employee, or independent third party) probably receives an above-average return on investment in the long run. More commonly, professional practices such as law, public accounting, medical, and engineering practices routinely are involved with the sale and purchase of minority interests as the professionals come and go. This process is called a buy-in and often is coupled with employment contracts. By definition, an employee stock ownership plan (ESOP) also involves minority interests. The buying and selling of such fractional interests (also called minority, nonmajority, or noncontrolling interests) are associated with unique considerations that directly affect the related value estimate.

Specifically, the purchase and sale of minority interests in small, privately held companies entails certain adjustments in value that pertain only to this particular situation. Two such adjustments must be made in estimating the value of a minority interest or noncontrolling interest:

Minority interest or lack-of-control discount

Marketability discount

The Business Valuation Committee of the American Society of Appraisers uses the following working definitions for each of these important discounts:

Minority interest discount: The reduction from the pro rata share of the value of the entire business to reflect the absence of the power of control

Marketability discount: An amount or percentage deducted from an equity interest to reflect the lack of marketability

The minority interest discount reflects the fact that ownership of only a small percentage of a company's shares gives the owner little or no authority over how the company is run. This lack of control leads to a discount in the value of such shares relative to the value a controlling interest block of shares would receive. In short, the inability to influence company decision making reduces the value of these minority stakes in privately held companies.

Alternatively stated, owning a controlling interest conveys more value to the holder than owning a noncontrolling interest. In fact, common terminology in this area includes the concept of a control premium, which is the theoretical opposite of a minority discount. As we shall see later, actual control premiums paid by acquiring entities of publicly traded securities serve as a basis for estimating minority discounts. In practice, the size of a control premium is a function of many factors, including the following:

Type of voting rights carried by the shares (cumulative versus noncumulative, whereby the latter grants the majority holder more power in selecting board members)

The relative distribution of ownership percentages (situations differ, e.g., two 40 percent owners and one 20 percent owner; three 33 percent owners; one owner with 49 percent, one with 1 percent and ten owners with 5 percent) and supermajority voting requirements (66 percent needed to approve corporate decisions)

Profitability and general attractiveness of the target corporation (better future, higher premium)

Existence of other suitors (bidding war creates higher premiums)

Other factors (e.g., state laws, Securities and Exchange Commission [SEC] disclosure requirements)

Quantitative Derivation of Premiums and Discounts

Our focus here remains primarily on evaluating minority discounts as part of our focus on the buying and selling (valuation) of small, privately held companies. For the sake of clarity, however, consider the following formulas that relate to one of the primary techniques used to calculate minority interest discounts while noting the different denominators:

$$\text{Control premium} = \frac{(\text{Controlling interest share price} - \text{Minority interest share price})}{\text{Minority interest share price}}$$

$$\text{Minority interest discount} = \frac{(\text{Minority interest share price} - \text{Controlling interest share price})}{\text{Controlling interest share price}}$$

It is important to realize that as a result of the nature of mathematical calculations, use of the same prices in both examples generates different percentages for the premium versus the discount. For example,

$$\text{Control premium} = \frac{(50 - 40)}{40} = +25\%$$

$$\text{Minority interest discount} = \frac{(40 - 50)}{50} = -20\%$$

A solution for this apparent inequality (25 percent versus 20 percent by way of the same change in differing directions) is found through the use of the so-called "midpoint formula," which calls for the use of a base figure located exactly halfway between the two base numbers (40 and 50). The resulting base number of 45 equalizes the percentage change in both directions to 22.22 percent (rather than 25 percent premium and 20 percent discount). Irrespective of this mathematical issue, these results can be interpreted in various ways. For example, the control premium reflects the takeover price paid by an investor as compared with the company's share price before announcement and execution of the takeover attempt. The minority interest discount, on the other hand, can be interpreted as the relative decline in value of a given share without any control or controlling influence on the company's operations.

Most such calculations that are made in connection with the valuation of small, privately held companies revolve around calculation of the minority interest discount (or the lack-of-control discount) as it applies to the buying, selling, or taxing of ownership interests that are small and noncontrolling. Stated differently, calculating control premiums is the means to the end of estimating the minority interest discount.

Marketability Discount Overview

The second adjustment made to the whole company value is the marketability discount, which is a function of the relative difficulty associated with trying to sell a minority interest in a privately held company to investors. Because of the lack of control and the great uncertainty involved with partial ownership of privately held companies, such shares generally are illiquid and difficult to sell (i.e., difficult to turn into cash without a loss in principal). There is no active market for minority shares in "main street" businesses (technically speaking, the business brokerage and middle-market segments) such as Joe's Garage, so this illiquidity is reflected in the marketability discount.

Procedurally, it is important to realize that these discounts generally are multiplicative, not additive. This means that the first discount is taken against the company value and then the second discount is applied to the originally discounted company value, thus softening the discount effect. For now, we shall assume that marketability discounts normally are not applied to the sale of whole privately held companies. The primary reason for assuming that whole company sales are not subject to the marketability discount is the fact that such illiquidity is already factored into the asking and deal price of the business through one or more valuation methods. Whether such illiquidity is factored into a multiple, discount or cap rate, rule of thumb, or evaluation of market comps, the difficulty associated with selling privately held companies (as opposed to publicly traded shares) is incorporated into the related analysis.

Our primary focus therefore continues to be the sale of minority interests and their corresponding discounts for lack of control and illiquidity applied against the whole company's FMV on a controlling and going-concern basis.

Analysis of Minority or Noncontrolling Interest Discounts

Use of terminology in this area can be problematic in certain instances. For example, the term *minority interest* generally is synonymous with *noncontrolling interest* in the eyes of the courts and many practitioners. There is potentially a huge difference between the two, however, reflecting the underlying reality of a particular set of circumstances. The important difference arises when a minority interest becomes a controlling interest. Can you imagine how this might happen?

A minority interest (less than 50 percent share of ownership) of as little as 2 percent could be a controlling interest if there were two other shareholders with 49 percent shares each. In other words, the 2 percent block of shares can control the company jointly by siding with either one of the 49 percent shareholders. This "swing block" can swing control one way or the other depending on the preference of the 2 percent owner. In addition, owners with 50 percent ownership may have a lack of control despite not being a minority interest. Thus, minority interests may be controlling, and nonminority interests may not be controlling. What about the case where there are three shareholders, each with 33 percent? Is any one of the three shareholders in control? Yes and no, depending on the issue and how the vote turns out between the three. Assessing a lack-of-control discount in this situation is not clear or simple, again depending on circumstances. Perhaps two of the three shareholders are married and always vote together. In this case, the couple would have a controlling interest, and the third party would not.

Other caveats exist for assessing control or lack thereof. One such caveat concerns the nature of the stock. On occasion, nonvoting stock is issued to raise additional capital from passive investors. In assessing control, only voting stock is relevant. In addition, different states have different statutes that protect the rights of nonmajority and noncontrolling shareholders. For example, many states give minority shareholders the right to receive "fair value" (not exactly FMV as it is often based on the concept of "equity" or "fairness") for shares that are sold in conjunction with a change in control of the business to the detriment of the minority shareholder.

Besides the nature of the stock (voting versus nonvoting) and state statutes (fair value rights), a company's bylaws or articles of incorporation may spell out certain rights, requirements, or constraints that affect control. Several states and many company bylaws contain supermajority clauses that require more than a 51 percent majority to approve certain transactions or events. A two-thirds majority may be required to sell the company, for example. Consider the situation in which one 40 percent owner and four 15 percent owners share ownership in a company. Under normal circumstances, the 40 percent owner would need only one of the four other investors to agree with his decisions to take action. The supermajority makes this more difficult, requiring two of the four to support the 40 percent owner.

In addition, the recent popularity of limited liability companies (LLCs) results in part from the flexibility allowed in allocating rights related to profit sharing, management duties, and ultimately control of the business. S-corporations, on the other hand, are much more rigid in that profits must be allocated in direct proportion to the ownership percentages, and each share receives one vote in most cases. LLCs allow allocations of profits and votes that are not on a straight pro rata basis.

Thus, when assessing minority interest discounts, it is necessary to analyze the particulars of the situation carefully to avoid the mistake of applying a discount against a minority share that actually has control characteristics. Although many appraisers tend to rely on average discounts based on real-world transactions, each situation is unique and must be independently assessed to reach the proper discount figure.

The issues and procedures surrounding the valuation of minority interests are among the most controversial of all in the valuation community. The most common sources of disputes related to minority ownership include taxation for estate purposes, settlement of divorce proceedings, and state laws concerning shareholder rights. It is important to understand that the rules of the game are different for each of these three distinct scenarios. Case law, individual judge characteristics and preferences, and the use of expert testimony characterizes most of these disputes that arise out of minority interest ownership situations. Remember that all valuation analyses should be performed and written with the targeted audience in mind.

The justification for minority interest discounts (also called noncontrolling interest discounts) generally is not subject to debate. In short, less control means less value. However, the question of whether such discounts are to be applied is a world away from the question of how to determine and apply them. The generally accepted fact is that minority owners have little to no control over the board of directors, company policies and procedures, and, importantly, the cash flow or earnings of the business. On the other hand, ownership of a majority or controlling interest transfers authority over all aspects of the business, including the following:

Select key officers and determine their compensation, duties, and benefits

Establish company objectives, goals, and company mission

Approve mergers, acquisitions, spinoffs, liquidation of assets, and so on

Declare and pay dividends, bonuses, and other distributions of cash

Make most other important decisions about the subject company

The following relationships should help to clarify the bigger picture relating to minority interest situations:

Lesser percentage ownership → Less control

Less control → More risk

More risk → Larger discount

Larger discount → Less value

Thus, a lesser ownership percentage ultimately is associated with less value. These relationships also hold in reverse (i.e., greater percentage ownership means more control, more control means less risk, less risk means lower discount, lower discount means more value). Now we move on to the more challenging aspect of minority interest situations.

How Are Minority Interest Discounts Calculated?

Now that we understand when and why a lack-of-control (minority interest) discount is to be applied, we turn to the actual process of estimating the size of the discount percentage. As you might have guessed, there is no single correct way to estimate the lack-of-control discount. Clearly, the final result depends on the unique circumstances at hand; different situations are associated with different degrees of lack of control.

General Factors to Consider

The following list describes key considerations that can either increase or decrease the derived discount:

Historical treatment of minority shareholders by majority owners, company management, and the board of directors

Sufficient number of minority votes to block certain important decisions or elect at least one member to the board of directors

Role played by nonvoting stock, relative distribution of shares, impact of state statutes in support of minority shareholders' rights

Amount and frequency of routine dividends or other cash distributions on a pro rata basis to all shareholders alike

Each of these factors should be evaluated when one is estimating the minority interest discount using any of the methods available to the valuator.

When looked at from the opposite perspective, different situations are associated with different degrees of control. Our focus should be on the lack of control, which could range from absolutely no control to minimal control under specific circumstances. Thus, the minority interest discount can be large or small. Our focus on lack of control (minority interest discounts) reflects the common occurrence of buying, selling, and taxing minority interests in privately held companies.

The important concept of minority interest discounts is grounded in actual transactions made in public exchanges such as the NYSE. Hundreds of studies have been completed that analyzed the difference in a company's share price under a minority ownership basis and a control (majority) basis. Shannon Pratt's Web site (*www.bvmarketdata.com*[sm]) contains the results of studies conducted with MERGERSTAT along with other market-based valuation information such as Pratt's Stats™ and BIZCOMPS™.

The MERGERSTAT study and most similar studies have empirically documented that purchasers of company stock on a 100 percent controlling interest basis pay a substantial premium compared with the preacquisition minority interest share price. As illustrated earlier, such control premiums represent the inverse of minority interest discounts. Historically speaking, the median control premium paid for publicly traded companies has hovered between 25 and 35 percent. As you recall, the minority interest discount based on the same share price data used for calculating a control premium is less than the premium because the discount is calculated with a higher denominator than that of the premium. Thus, reported control premiums that have hovered around 25 percent to 35 percent are associated with minority discounts in the range of 20 to 25 percent.

The MERGERSTAT control premium studies calculate premiums by comparing the publicly traded share price of a company on a date before any knowledge of a planned or actual takeover is presented to the public with the actual price paid at the conclusion of the takeover. Their basic calculation uses a five-day time period (specifically five active trading days) before the merger or acquisition plan is announced. It is important to note that the control premium and minority interest discount percentages just presented are averages from all industries.

By now, it should be clear that each industry and company situation is unique and should be analyzed on a case-by-case basis. MERGERSTAT offers the same data on an industry basis, which is generally preferable than using the overall averages. The industry average premiums and discounts are much more divergent, as should be expected. Even these numbers are not without criticism among professional valuators. Many experts believe that a large percentage (if not a majority) of the takeovers and related control premiums reflect much more than the element of control. They believe (and rightly so in the opinion of the authors) that such premiums also reflect potential synergism and economies of scale. This implication smacks of investment value, not fair market value. The experience of the authors confirms the fact that the highest prices paid by buyers often are a direct reflection of the benefits that will accrue to the new owner from improvements such as reduced overhead, expanded product lines, synergism, and economies of scale. Thus, it is safe to say that the average control premiums and their corresponding minority interest discounts tend to be overstated.

Now we turn to a review of the actual methods used to estimate minority interest discounts.

Proportion Method

Professional valuators use three primary tools for estimating minority interest discounts. The first method appears quite logical and flows directly from the valuation procedures we have learned in connection with the ARM approach. This first method calls for calculating the FMV of the subject company on a going-concern basis and then deducting the proper lack-of-control discount to arrive at the adjusted minority value. The essence of this method is as follows: Determine the value of a noncontrolling interest based on use of a control value as the starting point.

Comparison Method

The second approach is a type of market-based method that calls for direct comparison with similar historical minority interest values. The best source of comparative data for this method is prior minority interest sales in the recent past from the subject company. Certain types of businesses are routinely subject to the purchase and sale of minority interests, such as medical practices or law firms. Of course, there may not be any recent transactions or any transactions at all regarding the subject company. In addition, care must be exercised in ensuring that such in-house transactions were made at arm's length.

The next option for the comparison method involves a market approach method whereby similar company minority transactions can be evaluated and compared with the subject company. As in the guideline public company method described in Chapter Five, current share prices for publicly traded companies that operate in the same industry can be located, evaluated, and compared with the subject company's minority interest. All of the caveats and adjustments referred to in Chapter Five apply here, with one major difference. In the current case, we are comparing a minority interest with other minority interests instead of comparing a control (whole company value) value with minority interest share prices and their corresponding price to earnings (P/E) ratios. Theoretically, all methods should arrive at the same result.

Classical Method

If you are not satisfied with either of these methods, there is another choice in which you will use your basic valuation skills by attempting to estimate the value of the minority shares via estimation of all future income accruing to the minority owner and discounted back into present value (or capitalization of a historic measure of earnings or cash flow). In other words, it is possible to value the future benefits accruing to the minority owner directly by assessing the proportioned cash flow generation.

Your new-found valuation skills should lead you to the immediate conclusion that a lack of control over future cash flows increases the riskiness of such cash flows. Based on the ever-present risk–return paradigm, higher risk implies lower value. In terms of the ARM approach, this translates into a lower multiple applied against the derived cash flow measure. In terms of discounted cash flow or capitalization of earnings, this translates into a higher discount and capitalization rate. By now these relationships should be fairly clear, as summarized here:

Lesser percentage ownership → Less control

Less control → More risk

More risk → Lower multiple

More risk → Higher discount and capitalization rates

More risk → Lower value

Thus, a reduced ownership percentage (all other things held equal) is associated with less value.

Analysis of Marketability Discounts

In addition to a minority interest discount, the valuation of noncontrolling shares in a company probably will be subject to a second type of discount called a marketability discount. As noted earlier, this discount is based on the fact that minority shares in privately held companies are extremely difficult to sell in general (i.e., the market for minority shares is highly illiquid). Modern financial theory includes the premise that investors prefer liquidity. As a result, investments that are marketable are worth more than nonmarketable or illiquid investments.

In addition to assessing the general illiquidity of all minority shares in the context of modern financial theory, a practical viewpoint can be invaluable in deriving the proper marketability discount. Active business brokers and other intermediaries are fully aware that certain types of businesses and certain industries can be characterized as "hot" or "cold". Such characterization reflects the collective demand for and appeal of a given type of company in a given industry, a factor that could substantially affect the overall marketability discount. Two examples of the extreme positions here are video rental stores (extremely "cold" and hard to sell) and tax or accounting practices (very "hot," with hundreds of ready, willing, and able buyers for each practice that hits the market). Brokers know that obtaining a listing of an accounting or tax practice is as good as gold, whereas the prospects associated with listing a video rental store are dim.

Unsettled Issues

Among valuation professionals, there is a long-standing and evolving debate about when and how to apply a marketability discount. As evidenced by the frequency of this topic in professional valuation journals and newsletters such as the IBA's *Business Appraisal Practice* and Mercer Capital's *BizVal.com,* it continues to be a contentious issue among valuators and the courts. The major unsettled issues include the following:

> Should a marketability discount be applied to the sale of whole privately held companies (as opposed to minority interest sales only)?

> Should the use of restricted stock and pre–initial public offering (IPO) studies be used to estimate the marketability discount, or should the quantitative approach associated with the QMDM be used?

In addition to directly addressing these two questions, the next section contains important information about discounts and the legal system.

Applying the Marketability Discount

Generally speaking, there appears to be agreement that the marketability discount should be applied only to minority or noncontrolling stakes based on the argument that the whole company (control) value that serves as the base for adjustment should already reflect this illiquidity via the chosen valuation methods. Although this may not always be the case, it seems to be common practice to apply marketability discounts only to minority interests.

Those who argue in favor of applying marketability discounts directly to the company's control-based FMV claim that such illiquidity costs can be estimated properly via one of two methods. The first method is conceptually appealing and amounts to estimating the complete cost of taking a company public through an IPO. To correctly estimate these costs, experts should be contacted to gauge the current expenses associated with legal review and document preparation, accounting review and audited statements, investment banking fees related to selling the shares to the public, and any other regulatory-related costs such as filing and annual reporting fees.

The second method is not quite as involved and could be completed in very little time. This method for estimating the marketability discount for a whole operating entity calls for estimating the costs of selling the company through an intermediary such as a business broker or a middle-market specialist. The primary fees here include the commission paid to the intermediary, legal costs associated with preparation or review of all purchase documents, closing costs, and other miscellaneous expenses incurred by the seller such as the cost of completing an environmental audit, the cost of a land survey and title insurance if real estate is involved, and any other costs that might be shared with the buyer such as loan underwriting and documentation fees. Another important cost involved with selling a business is time.

Discounts and the Courts

The application of both minority interest discounts and marketability discounts often is the primary focus of valuation disputes that make their way to the courts. Given that each of these discounts can be 40 percent or more, it is easy to see why they can become a source of great debate. Their derivation and application in this regard generally are presented in an adversarial manner, with a judge making the final call as to their size. It is not uncommon for the cumulative impact of these discounts to erase 60 percent or more of the value related to the subject company's shares.

Settlements of these disputes often revolve around the presentation of theory and fact by each side's expert testimony. The use of such testimony is subject to the judge's opinion as to its credibility, so it is important to use experienced valuators to protect your interests. Regarding the admissibility of expert testimony, there is an important rule of evidence in federal courts known as Rule 702. This rule provides guidance as to what type of professional, expert-oriented evidence (valuation analysis) can be admissible in federal courts. Rule 702 states,

> If scientific, technical or specialized knowledge will assist the trier of fact to understand the evidence to determine a fact in issue, a witness qualified as an expert by knowledge, skill, experience, training or education, may testify thereto in the form of an opinion or otherwise if:
>
> a) The testimony is based on sufficient facts or data
> b) The testimony is the product of reliable principles and methods, and
> c) The witness has applied the principles and methods reliably to the facts of the case.

The Supreme Court tried an important evidence-related case in 1993 (*Daubert v. Merrell Dow Pharmaceuticals*) that led to the creation of the so-called Daubert factors. These factors can be used by a judge in determining the admissibility of evidence under Rule 702. They are presented here in summary form:

> Can the theory, technique, or tool in question be adequately tested in practice? Has it been?
>
> Has it been printed in major publications and peer reviewed?
>
> Is there a known error rate (actual or potential)?
>
> Are there documented and accepted procedures and standards in support of its application?
>
> Is it generally accepted by the professional or technical community wherein it is applied?

The primary reason for covering this legal issue here is to simply make entrepreneurs aware of the availability of expert witnesses in support of their valuation interests if a dispute ends up in a court of law. Such experts must be carefully chosen, or a judge might declare their opinion inadmissible. Should you find yourself in a valuation-related court case, there is no substitute for careful and thorough preparation with the support of legal counsel and expert valuation witnesses. Common situations that end up in court include disputes over estate taxation, divorce, and damages resulting from seller or broker misrepresentation.

Estimating the Marketability Discount

Interestingly, the answer to the second question posed earlier can be presented in relation to the important role played by the courts in settling discount-related disputes. In fact, Rule 702 relates directly to a recent trend in business valuation that concerns the QMDM (created by Z. Christopher Mercer). This model is gaining ground in the courts and among professional appraisers as a generally accepted, highly quantitative method for determining marketability discounts. Because this model meets the Daubert test for admissibility into evidence, it will undoubtedly continue to infiltrate important precedent-setting court cases involving marketability discounts.

The creation of the QMDM model was a direct result of dissatisfaction with traditional methods used to calculate marketability discounts. These traditional methods revolve around two distinct theoretical foundations. The first method involves estimations of the costs associated with going public or selling the company through an intermediary, which are interpreted as the cost of making the subject company shares liquid and marketable. The second method involves analysis of pre-IPO and restricted stock studies performed by dozens of practitioners over the past several decades. The essence of these studies is the belief that comparisons of a company's share price before and after the company goes public and comparisons of a company's share price before and after the holding period for restricted stock ends reflect the degree of illiquidity associated with the subject company's privately held shares.

For example, the pre-IPO situation appears to be logical in that the primary difference between the company's share price before and after the IPO is the increased liquidity offered by public trading on an organized exchange. However, careful analysis of this relationship creates some doubt about its reliability. Other factors that affect a company's share price may also change during this period (e.g., unfavorable earnings report or forecast, filing of a major lawsuit, rising interest rates, or changing regulatory enforcement patterns).

Restricted stock (also called letter stock) is identical in every respect to a publicly traded stock except for restrictions on open market trading for a certain period of time. For example, companies can raise capital through the sale of restricted shares to qualified investors without jumping through all the hoops associated with a traditional IPO. The restriction in many cases is a two-year holding period, during which the shares cannot be bought or sold. Comparing the price of the restricted stock with otherwise similar stock should provide solid evidence as to the marketability discount applicable to such minority interests.

For a variety of reasons, each of these methods has been successfully challenged in the courts, with diverse interpretations from many different judges across the country. The relevance of the QMDM is a result of its quantitative nature that addresses directly the pertinent issues related to liquidity and marketability. Current disputes revolving around marketability discounts should be based in part on use of this model because of its wide and growing acceptance among valuation professionals.

How Are Marketability Discounts Calculated?

As alluded to earlier, there are three general schools of thought (tools) available to the valuator in need of estimating and applying a marketability discount for minority interests.

General Factors to Consider

When evaluating the subject interest for illiquidity, the following factors should be considered regardless of the chosen method:

Quantity and quality of potential buyers of the minority interest

Legal restrictions placed on the shares regarding their potential sale or transfer (e.g., holding period)

Relative size of the block of shares compared with a controlling block size

Contractual clauses included in bylaws or buy–sell agreement (e.g., redemption policy or mandatory pricing formulas)

Cash distributions and dividends paid historically to the holders

Probability, timing, and cost of possible public offering

Financial condition of business and appeal of industry

Blockage power of the interest

Actual historical sales of company stock or similar company's stock

Quality of management and replacement management

Restricted Stock and Pre-IPO Studies

One traditional approach has revolved around pre-IPO and restricted stock studies conducted over the past several decades. To the extent that the marketability
discount reflects the cost of illiquidity inherent in shares that are not traded in
public markets, use of public stock data appears to be a logical starting point for
assessing such a discount. The discount in effect compensates the buyer for this
lack of access to a publicly traded market.

Historically speaking, one of the more common techniques for estimating
marketability discounts was based on a comparison of the common stock and
restricted stock (also called letter stock; typically must be held for at least two
years) sold by the same company. Letter stock is issued as part of a limited public offering to qualified investors made in such a way as to minimize the related
offering costs. In short, substantial capital can be raised without the time and
costs associated with a traditional IPO or other equity offering. Because the
only difference between common stock and restricted stock from the same
company is the marketability constraint found in the holding period (and possibly the timing of issuance), any price difference can be deemed a reflection of
the illiquidity of the restricted stock.

A major study was conducted by the SEC and presented to Congress that
was based in part on the comparison of discounts associated with letter stock
with the price of otherwise identical but unrestricted stock on the open market. The study presented the amount of such discounts as found on four major
stock exchanges:

NYSE

AMEX

Over-the-counter (OTC) reporting companies

OTC nonreporting companies

The difference between reporting and nonreporting companies is based on
the required filings from each category. Reporting companies were required to
file periodic reports such as 10-Q and 10-K, whereas nonreporting companies
were subject to substantially less reporting. The amount of the discount rose
down the list from the NYSE (smallest) to the OTC nonreporting (highest).

The OTC nonreporting companies were primarily in the 30 to 40 percent range, with 56 percent of these companies generating a discount of 30 percent or more. Slightly more than 30 percent of the OTC reporting companies generated discounts greater than 30 percent, with 52 percent showing discounts greater than 20 percent. The majority of other such studies led to average discounts in the 30 to 40 percent range. The implications are crystal clear. The less liquid the shares are, the greater the marketability discount.

Estimation of IPO Costs or Intermediary-Facilitated Transactions

As described earlier, this method is alarmingly simple. If the valuator is honest in the calculations, generating an estimate for the cost of going public should not be too difficult. By purchasing a book that covers the IPO process, one could easily reach a credible estimate of the related costs (e.g., legal, accounting, brokerage, printing, consulting). A basic Internet search could also lead the valuator to the needed information for such a calculation.

Alternatively, estimating the costs associated with listing, marketing, and selling a business on the open market can give the valuator another estimate of a marketability discount. These costs would consist primarily of commissions to a broker or middle-market specialist, legal fees to prepare or review the purchase contract, escrow charges, and other miscellaneous expenses such as payment for title insurance and an environmental audit if real estate is involved. In reality, the second most substantial cost is nonmonetary. The time needed to meet with a broker, attorney, potential buyers, and escrow personnel can add up quickly.

Use of the QMDM

This chapter has alluded to this increasingly relevant tool for estimating marketability discounts related to minority interest shares in privately held companies. Recent court findings have placed in doubt the automatic use of restricted stock studies to determine marketability discounts. In *Estate of Frank A. Branson v. Commissioner,* the judge rejected the use of specific restricted stock studies in a direct manner that brings into question the relevance of their usage in the future. It is not only an issue of whether they should be used but also of how they are used.

If restricted stock studies are no longer useful, what is? Many professionals believe that the QMDM will fill the vacuum left by the dismissal of the restricted stock method. According to the creator of this model, Z. Christopher Mercer, the marketability discount is the valuation discount necessary to entice the prospective investor in an illiquid security to purchase it rather than a similar investment that is readily marketable. If you are interested in purchasing his book, *Quantifying Marketability Discounts,* go to *www.bizval.com* or to one of the all-purpose valuation Web sites listed at the end of Chapter One. As noted earlier, this model is thoroughly covered in valuation newsletters and journals, including Mercer Capital's own BizVal.com publication. A succinct article covering the essence of this model, titled "The QMDM Revisited," has been written by Mercer and can be found in the January 11, 2000 edition of the *E-Law* newsletter published by Mercer Capital (also available at *www. bizval.com*).

The QMDM is well grounded in modern financial theory and offers a logical approach for estimating a privately held, minority interest stock's marketability discount. It is based on assessments of questions that relate directly to the question of liquidity in relation to the minority stock holding. The model primarily seeks answers to the following questions:

During the expected holding period of the minority interest, what amount of cash payments are anticipated in the form of dividends or other distributions?

Are the anticipated cash payments likely to grow during this holding period?

What amount of time is expected to pass before a more liquid status for the investment is probable?

In addition to the cash payments during the expected holding period, is an increase in its FMV likely? How much?

Based on the risks associated with this type and amount of investment, what is the necessary rate of return compared with similar investments that are actively traded in a fluid market setting?

Rather than estimate the marketability discount by comparing the subject interest with an entire group of similar transactions, this model delves directly into the economic reality behind the specific investment at hand. This critical difference explains its rapid rise to the forefront of marketability discount discussions among professionals.

However, the same questions apply to the use of the QMDM as to the use of the restricted stock studies mentioned earlier (not only whether the model should be used, but how). A recent case in which the opposing valuators used different methods (one used restricted stock studies and the other used the QMDM) led to the judge criticizing both methods. Importantly, many experts believe that the judge did not find fault with the method but with the facts applied to the model. Specifically, the answers to the five QMDM questions presented earlier were deemed improper, not the model per se. Evidence in support of the QMDM is found in the fact that the judge made a final determination of the marketability discount that was very close to that generated by the model (judge used 20 percent instead of QMDM's 15 percent and the opponent's 35 percent).

Concluding Remarks

The controversy behind calculating and applying marketability discounts will continue into the near future. Therefore, it is important for any business owner who becomes involved in such a dispute to seek competent professional guidance to take advantage of recent developments in this dynamic area of business valuation. Given this evolution of acceptable methods and the substantial impact that the two types of discounts can have on the value of noncontrolling interests, careful analysis and attention to detail are necessary to ensure credibility and a favorable outcome if the exposure to these discounts leads to litigation or other types of dispute resolution. State laws involving minority shareholders, for example, vary from state to state and also tend to change over time.

For example, in a recent court case in South Dakota (*First Western Bank Wall v. Olsen,* January 2001), the appellate court upheld the trial court's refusal to apply either a minority interest discount or a marketability discount. To encourage investment in minority, noncontrolling corporate interests, the court prevented unjust enrichment for the insider majority holder. The court argued that the minority shareholder is entitled to full proportionate value when cashing out upon sale of the company. The court also argued that there was a ready and available market for the minority shares, provided in fact by the majority shareholders.

Another recent case that made its way to the Eighth Circuit Court of Appeals (*Swope v. Siegel-Robert, Inc.,* 2001) from the state of Missouri also disallowed both minority interest and marketability discounts in a dissenting shareholder (minority shareholder) rights case, giving great momentum to the recent trend toward such blanket exclusions in minority shareholder situations. In dissenting shareholder stock appraisals in the state of Missouri, fair value is not the same as fair market value because the dissenting minority holders cannot be considered ready, willing, and able; that is, they are "unwilling sellers with no bargaining power."

If the court imposed a minority or marketability discount, the controlling majority holders would again be unjustly enriched. The Missouri appraisal statute was created specifically to protect minority stockholders in closely held corporations by ensuring their receipt of full proportionate value of the stock upon sale of the company. The Eighth Circuit Court noted that the purpose of the Missouri appraisal statute is to protect minority stockholders in closely held corporations. The statute seeks to compensate dissenting shareholders for full proportionate value of the stock.

Interestingly, the Eighth Circuit Court also looked to Delaware corporate law and Delaware's courts and legal system for its extensive experience and expertise in the subject matter, finding its position both reasonable and convincing. The court noted the "compelling logic of the current trend toward disallowing" minority and marketability discounts in dissenting shareholders' fair value appraisals and found that the Missouri Supreme Court would follow this trend. However, another Missouri statute illustrates the often nebulous nature of such situations by requiring that the application of discounts be evaluated and applied on a case-by-case basis, leaving the door open for alternative findings in the future.

The main point is that state laws can override valuation custom when it comes to minority shareholders. A careful and current review of recent case law on a state-by-state basis is necessary in many situations involving minority shareholders. Importantly, note that the treatment of minority shareholders for tax purposes is very different from that for dissenting shareholder purposes. The IRS almost routinely allows discounts for lack of control and marketability if the conditions are correct. The debate here is oriented more toward how rather than whether to apply discounts, as evidenced by the rise of the QMDM in recent years.

Hypothetical Example of Multiplicative Discounts

Let's close with a simple hypothetical example of the power of these discounts over minority interest values. Assume that the control value of 100 percent of a company's shares is $1 million. Assume further that after diligent efforts and calculations, discounts of 35 and 30 percent, respectively, are determined to be appropriate for minority interest (lack of control) and marketability purposes. Note the dramatic reduction in value:

100 percent control value:	$1,000,000
Less minority interest discount:	-$350,000
Pre-marketability discount value =	$650,000
Less marketability discount	-$195,000
Final discounted value =	$455,000

The multiplicative and cumulative impact is nearly 55 percent.

CHAPTER 8

ARM Approach Case Study and Words of Wisdom

If you have carefully read the material in the previous chapters, you are prepared to put your new skills, insights, tools, and techniques to work through the innovative ARM Approach Questionnaire. This questionnaire will help guide the valuator through the three components of the ARM approach in a manner that facilitates understanding of the subject company and industry while moving toward a value estimate.

In this chapter, a case study is presented for purposes of completing our analysis of business valuation and the ARM approach. The discussion is primarily procedural in nature to facilitate the proper use of the questionnaire in any valuation situation. In other words, rather than focus chiefly on the valuation *techniques,* this chapter focuses on the valuation *process* via the ARM approach. Instead of being given fish to eat, we will focus on how to fish under various conditions.

The ARM approach is intended to allow even first-time valuators to arrive at a credible estimate of business value without expending an excessive amount of time and energy. The ARM Approach Questionnaire has been developed specifically to guide the novice through potentially complex and overwhelming situations. While completing the questionnaire, do not hesitate to return to relevant chapters, the CD-ROM materials, or one of the many referenced Web sites to strengthen your general valuation knowledge.

It is also important to realize that not all questions must be answered to complete the valuation process. It is up to the valuator to decide how much detail should be incorporated into the analysis of the company and industry. For example, it is possible to base the entire review of the company and industry around the "pluses and minuses" analysis as opposed to addressing every area covered in Section Three (e.g., you can complete Sections One, Four, and Five only). Completing Sections Two and Three may be sufficient for proceeding to Section Four and the actual valuation analysis, particularly if they are completed in conjunction with the Five-Page Tool. The point is that with experience, the valuator will gain the confidence to selectively use the various sections of the questionnaire and Five-Page Tool.

Given the importance of understanding the value of an entrepreneur's often lifelong endeavor, finding additional time to review some of the useful Web sites sprinkled throughout the book will surely help. By understanding how a business is valued, owners will better control their company's future (value) as they plan an exit strategy. Alternatively, potential owners will be able to influence (or at least justify) the price paid upon acquisition. By tracking current developments in a given industry, both buyers and sellers can more effectively assess business value. In short, you can create value by understanding value. For additional valuation insights (including links to industry analyses and reports), seek out these informative sites:

www.BVResources.com[sm]

www.valuationresources.com[sm]

www.vrbusinessbrokers.com[sm] or *www.scottgabehart.com*

If you are a potential purchaser, bear in mind that the items on the questionnaire also relate directly to the important process of due diligence. A buyer should not rely on the presentation of the seller or seller's broker alone, given the importance of such a transaction. In practical terms, most offers are made subject to contingencies (all offers should be subject to contingencies) that include verification of the income and cash flow figures presented by the seller.

Consider the questionnaire an important component of due diligence. If your review of books and records leads you to the conclusion that the actual cash flow is less than presented, you have the right to withdraw your offer or submit a revised offer at a lower price. Completing the questionnaire is important for many procedural reasons beyond simple business valuation. Do not hesitate to ask the seller key questions repeatedly and in differing terms.

To put some teeth behind the seller's responses, consider adapting one or both of the seller's disclosure statements available through the author's first book, *The Upstart Guide to Buying, Valuing, and Selling Your Business,* published by Dearborn Financial Publishing (available through the publisher, at major bookstores, and at *www.scottgabehart.com*). As the title of this book implies, its content is deal-oriented and contains dozens of useful contracts, worksheets, checklists, forms, and clauses, all related to the buying and selling of companies. The disclosure statements found in this book generally lead to additional insights and clarifications that may have otherwise been overlooked.

If you are an owner interested in selling, you will be directed toward the key value determinants that you can approach aggressively in your efforts to improve the company and its value. You will also be preparing yourself to answer many probable questions that will arise from a buyer's investigation of the company. You can gain an element of control over the valuation discussion by understanding the valuation process within the ARM approach. Once again, by understanding business valuation, you can strategically increase business value and ensure the ultimate receipt of fair market value (FMV) upon sale.

Both buyers and sellers can improve their relative standing by understanding the valuation process. This may appear to be a zero-sum game, but it need not be so. If both parties are equally educated on the valuation process, the chances for reaching a mutually beneficial agreement are increased and the chances for more creative solutions increases (e.g., sale of a business subject to an earnout formula, which allows both sides to profit from increases in future sales and cash flow). Finally, ensuring that the deal price is fair to both sides greatly reduces the probability of future litigation.

We now turn to use of the questionnaire and the Five-Page Tool, both of which should be followed closely from the beginning of the valuation effort. Regardless of the purpose for the valuation, the questionnaire will lead you to a credible value estimate if properly followed. This chapter concludes with a potpourri of valuation insights, tips, rules, pointers, issues, thoughts, and concerns that you should review from time to time to help reinforce the fundamentals of business valuation.

ARM Approach Case Study

Having diligently worked your way through the first seven chapters of this crash course on business valuation, you should be well equipped to apply this new or heightened knowledge to the valuation of almost any type of privately owned company. To complete the learning process, we apply the ARM approach to a real-world scenario. Given the incredibly diverse collection of business types, it is impossible to present case studies for every possible situation.

To broaden the practical coverage, relevant industry information and related valuation peculiarities have been introduced throughout the book for businesses such as restaurants, Internet-based companies, accounting practices, medical practices, and manufacturing businesses. In addition to this industry-specific information and the case study presented in this chapter, additional valuation analyses are included on the CD-ROM that accompanies this book. This CD-ROM also holds dozens of industry-related association and organization Web site addresses and other contact information.

Case Study Coverage

In the proverbial real world, it is not only types of businesses that differ (e.g., retail, service, manufacturing); the application of business appraisal techniques and their corresponding reporting formats also differs dramatically from one professional to the next. Another valuation analysis is included on the CD-ROM attached to this book to accustom the novice valuator to various reporting styles and valuation techniques. As stressed throughout the book, the CD-ROM is an integral part of this publication. Besides the second valuation case study, relevant and important extensions and insights into cash flow analysis, rules of thumb, and the asset or cost approach to business valuation are included on the CD-ROM. This supplemental and diverse array of valuation techniques, perspectives, and insights will help prepare the entrepreneur and novice valuator maximize their understanding of the dynamics behind business valuation.

The Tradeoff Between Time and Results

Business valuation estimates are the result of careful analysis of the subject company and industry through various efforts designed to thoroughly yet efficiently gather the relevant documents and information necessary to produce a credible outcome. Actual business valuation procedures vary from person to person and from situation to situation because of the diverse set of options available to the valuator. There are dozens of valuation techniques, each with a number of spin-off versions based on differing procedures and assumptions, all of which ultimately fall under the three classical valuation approaches introduced early in this book.

Whether one uses the ARM approach or a collection of other methods, every known valuation technique contains at least one major subjective aspect that causes the estimates to vary from one valuator to the next (even if the exact same technique is used). Not only are the individual techniques subject to the individual assessments of each valuator, but the entire valuation process can vary dramatically from one party to the next.

The practice of business valuation can range from overly simplistic to unnecessarily complex. It is not simply a matter of investing time, however, as a valuation effort that takes one hour for a skilled valuator may generate as credible a result as one that takes another skilled valuator one week or one month. Where a given valuator ends up on this spectrum of involvement is a matter of choice. The difference between the two extremes is often a matter of certainty or probability; that is, the more thorough the coverage (all facts are verified, industry is completely researched through today's current events, dozens of questions are answered, disclosure statements are signed, all comp sources are analyzed, complete financial statement analysis is conducted, industry participants are interviewed, and so on), the more certain the valuation result. A brief analysis may turn out accurate, but it will be based on numerous assumptions that may or may not be true. Only a thorough, rigorous, and properly executed valuation will normally ensure a credible valuation result.

Unfortunately, the real world does not always permit such a complete examination because of time and financial constraints. Just as any user of financial statements would prefer audited ones, so too would a business appraiser. Most business owners must be satisfied with compiled financial statements (as opposed to reviewed or audited) for analyzing their financial performance and presenting information to outside parties for applicable business purposes. Although audited statements are preferable to compiled statements, this does not mean that compiled statements are worthless or should be ignored.

The Middle Ground of the ARM Approach

In developing the ARM approach, we have attempted to find a useful middle ground between the two extremes of simplistic and brief versus complex and comprehensive. A credible valuation estimate almost always includes a certain amount of reliable information, much of which is not readily available.

Adjusted cash flow (ACF) must be calculated in the proper manner, and some research may be needed to determine which, if any, rules of thumb are relevant for the subject company. Market comp data must also be sought out through one or more of the major databases. Each of these requirements also calls for the assessment and application of the unique aspects of the subject company and industry, all of which takes time and effort on the part of the valuator.

Experienced valuation professionals know quite well that the more time they invest in evaluating a company or an industry, the more credible their final value estimate will be (up to a point, of course). Time is a scarce resource, however, so limits must be placed on the number of hours or days that can be devoted to the valuation effort.

Regardless of the purpose of the valuation effort or the type of business, the ARM Approach Questionnaire and the Five-Page Tool can be customized and applied to practically any situation. It is possible to ignore certain questions and issues addressed on the questionnaire, and it is possible to restructure or amend the questionnaire with a simple word-processing program. One of the most common types of adjustment is to tailor the pertinent questions and issues to a specific type of business within a specific industry (for example, a service business within the landscaping industry or a retail business within the upscale gift industry).

People who are active in a certain industry almost instinctively know the critical issues and concerns that affect business value. It is a simple matter of incorporating these details into the flow of the questionnaire and the Five-Page Tool on a case-by-case basis. In many instances, however, the questionnaire as written will suffice. Removing irrelevant or unnecessary components will help suit the questionnaire to the subject company. As is true with many endeavors in life, the more experience one obtains, the better one becomes at mastering the outcome.

Case Study Information

The following facts, insights, applications, and interpretations relate to the ARM approach. Before proceeding further, it may be wise to return to Chapter Three and review the ARM Approach Questionnaire and the Five-Page Tool. Because of space limitations, only the key and material aspects of the subject company and industry are presented.

You should use the Five-Page Tool and the ARM Approach Questionnaire in full from start to finish until you develop the necessary skills and knowledge to allow a condensed approach or selected application of the important aspects of the valuation process. When you address the various issues in the questionnaire, it may become obvious that a certain area is irrelevant for the subject company. This type of judgment call permeates the entire valuation process. In addition, you are encouraged to surf the Internet and review materials found on any of the key valuation-related Web sites presented at the end of Chapter One, in the questionnaire, and throughout the book. Because so much of the earlier coverage was devoted to service businesses, the case study presented in this chapter involves a manufacturing business. The CD-ROM contains additional valuation analyses that address other businesses as well.

For the sake of clarity and learning, comments are provided throughout the case study that are chiefly explanatory rather than directly related to the subject valuation. For example, after the bulk of the background information is presented, a brief analysis of each of the five major sections of the questionnaire follows.

To maximize the usefulness of this experience, you should prepare the Five-Page Tool worksheets before reading further. It is impossible to present all potentially available and relevant information about the subject company in a few short pages, so it is expected that several questions will arise that theoretically should be answered by the business owner. Because this is clearly impractical, it is suggested that you compile all the necessary questions and then, at the appropriate time, make your own credible responses and consider them as assumptions relative to the valuation process.

General Comments About Valuation of Manufacturing Companies

As a link between the previous discussion regarding the usefulness of the ARM approach to business valuation and the following company-specific information related to the case study, a few comments regarding the valuation of manufacturing companies may prove helpful.

Despite increased global competition, manufacturing in the United States is enjoying a renaissance, with output at record levels as productivity continues to grow via ever faster hardware and smarter software. Productivity growth in the 1990s mirrored the incredible rates seen in the 1960s, with a slowdown occurring for the first time in 2000 (as of early 2002, the downturn in this sector appeared to be reversing course as the overall economy emerged from recession).

Approximately 99 percent of all manufacturing companies employ fewer than fifty people, meaning that the number of such privately held companies is enormous.

There is an incredible demand among business buyers for manufacturing businesses, making this one of the few true seller's markets. For this reason and others, multiples paid for manufacturing companies are higher on average than for other similarly sized businesses. Substantial hard assets and other barriers to entry contribute to the higher average multiples as compared with service or retail businesses. Many entrepreneurs recognize the inherent value in producing goods, making it the business type of choice for some of the nation's most savvy operators.

According to Sam Stapley (designated broker for the VR Business Brokers office in Scottsdale, Arizona), an entrepreneur and business broker with more than forty years of experience, manufacturing companies ultimately must be valued based on evaluation of cash flow (despite the presence of substantial assets). In other words, the value of the assets is found ultimately in their ability to contribute to revenue or cash flow generation. Thus, rules of thumb or other valuation techniques based on assets should take a second position behind cash flow techniques.

Valuation factors and considerations unique to manufacturing companies include the following:

Patents, trademarks

Work in progress, deposits, and advanced billings

Inventory valuation, cost of goods sold, and gross profit

Condition of assets, deferred maintenance, and depreciation

Contracts with customers and concentration of customer base

Availability of raw materials, supplier contracts, and number of sources

Key employees, unions, and benefits

Sales trends, product mix, new products, and backlog

This list is by no means all-inclusive, but it does include many of the more important considerations for evaluating a manufacturing company. Review the lists in Chapter Five to assess the overall pros and cons of a subject company. In regard to risk assessment, Nancy Fannon (CPA, CBA, BVAL) of American Business Appraisers in Portland, Maine, presents the following major risk categories in a recent article found on the Business Valuation Resources Web site (*www.BVResources.com*sm):

Increased global competition

Technological obsolescence

Functional obsolescence

Product liability

Consolidators and roll-ups

Supplier partnerships

Issues such as lower-priced inputs, technological advances, product diversification, class action lawsuits, larger competitors, and supplier pressures regarding the flow and control of inventory can make or break the typical privately owned manufacturing company. Thus, company value is a function of how well these risks are managed. In her article called "Thousands of Manufacturing Companies to Value Means the Appraisers Need to Assess Their Risks" (published as a guest article on Shannon Pratt's Business Valuation Resources Web site at *www.BVResources.com*sm), Fannon outlines several factors that the typical buyer evaluates when considering the purchase of such companies. In addition to many of the factors listed earlier in this segment, she cites the following issues of concern for the typical buyer:

Appraisal of equipment

Likelihood of customer departure under new ownership

Off-balance-sheet liabilities and contingent liabilities (e.g., lawsuits, warranty repairs)

Management strength and remaining middle managers

Capacity constraints

Fannon concurs with Stapley's opinion that the income approach techniques typically are the most important for valuation purposes. Although most buyers find great comfort in the presence of real or tangible assets and seek to understand their value (FMV or liquidation value [LV]), their ultimate importance lies in their ability to help generate revenues and cash flow for the owners. Specifically, she states that because of the common presence of substantial debt (leverage), discounted cash flow analysis on a debt-free basis using the company's weighted average cost of capital (WACC) is most appropriate. A debt-free basis is preferable in order to eliminate the impact of a company's leverage on the value of equity (ownership interest). Practically speaking, this means that interest expense is included in cash flow (interest expense × (1 − tax rate) for use of after-tax measures of cash flow) and the market value of the related debt is subtracted from the overall derived value to estimate the "equity" or debt-free value of the company.

Regarding the market approach to valuation, the primary challenge is to find truly similar companies. Most manufacturing companies are subject to unique developmental outcomes in terms of their current state of technology, mix of labor and equipment, product development and diversification, and marketing channels. In other words, even companies manufacturing the exact same product will be at different phases in their company life cycles and product life cycles, making direct comparison difficult if not undesirable. However, as explained in the ARM approach, the ability to locate and use market data for dozens of similar companies (similar industry, size, and geographic markets served) allows the valuator to use a shotgun approach by generating average multiples for comparison with the subject company. As noted elsewhere, such multiples have been amazingly stable over the past decades, hovering around 50 percent of gross revenues for manufacturing companies in general.

Rules of thumb may also play a role in valuing manufacturing companies if used with caution and discretion. The best sources for these rules of thumb are discussions with active industry participants (e.g., owners, consultants, brokers,). Such rules typically are revenue- or cash flow–oriented and reflect the tendencies found in actual historical sales. As described in Chapter Five, such rules of thumb are actually a combination income and market approach; that is, they are based on prior market sales but described in terms of revenues or cash flow. Manufacturing businesses with substantial "hard" assets should also be evaluated with at least one method that directly accounts for their "fair market value". Typically, this involves a rule of thumb similar to the following:

1 to 2 times ACF plus FMV of Assets

This method is simple and often credible for smaller manufacturing companies. Naturally, as the cash flow rises, so too will the proper multiples. As explained near the end of Chapter Five (section titled "Applying the Guideline Public Company Method"), another rule of thumb exists that does not depend upon the calculation of cash flow. This method involves the assessment of the relationship between a firm's hard assets and business value by way of market comp data.

By comparing the difference between historical purchase price and the value of the related identifiable tangible assets (FF&E plus inventory), the average price paid for a company's "goodwill" can be established. In the case described earlier, buyers paid 42 cents for each dollar of "hard" assets, i.e., the average business in this industry was worth approximately 1.42 times the value of the hard assets. This innovative approach provides the valuator with a method for assessing company value directly in terms of tangible assets. When utilized in conjunction with other methods (ARM Approach), the valuation outcome is potentially much improved.

Bearing in mind the many assumptions that permeate the valuation process (e.g., asset sale versus stock sale), most rules of thumb for manufacturing companies related to cash flow are two to six times ACF. Important considerations here include the specific measure of cash flow used (e.g., ACF, earnings before interest and taxes [EBIT], earnings before interest, taxes, depreciation, and amortization [EBITDA]) and the magnitude of the cash flow (higher cash flow, higher multiple). The common rule of thumb just cited is more important when the subject company's cash flow is less than normal (less than $150,000 for manufacturing businesses), helping to focus on asset values (one to two times ACF plus assets).

Naturally, this method tends to miss the mark if the subject company is earning substantial cash flow (more than $500,000), but it provides a meaningful result for smaller operations and as part of a basket of valuation techniques. Generally speaking, it is always prudent to use more than one valuation method when valuing companies of any type or size.

Overview of the Subject Company*

The subject company has been in the business of manufacturing monuments and markers primarily for sale to golf courses in addition to developers of master-planned communities and park and recreation departments around the world for more than twenty-five years. In 1977, the company changed its name to *Granstone* to more effectively capture the essence of its business (aggregate and resin markers and monuments that resemble a combination granite and sandstone). Among other achievements, the company has earned preferred vendor status with many of the world's top residential development companies and golf course operations. The company has operated out of the same 5,750-square-foot leased building for more than fourteen years in Springfield, Illinois, with a current lease (at market rates based on a consumer

---

*The subject company name and associated information are fictional but representative of similar companies operating in similar industries; that is, it is a composite of many real companies that operate in similar markets. The name, location, and financial results are entirely fictional and not related to any specific company and should not be construed as bearing a resemblance to any particular company.

price index [CPI]-level increase in rent each year) that extends five years through the year 2006.

An average order size of approximately $10,000 to $15,000 during the fiscal year 2000 (ending June 30, 2000) led to total revenues of nearly $850,000, representing an increase of approximately 25 percent over fiscal year 1998 levels. The company's ACF was approximately $294,000 (after subtracting replacement salary for second officer active in the business) for the fiscal year ending on June 30, 2000. A favorable financial aspect of the company's operations is its policy to receive 50 percent of the contract price up front and before manufacturing, helping the company to cover not only the direct costs but also a portion of fixed costs before expending resources.

The bulk of sales (more than 80 percent per year) are made in relation to golf course operations, whether as independent golf courses or as part of master-planned communities. The company caters to a mix of new and repeat customers, serving approximately fifty major customers during a typical year. According to the Golf Research Group, there are more than 15,000 golf courses in the United States alone. Europe is another lucrative market, with more than 5,000 courses and growing rapidly. The park and recreation department sales are one of the highest upside potentials for the company because of their great number and the increasing awareness of the product's durability and long life cycle. Finally, a brand new product called Tote-a-Tool also presents upside potential for the company's revenues.

Although the asset figures found on the company's balance sheet appear to be minimal, additional assets that are not listed add value to the company and the proposed deal. For example, the company maintains the molds used in producing golf course markers and has invested substantial time and money in a brand new peripheral product called the Tote-a-Tool. As of January 31, 2001, the company's total assets were approximately $283,000 (approximately $235,000 in cash and receivables, which will remain the property of the seller) in book value. Inventory was approximately $40,000, and the FF&E was estimated to have an FMV of approximately $25,000.

Business and Industry Analysis

As noted in the executive summary, the subject company known as Granstone, Inc., manufactures and sells a wide variety of markers and monuments to golf course operators, master planned community developers, government-related parks and recreation departments, and sports arenas across the United States and around the world. Specifically, they operate in the specialty signage design and fabrication industry and ultimately compete with manufacturers of wood, pure granite, plastic, neon, and metallic signage. Established in 1975, the company has grown with changes in technology, with the end result being the capture of significant market shares in their target markets.

As noted earlier, most company sales are related to golf course operations (more than 80 percent), whether made to independent golf course operators or to golf course operations contained in master planned communities. The number of golf courses in the United States is a staggering 15,000 or more (according to the *Golf Research Report*), with approximately 450 new courses each year. The European market took fifty years to grow from 1,000 to 2,000 courses but only four years to go from 4,000 to 5,000 (according to *Golf Weekly*). The growth of master planned communities is a function of both the general state of the economy and demographic changes. Despite a recent slowing in new home starts across the country, the current level is near historical highs. Falling interest rates once again are encouraging continued growth as the Federal Reserve attempts to forestall a pending recession in the United States.

The owner and buyer believe that a large upside potential exists regarding sales to parks and recreation departments because of a change in perception among government officials about the relative cost of the Granstone products. Specifically, it is increasingly accepted that although Granstone products have a higher price per unit, the materials are such that they can last forever (barring unnatural attempts to deface or steal) or at least substantially longer than cheaper alternatives. In short, the life expectancy of the Granstone product is sufficiently longer than substitute products such that the cost per year or period of time in use is comparable or superior. This fact, combined with the favorable appearance, custom applications, and high quality, are increasing the perceived attractiveness of the products. With thousands of park districts across the country, an aggressive marketing effort targeting this niche should generate favorable results.

According to the prospective owner, other potential niche opportunities exist in the architect and builder community (e.g., street signs, entrance signs) and in the outdoor putting green and sand trap market (jointly marketed with their new Tote-a-Tool product). However, it is important to stress that the prospective owner has made it quite clear that the primary emphasis will remain the golf course community. Approximately 450 new golf courses have been built every year in recent history, with no decline expected in the near future.

The essence of their product is its natural-looking beauty achieved by an advanced material that is the product of extensive research and development. Their Granstone (trademarked) markers and monuments can be custom made in terms of shape, size, design, and color to suit the specific needs of their diverse customer base. The company employs a number of experienced graphic artists to generate customer-specific logos with raised or recessed lettering.

In addition to a uniquely favorable appearance of granite or sandstone, the product is durable and low-maintenance. The durability and low-maintenance features are major selling points to golf course superintendents, who are always under pressure to minimize operating costs of all types. The finished product resists chipping, cracking, and peeling caused by sun, rain, wind, cold, and snow because it is treated with a special compound as part of the routine manufacturing process.

Perhaps most important of all is the comparable pricing of the company's products compared with their competitors (e.g., wood, pure granite, plastic, metal, synthetics) in terms of durability and product life expectations. For example, industry participants estimate that Granstone is approximately 10 to 15 percent cheaper than pure granite and less expensive to ship because of its lesser weight. In general, however, the Granstone product line caters more to the upscale, trendy golf courses because of its uniquely attractive appearance. To reiterate, although their pricing is above average, it is the contention of the company that the cost per unit of time in service is comparable to that of wood, pure granite, plastic, and other synthetic and metal alternatives.

The relevant industry in which the subject company operates is not readily classified because of the combination of manufacturing with a unique material and selling directly to the end user (in addition to sales made through approximately five manufacturer's representatives). Thus, the company can be described as a manufacturing company with direct sales primarily to the end customer (roughly 20 percent of all sales are made through the distributors). A more precise definition would be a manufacturer of specialty signage. The SIC code number 3993 (manufacturing of signs and advertising specialties, under the general category of miscellaneous manufacturing) appears to be the most applicable description for the subject company. No specific companies producing similar products were linked to this SIC code in the Hoover's Web site, but an Internet search produced numerous hits related to the subject market. Note that this SIC code has been replaced with the NAICS code 33995 (sign manufacturing), effective in 1997.

An Internet search using the Yahoo search engine revealed that there are a large number of "sign" manufacturers, "monument" manufacturers, and "golf course sign and marker" manufacturers (in terms of frequency, sign manufacturers were found in greater numbers). The sign manufacturers are organized and represented by such groups as the International Sign Association, chartered to "promote and advance the sign and graphics industry through education, research, and continuous improvement of our members' products and services." Legal insights into the sign industry can be found on the Web site *www.*

signlaw.com, an informational Web site on American law covering signs, billboards, outdoor advertising, and related fields. The monument industry is represented in part by the nonprofit organization Monument Builders of North America, chartered to promote memorialization in a viable, innovative, and diversified business for its membership.

To the best knowledge of the owner, prospective owner, and broker, no other company uses a Granstone-type product. However, several companies are manufacturing customized, true granite golf course markers and signs, such as Great Lakes Granite Works, located in Michigan. The primary disadvantage of true granite is that it is more susceptible to breakage than the Granstone product (and it is limited in terms of color). Wood, metal, and plastic golf course markers are also manufactured by a number of companies across the United States, such as Prime Golf in Florida (acrylic, granite, wood, and aluminum signs). However, according to the owner, the value of the synthetic product manufactured by the subject company generally exceeds the alternatives; that is, the cost per unit of time in service is similar if not superior. Overall, the Granstone advantages are cost- and appearance-oriented because the product is more durable and subject to creative logo and legend insertions of practically any color or size.

There are many niche businesses in the golf signage industry, including the following:

XYZ Production: Creates personalized signs for each marker, using a software program to create the unique cover that is laminated on each sign

ABC Enterprises: Places an aerial photograph of each hole on tee markers to aid golfers in their play

Golf World: Uses DuPont Corian (trademarked) solid surface products to extend life of markers that feature graphics inlaid with durable resins

Marker World: Currently located in more than 1,000 golf courses in the United States alone, the Marker World system speeds up play to maximize golf course revenue (yardage markers only)

Overall, it appears that the closest alternative to the Granstone approach is the Golf World product (DuPont surface products are used to enhance durability and life of marker). Most companies that are in this broad market do not readily place pricing information on their Web sites, but sample pricing information obtained via the valuator's search confirmed the following general conclusions:

Granstone granite is cheaper than true granite.

Granstone products were above average in price.

The overall price was a function of both material and the type and amount of information placed on the materials (e.g., logos)

The Granstone granite and synthetic sandstone products are flexible in that legends and logos may be applied in many different ways (e.g., sandblasting, silk screening, decals, or metal, foam, or plastic graphics). Each sign is approximately 2 inches thick and weighs approximately 10 pounds per square foot.

In conclusion, the future of the industry and the company appears to be quite favorable.

Current Owner and Employee Information

The company is fully owned by Ed Rock and his wife, Tanya. Ed serves as the company's president and chief executive officer, whereas Tanya is minimally involved with general office duties (only ten hours per week). Ed has been chiefly responsible for marketing and finance but has intentionally reduced the amount of active marketing over the past two years because of failing health (other than attending trade shows). In general, the most valuable aspect of the company's personnel is its extremely high average tenure. Of the five salaried employees, the average tenure is nearly ten years.

The owner is assisted in great part by his son, Tony Rock, who has been with the company since the mid-1980s and would consider staying on with the new owners as a salaried executive with substantial responsibilities. Tony has been in charge of manufacturing operations for more than ten years and is responsible for all areas of research and design, manufacturing processes, administrative management, and customer service. Of great importance is his understanding of the unique blending processes used by the company in relation to its proprietary manufacturing efforts. He could be considered the glue that holds the company together as he interacts with company personnel at all levels and attends important trade shows to support the company's marketing plan.

Typical staffing levels hover around eight full-time employees earning annual salaries between approximately $27,000 and $54,000 (Tony has a base salary of $80,000, which will be reduced to $40,000 plus an incentive of 2 percent of gross revenues under the new ownership). Two of the most important employees are the company's full-time production specialist (graphic artist) and office administrator (approximately $54,000 and $44,000, respectively), both of whom have been with the company for many years. The artist is highly skilled and can create customer-specific logos and legends and is supported by two other graphic artists capable of using the computer-aided design software. The office administrator not only is responsible for all clerical functions but also has developed strong working relationships with many key customers.

Other employees are responsible for shipping, molding, sandblasting, finishing, and general production efforts, earning annual salaries between $26,000 and $40,000. The tee marker production workers earn an hourly wage of $10. For the year ending June 30, 2000, the labor component of cost of goods sold totaled approximately $160,000 (approximately 10.5 percent of sales), and clerical support totaled approximately $28,000 (including payroll tax, amounting to approximately 3.4 percent of total sales), together running at approximately 14 percent of sales (excluding employee benefits and officer compensation for Tony and Ed Rock).

Looking forward, it is important to understand the value of continued employment of the company's key personnel, especially Tony Rock. Upon closing, he is willing to remain employed with the new company as vice president of manufacturing working for an annual base salary of $40,000 plus 2 percent of all gross revenues and a standard benefit package. Given his in-depth and unique understanding of both the manufacturing process and the customer base, this fact is a critical determinant of the company's present and future value.

Lease Information

The company currently operates out of a 5,750-square-foot leased premise located in Springfield, Illinois. Springfield is the home of Sangamon State University and is located almost halfway between Chicago, Illinois, and St. Louis, Missouri, two of the nation's busiest commercial centers with large airports. The current lease rate of $2,706 (includes sales tax but excludes common area maintenance charge [CAM]) terminates in July 2001 and will rise by a few hundred dollars thereafter. According to the broker, the CAM-related charges are found in the repairs and maintenance category of the income statement, which during the year ending June 2000 amounted to only $928.

It is noteworthy that the current lease covers approximately 80 percent of the subject building, with the remaining space available to the owners via a right of first refusal if the current tenant vacates the premises. It is the opinion of the owner that additional sales equal to 20 percent of the current sales level are possible with the currently available space. However, a second shift could alleviate a space shortage and allow sales increases to approximately 70 percent higher than present levels. Total rental payments for the year ending in June 2000 amounted to approximately 4 percent of sales ($33,000).

Financial Analysis

The subject company appears to be in strong financial condition, as reflected by the consistent generation of profits and positive cash flow for the owners and minimal debt on the balance sheet. Note once again that the company's fiscal year runs from July 1 to June 30; that is, the references in this discussion to the year 2000 are based on the fiscal year ending June 30, 2000. As of January 31, 2001, the company maintained a debt level (excluding an income tax liability) of approximately $30,000. Besides the acquisition-related debt, the new owner will start his tenure almost debt-free (truck loans are being assumed).

Revenues

2000	$849,192
1999	$829,985
1998	$684,019

Although revenues appear to be flat over the past two years, it is important to understand that the owner has drastically reduced the amount of aggressive, in-person marketing and sales efforts during this two-year period. A favorable interpretation regarding revenues would be that the 2000 sales level is approximately 25 percent higher than that of 1998. The revenues generated during the first seven months of the current fiscal year are lower than year-earlier measures, but the owner has stated that recent above-average orders have been placed that will help bring the revenue level in line with last year. Overall, the owner expects the 2001 fiscal year sales to approximate the 2000 fiscal year level.

The owner has stated that he has not made substantial in-person marketing calls for more than four years. Because of the growth of the company, responsibilities at the home office, and his age (owner is now sixty-five, and his immediate family has experienced serious health problems when approaching this age), the overall marketing effort of the company has slowed.

In addition to trade shows, direct mail, and other advertising efforts, the company works with several manufacturer's representatives (approximately twelve) to promote the sales of company products across the nation. Total commissions paid in the 2000 fiscal year were approximately $34,000, compared with a total commission payment of $21,000 in the previous year (representing approximately 4 percent and 2.5 percent of total sales, respectively, in 2000 and 1999). It is estimated that approximately 20 percent of all sales are generated through these reps, who are paid a commission of approximately 20 percent (higher than average for this type of arrangement).

As explained earlier, the average sale made to their golf course customer base is approximately $10,000 to $15,000, with the single largest order coming in at approximately $33,000 during 1999 (equal to approximately 4 percent of total sales). No single customer generates more than this 4 percent figure, with the top five customers in a given year averaging approximately 8.5 percent of total sales, indicating that the customer base is diverse.

The largest single customer has been the Grand Development Companies, which use the subject company's products for all of their new golf communities (including street signs for their neighborhoods). The largest group of customers is found through the International Golf Corporation, the world's largest owner and operator of golf courses (more than 500 courses around the globe). Because of their organizational structure, however, each course is independently operated by its respective management team, which means that each course must be negotiated with on a case-by-case basis.

The subject company's important designation of preferred vendor status for both the International Golf Corporation and World Golf (World Golf operates approximately forty courses and is growing rapidly) will help ensure a steady flow of new orders into the coming years. The value of the preferred vendor status is found in the fact that these customers must choose among this elite group of vendors to purchase specific types of product or risk negative consequences by upper management.

Another revenue generator is found through reorders that occur as golf courses go through new management teams or run through their normal operating cycles in search of an improved or unique appearance to improve the golfing experience. The larger products such as entrance signs, directional signs, and tee markers tend to last a very long time if not forever. They are replaced if management seeks a facelift or redesigns several holes. Tee box rocks or markers are replaced more frequently because of theft or lawnmower damage or as part of a general overhaul. There are typically 180 markers per course, so the replacement numbers can be substantial.

A major unknown at this time is the unfolding situation concerning the company's new product, called Tote-a-Tool, which became a part of the subject company's operations during January 2001. This unique product is a beltlike apparatus worn around the waist and over the shoulder, used by professional golf course maintenance crew members or landscaping crew members that protects and conceals unsightly tools, parts, fluids, and other frequently used materials. Granstone is the exclusive distributor of the product for the next three years, featuring a patented design with a durable yet flexible material used for military operations. The durability of the product nicely complements the Granstone product quality (i.e., the new product is consistent with the overall theme and company niche in the golf course industry). By organizing and safekeeping the tools and other frequently used maintenance-related materials, the product reduces operating costs and increases profitability.

The product can be evaluated on the company's (fictional) Web site (*www.*

Granstone.com). The company hopes to increase overall revenues by as much as $50,000 during the first full year of sales. After introducing the product at a major landscaping trade show in January and to the golf course superintendents' trade show in February, the new owner plans to send a mailing to all existing Granstone customers (purchasing agents and other relevant contact personnel) to promote the new product as fully as possible.

The owner has developed a comprehensive business and marketing plan with the assistance of family members to help boost future sales and profits related to all products. Several major steps are planned for immediate execution, including the following:

Refocus on and enhance sales to golf course–related customers, including master planned communities around the world

Actively pursue the parks and recreation departments because of a perceived opening in this market for both Granstone and Tote-a-Tool products

Approach architects, builders, contractors, and others to generate non–golf course sales of signs (in addition to markers and monuments)

Develop the manufacturer's rep channel or abandon and reallocate these resources toward in-house sales personnel development

Generate high-quality direct mailings to all current Granstone customers and other potential customers such as building maintenance, apartment complex maintenance, and other similar businesses

Attend golf course superintendent and maintenance-related trade shows promoting the sale of the new Tote-a-Tool product

Expand into the sale of other golf course maintenance tools such as rakes to combine with the sale of the Tote-a-Tool product (cross-marketing)

In conclusion, continued growth in the golf course industry around the world, increasing acceptance of the product and its durability, promotion of the new Tote-a-Tool product, and more aggressive penetration into the parks and recreation and various maintenance-related departmental budgets should help propel the business to increased levels of revenues.

Adjusted Cash Flow

Most entrepreneurs and valuation professionals agree that the primary determinant of business value is a business's ability to generate income or cash flow for its owners. Many important valuation techniques rely on various measures of cash flow for estimating a company's FMV. Variations in these measures account for the following:

Pretax or after-tax

Deducting manager's salary or adding owner's compensation

Incurring capital expenditures

One-time expenditures

Time value of money

Changes in working capital

Many business brokers, entrepreneurs, and business valuators alike use a measure of cash flow known as adjusted cash flow (ACF), which is often called "seller's discretionary cash" or simply "net". Regardless of the term used, it is typically calculated as the sum of net income plus owner's salary and perks, depreciation and amortization expense, interest expense, and any one-time or nonrecurring expenditures.

Over the past three full years, the subject business generated the following ACF amounts:

2000	$294,212
1999	$282,584
1998	$155,050

These figures are calculated as follows.

The primary measure of earning power in this report is ACF. Regardless of the title given to this measure, most valuation professionals and business brokers use a similar format for calculating this important figure, such as Shannon Pratt's widely cited book *Valuing a Business*. In basic format, ACF is the sum of the following:

ACF ($)	Fiscal Year 2000 ($)
Pretax income	33,282
Officers' salary (two officers)	261,400
Officers' payroll taxes (estimate)	24,000
Depreciation and amortization expense	11,600
Interest expense	N/A
Owner's insurance (health, life)	2,680
Personal auto expense	N/A
Travel and entertainment (T&E)	1,250
Total	$334,212
Less replacement salary	–$40,000
Final ACF	$294,212

Similar calculations were made for 1998 and 1999 as well, with the results presented earlier in this report. Because it is customary to calculate ACF based on the efforts of a single owner working the business full-time, the replacement salary adjustment was made to reflect the amount of wages that would be paid to replace the second owner's work effort. The addbacks for T&E are extremely conservative in nature, and although the trucks are used in part for personal reasons, no addbacks were made to remain conservative in the overall approach.

Note that some valuation methods, as per Small Business Administration (SBA) Guidelines, use a different measure for earnings power (e.g., the discounted future earnings method, which is based on after-tax income and reduced by the required owner's compensation, and the capitalized adjusted earnings method, which is based on historically adjusted and averaged earnings).

Although the valuator has used primarily the ACF figure based on the most recently completed fiscal year ending June 30, 2000, the ACF for the first seven months of the current fiscal year is nearly identical on an annualized basis. Note again that the discounted future earnings method uses a weighted average of prior years for the base year as opposed to the latest period only (as does the capitalized adjusted earnings method) and an after-tax measure of cash flow.

The valuation results in this report are based on the typical terms of an asset sale despite the fact that the transaction is a stock sale. Accordingly, a key assumption is that the business will be delivered free and clear of all debts but the seller will retain all cash, deposits, and receivables as of the time of closing (valuation). Important assets as of January 31, 2001, are as follows:

Item	Fair Market Value
Inventory	$39,500
Furniture, fixtures, and equipment (FF&E)	$20,000
Molds	$10,000
Written-off assets and leaseholds	$ 5,500
Total key assets	$75,000

The valuation of fixed assets is always subject to debate and wide variations in interpretation from one valuation professional to the next. Most lending institutions take a very conservative stance in this area, but in terms of estimating the FMV of going concerns, higher values typically are assigned to the FF&E when compared with bank valuations.

Allocations of purchase price between buyer and seller, on the other hand, may be more motivated by tax considerations than a desire to capture the true market values. Also, to the extent that much equipment is expensed (e.g., Section 179 expense) rather than capitalized, the book value from financial statements tends to understate its true value. Finally, most businesses use their tax depreciation schedules for book purposes as well, which means that there is a tendency to depreciate assets as quickly as possible to minimize taxable income and take advantage of the time value of money. From a replacement value perspective, the cost probably would exceed $100,000 in today's dollars.

A common rule of thumb used by valuation professionals in lieu of formal equipment appraisals is to estimate the value of FF&E as being halfway between original cost and current depreciated book value. Because the equipment of the subject company is approximately seven years old or less, it is in good working condition and has been subject to ongoing routine maintenance according to the owner. Using this rule of thumb generates a value for FF&E of approximately $75,000. Leasehold improvements and fully depreciated or expensed assets are estimated to have an FMV of approximately $55,000, and the company's extensive collection of molds (can be used for reorders) has a conservative value of approximately $10,000.

Other key assumptions include the following:

A replacement salary for the second officer was estimated to be $40,000, including payroll taxes and benefits.

The owner stated that there were no past, present, or probable lawsuits, worker's compensation claims, or other material or detrimental events relevant to the company's FMV.

Questionnaire results (sixty initial questions and approximately forty follow-up questions) contain numerous relevant assumptions and useful information (available upon request).

Note that the ACF measure of cash flow is used at least in part for three of the valuation techniques included in this report. In addition, however, the discounted future earnings method uses an after-tax measure of earnings, and the capitalization of income method uses a weighted average after-tax cash flow figure.

In regard to the impact of the potential buyer on the future revenue and cash flow performance of the subject company, note the following important observations:

Buyer has twenty years of manufacturing experience with similar companies using similar processes with resins and epoxies.

Buyer has ten to fifteen years of marketing and finance experience in companies with worldwide operations using similar manufacturing processes.

Buyer started a company known as Arbeit, Inc., in 1989, achieving significant success and selling out to a German company in 1993.

The manufacturing processes and equipment used at this company were similar to those used at Granstone.

In management positions with Aerospace, Inc., subsidiaries, buyer grew the division from $10 million to $100 million based on similar manufacturing processes.

The buyer appears to be an ideal fit based on extensive managerial experience in all fields, particularly nearly identical manufacturing process experience. His background and experience coupled with the existing employee base and the willingness of the current owner's son to continue working as vice president of manufacturing bode well for the company's future.

Additional Commentary on Assets and Liabilities

Based on the decision to sell the company as a stock sale (as opposed to an asset sale), most assets and liabilities typically are included in both the sale and the valuation analysis. Generally speaking, a stock sale is premised on the fact that the seller will deliver all assets and liabilities as-is, including cash and accounts receivable and all debts. In this particular case, however, the stock sale excludes the cash, receivables, and liabilities such that it is more like a traditional asset sale. The noteworthy differences between a stock sale and an asset sale include the following stock sale factors:

Buyer inherits the seller's existing depreciation schedules for fixed assets (already nearly fully depreciated but minimal in overall amount)

Buyer assumes all unknown and contingent liabilities, unless specifically excluded by contract

Buyer assumes all existing contracts with employees, customers, and suppliers in their current condition

A review of the company's balance sheet as of January 31, 2001, indicates that most of the company's assets (total assets equal $284,000) are in cash and accounts receivable ($110,000 of $235,000 are accounts receivable), which will remain the property of the seller. The company's total current liabilities are approximately $130,000, made up primarily of accounts payable ($55,000) and customer deposits ($40,000). As mentioned earlier, the only debt facing the company relates to the company trucks ($30,000). This liability will be paid out of closing funds.

Additional Comments on the Income Statement

As described earlier, the company's sales were steady over the past two years at a level approximately 25 percent higher than that of three years ago. It is probable that the company's sales will rise modestly in 2001 as their new product is aggressively introduced. It is also likely that the company's advertising and promotion expenses will rise above current levels (from approximately 2.5 percent of sales to as high as 4.5 percent of sales) to introduce the new product and expand infiltration of the parks and recreation markets.

The company's historic gross profit margin has hovered around 60 percent (cost of goods sold [CGS] equals 40 percent), providing a contribution margin of about 40 cents for each dollar of sales. Total general and administrative (G&A) expenses have been approximately 56 percent, leaving around 4 percent of sales for pretax income. Rent expense has also been fairly constant (about 4 percent of sales), with other major expenses coming in the form of officer salaries (30 percent), shop and office supplies (4.5 percent), payroll taxes (3.5 percent), and clerical salaries (3 percent).

Looking ahead, the new Tote-a-Tool product might turn into a cash cow given its high gross profit margin of nearly 80 percent at current pricing levels. Despite the increased advertising expense involved with promoting the new product, it is anticipated that bottom-line profits will rise significantly as a result of its appeal and high contribution margin.

Economic Analysis

State of the U.S. Economy

The U.S. economy is in its tenth year of economic expansion, a period of economic growth rarely matched in the nation's history. Both inflation (approximately 3 percent) and unemployment (4.1 percent) remain near 25-year lows despite a recent slowing in gross domestic product (GDP) growth (1.1 percent revised growth rate in fourth quarter 2000). The equity markets, until very recently, were near all-time highs despite the slowing economy and falling corporate earnings. As the Dow Jones Industrial Average has dipped below 10,000 for the first time in a few years, the economic climate appears to be worsening (at least in the eyes of investors), but the appearance of a recession is still questionable.

In the second quarter of 2000, GDP growth registered an approximately 5.5 percent real growth rate, and unemployment stayed below 4 percent. The

CPI has also stayed well below the troubling levels of the 1970s and 1980s, partially in response to the increase in interest rates engineered by the Federal Reserve Bank over an eighteen-month period ending near the end of 2000. This increase in bank rates in pursuit of what Alan Greenspan calls a soft landing is what many believe is responsible for the recent slowing in GDP (fourth quarter 2000 grew at a revised 1.1 percent only). On the positive side, as a result of this slowdown, the Fed has reversed course and lowered interest rates twice in 2001, and the president and Congress are debating not whether but how much of a tax cut to enact.

In conclusion, most economists believe that the recovery will continue despite the recent problems. Expansionary fiscal (tax cuts) and monetary (lower interest rates) policies should help steer the economy into further years of economic growth.

State Economy

Anyone familiar with the Illinois economy is aware of the fact that general prosperity is evident by many visual and statistical measures. New construction at high levels can be seen throughout the state, and Illinois continues to be one of the leading exporters in the nation because of its proximity to Canada.

Illinois has enjoyed almost nine years of economic growth with low inflation, and the state unemployment rate has remained near to slightly above the national average. Recently, however, there has been a minor reversal of the strong growth patterns as reflected by various indices and anecdotal evidence such as layoffs and plant closings. What is currently occurring probably is a slowdown in the rate of growth, not a negative growth rate. As in the U.S. economy, there are signs of a slowdown (e.g., fewer new home starts, corporate layoffs at Motorola) in Illinois. However, it appears to be a matter of returning to what might be perceived as more normal growth rates.

Local Economy

The local economy in Springfield, Illinois, is highly dependent on both agriculture and state government (capital city). Whereas state government continues with steady employment levels, agriculture markets have prospered in recent times because of a combination of record harvests and stable prices (resulting in part from growing international demand for food-related products such as those produced by A.E. Staley in Decatur, Illinois, approximately 45 miles from Springfield).

Unemployment remains low compared with that of the 1970s and 1980s, and sales of new and existing homes have also risen steadily since hitting bottom in the early 1990s. Although a reduction in the rate of economic growth is likely in the Springfield area, it is again a matter of relative perception because growth probably will continue, albeit at a lower rate.

Economic Outlook

Whereas most forecasters expected continued moderate growth in GDP coupled with moderate inflation, some forecasters such as Infometrica forecasted a recession in 2000 brought on by rising inflation and rising interest rates. Although Infometrica was close to being correct, a recession did not take place (only a slowdown in growth rates). Because a recession typically is defined as two or more consecutive quarters of economic decline as measured by GDP, it is unlikely that the year 2001 will be a recessionary year because of the upcoming fiscal stimulus of tax cuts and continued reductions in bank lending rates. Upon weighing the current evidence about the future of the U.S. economy, it appears that at least modest growth will continue during the new millennium. As the federal tax cuts begin to take hold (approximately $1.4 billion over ten years, weighted heavily towards earlier years) and the Federal Reserve continues to drop interest rates (down almost 3 percent since the beginning of the year 2000), the economy probably will respond in such a manner as to prevent a recession from taking hold in the near future.

Valuation Analysis

It is time to begin the actual valuation process for our hypothetical subject company. You should have already prepared the five worksheets for the Five-Page Tool, listing the key findings related to cash flow, assets, pluses and minuses of the company, key assumptions, and any questions that warrant further attention. Having done this, you are well prepared to walk through the questionnaire and complete the necessary analysis to reach your valuation estimate. Rather than reproduce the questionnaire again at this juncture, you can print a copy from the attached CD-ROM and then work your way through the five sections.

Naturally, we begin with Section One. As a practical matter, it is advisable to print a copy of both the full-scale, complete questionnaire and use it concurrently with the condensed questionnaire. The idea here is to read from the full version and place your responses on the condensed version. This will allow optimal understanding and clarity.

Section One

Because Section One begins with a reference to the Five-Page Tool, a few comments are in order. The importance of this part of the valuation analysis cannot be stressed enough. This tool provides the foundation on which the questionnaire is completed and the valuation estimate is grounded. To begin the Five-Page Tool, you must have requested and received the financial statements (preferably tax returns and other company documents). Section One spells out the typical documents needed to complete the valuation analysis, so double check this list each time you begin a valuation effort. Reviewing the income statement and the balance sheet line by line while constructing a preliminary ACF analysis and asset valuation overview will direct you immediately toward key valuation factors and insights. As you construct your initial ACF model, jot down immediately any major assumptions you have made and any questions that arise that are relevant to the ACF calculation or any other aspect of valuation (e.g., pluses and minuses that stand out right away such as a favorable trend in revenues or an apparently high gross profit margin). You should also begin formalizing and visualizing your understanding of the company's operations and the industry in which it operates.

After the Five-Page Tool worksheets are well under way (including your initial thoughts regarding the relative pluses and minuses of the subject company and industry), it is time to begin forming the framework in which the valuation will unfold. For example, it is important to quickly address the following questions:

What is the purpose of the valuation?

What is being valued?

What are the standard and premise of value?

Summarize the intended valuation effort in one sentence (e.g., "valuation of XYZ company for purposes of establishing its FMV in order to make offer to purchase business as an asset sale").

If a bank loan (SBA) is involved, include a reference to this in your one-sentence description as well. The idea is to summarize the key environmental elements surrounding the valuation process so as to properly assess the business value in light of the intended audience.

Section Two

Section Two is designed to quickly cut to the chase and capture the key facts and conditions of the subject company and industry. In general, it is preferable to ask the business owner to fill out this section (and the next section) in conjunction with your efforts to address these initial questions. In fact, certain questions can be properly answered only by the owner (or the company bookkeeper, CPA, or other key employees) such as probable capital expenditures, level of working capital needs, verification of sales revenue, and recent or pending material changes. The process of involving the owner will also allow you to get to know the seller and assess his credibility and general demeanor. To the extent that you probably will be a type of partner throughout the training period or as long as there is an outstanding note payment, it is wise to carefully gauge the personality and credibility of the seller. Be careful.

This section also allows the valuator to continue improving her understanding of the company, particularly its ability to generate cash flow (ACF). Because you have already begun your ACF analysis as part of the Five-Page Tool, the responses here from the owner will help confirm or explain the actual contributors to cash flow in the framework described in Chapter Four (ACF is a measure of the pretax, cash-equivalent benefits accruing to a single owner working the business on a full-time basis). Making the necessary adjustments if the business is absentee-run or fully operated by family members normally entails feedback from the owner to ensure a correct evaluation.

Information obtained during the Section Two analysis will further develop your understanding of the unique features (pro and con) of the company and industry. Based on the owner's response to Section Two questions (particularly numbers 5, 9 to 11, 13, 14, 19, and 20), an excellent opportunity exists to update your Five-Page Tool worksheet listing the pluses and minuses of the subject company and industry. The contents of this worksheet will play a pivotal role in developing the applicable multiples to apply to ACF, rules of thumb, and market comp analyses.

Section Three

If time is a concern or if you are merely curious about the value of your business, it may not be necessary to address every question in Section Three. For that matter, several questions may be irrelevant or simply unnecessary for certain types of businesses and under certain circumstances. Alternatively, it may be that a quick review of the questions will lead you to the conclusion that only a handful are truly important or relevant. There is certainly no harm in addressing all questions to the extent that the more one knows about a given business, the more probable it is that a credible valuation estimate will emerge.

Once again it may be prudent to request the assistance of the owner or one of several possible representatives of the owner such as the company's CPA, attorney, consultant, broker, or key employee. To a certain extent, most business owners would be pleased if not impressed to see a prospective owner asking for their feedback. Of course, there are always limits to what is considered helpful or reasonable. If the owner continues to operate the business during the valuation period, he will find it difficult to spend too much time answering questions that seem to go on and on. It is advisable to limit the number of questions that you ask business owners under these conditions so as to not irritate them. If you spread the questions around to different people, no one person will be overwhelmed.

Section Three is concerned with not only the subject company but also the subject industry. Diligently investigating the key features and current trends in an industry is as important as evaluating the subject company. Such research typically can be done without the aid of the business owner. Consider tapping into one of the many Web sites presented on the questionnaire to help in this regard.

In addition to evaluating the company's products or services and competition, this section should foster a more complete understanding of the company's balance sheet and income statement. Because dozens of different aspects of the company and industry are addressed in this section, you should not be surprised if you begin to feel overwhelmed. Herein lies another important feature of the Five-Page Tool. As you make your conclusions about the questions chosen for investigation, make sure to include them on the most relevant worksheet. For example, if it is determined that the subject company is facing a real capacity constraint, list this as a minus on the "Key Valuation Factors" worksheet. If you are uncertain as to the capacity constraint and need further clarification or insight, jot down a question on the "Questions" worksheet. If you are forced to make a major assumption, include this on the "Major Assumptions" worksheet (e.g., "It is assumed that the current outstanding lawsuit involving a worker's compensation claim will be satisfied without any impact on future insurance rates").

Section Four

We now move into the actual valuation process based on the many findings, assumptions, terms, and conditions discovered through the first three sections of the analysis. This section includes a series of questions and analyses divided into the three distinct ARM-related components (ACF multiples, rules of thumb, and market comps). Thus, the first seven questions involve ACF, the next ten questions involve rules of thumb, and the final seventeen questions pertain to the use of market comp data.

ACF Multiple

It should not be surprising that the first step in Section Four calls for finalizing the calculation of the subject company's ACF results over the past few years. As stressed throughout this book, cash flow accruing to the owner is the primary determinant of business value. It is critical that the ACF result prepared here be as accurate and complete as possible given its role in facilitating value estimations via each component of the ARM approach. Take a step back and review the chapter outlining the finer points behind this calculation (Chapter Three) and remind yourself why this figure is so important. Depending on the purpose and audience for the valuation, either three years or five years of historical analysis is necessary. For example, if you know that the SBA ultimately will be involved, you may as well make your calculations for the past five years instead of three years.

The next series of steps involves analyzing the company and industry within the "pluses and minuses" context of the first worksheet in the Five-Page Tool. The combination of consultation with the owner, the valuator's independent review of the company, and various types of industry research, you will be able to finalize your "Key Valuation Factors" worksheet to apply in later steps. It is once again a matter of choice as to how detailed the analysis becomes, depending in large part on the purpose of the valuation.

The industry research should include at least a basic financial statement analysis made up of both trend analysis and comparative analysis with industry averages through one or more of the sources listed under question 3 of Section Four. Whether any of the managerial tools or techniques are used is also a matter of choice. To the extent that a strengths, weaknesses, opportunities, and threats (SWOT) analysis is similar to our "pluses and minuses" approach, perhaps a review of the Porter five forces may be a useful technique. Walking through the premises is a must and should have already occurred earlier in the analysis.

Question 5 in the first part of Section Four (related to ACF multiples) provides the valuator's first estimate of value. This question forces the valuator to consider the important empirical relationship between the magnitude of ACF and the corresponding multiple. The final two questions lead the valuator toward a finalized "Pluses and Minuses" worksheet to be used for generating the estimate of the proper multiple to apply to the company's derived ACF figure.

Rules of Thumb

The next ten questions walk the valuator through the use of rules of thumb (if applicable). Because most rules of thumb involve either ACF, gross revenues, asset values, or some combination of these three figures, listing these amounts for the past three to five years in a grid format is a good start to using rules of thumb. In addition, the valuator will once again face a condensed view of the historical performance of the subject company in regard to the most important success indicators.

It is now necessary to see which rules of thumb are used for the type of company at hand. If the valuator determines that no rule of thumb is commonly used, there is no need to prepare the related grid. However, preparation of this grid is useful in itself (if it has not already been prepared as part of the Five-Page Tool). At a minimum, practically every business type can be valued with a generic rule of thumb involving ACF, gross revenues, or assets. More important, however, are the situations in which the use of such rules is a critical determinant of asking prices and the resulting market prices (e.g., accounting and tax practices, restaurants, ISPs, and other service businesses).

Questions 5 through 7 direct the valuator to assess the subjective element of the relevant rule of thumb and evaluate its application in the context of the strengths and weaknesses (pluses and minuses, pros and cons, opportunities and threats) of the subject company. The ever-growing worksheet of pluses and minuses should be updated and used in selecting the appropriate multiple for the rule of thumb at hand.

After this process is completed through question 8, the valuator is asked to apply the "reality check" or "payback" method to the subject company to preliminarily assess the reasonableness of the initial two value estimates (ACF multiple and rule of thumb). The final step involves assessment of the company's probable future cash flow in relation to the typical amount of debt service that would be present under normal seller financing terms. This is basically another type of reality check to the first two value estimates, serving primarily to assess the viability of obtaining seller or bank financing.

Market Comps

Last, but not least, we turn to a review of market comparable data. The first five questions are intended to facilitate the classification of the subject company into its proper segment for purposes of selecting the most pertinent source of market comp data. The remaining questions are self-explanatory and lead the valuator toward the optimal database and assessment of the subject company compared with the norm or average business in this market segment.

As is true for the first two components as well, the ultimate factor in estimating business value is the valuator's overall assessment of the unique pluses and minuses of the subject company as compared with the average business of its type and size. Thus, the "Key Valuation Factors" worksheet must be diligently and continuously developed and updated throughout the entire valuation process, reflecting the valuator's opinion and interpretation of the company's unique features.

Section Five

This section is intended to finalize the valuation results via a rational allocation of the three value estimates derived in each component of the ARM approach (ACF, rules of thumb, market comparables). Calculating and comparing the arithmetic mean of the three distinct value estimates with a weighted-basket allocation of the three values in line with the valuator's assessment of the relative reliability and credibility of each result serves only to spur the valuator's thought process as to what the FMV of the subject company is. Although there is no generally accepted valuation principle in this regard, most professional valuators will use a rational and documented weighting to derive their final value estimate.

The primary concern of the valuator at this point in the valuation process should be credibility in the eyes of the target audience. Whatever your final valuation estimate may be and however it may be determined, remember that you may need to defend your estimate and each of the many steps that led to the final value estimate. If you keep this in mind throughout the entire process, you will be more likely to present a logical, reasonable, and supportable valuation figure that is more likely to be accepted by the reader.

To the extent that business valuation takes on meaning only in the heat of the battle, you will be well served by the ARM approach if you bear this important fact in mind. Being able to explain your major assumptions and determinations in a believable fashion is key to reaching your valuation-related objective, whatever it might be. The ARM approach and the Five-Page Tool will give you the tools to win such battles of any type.

Final Comments

Congratulations are in order for those of you who have read each of the chapters and used the ARM Approach Questionnaire and Five-Page Tool. If you have devoted your time and energy to grasping the material that makes up the ARM approach to business valuation, you can feel confident that you will be able to review practically any type or size of business and generate a credible estimate of its FMV. By learning the finer points of each component, you have built a valuation foundation that will serve your interests well in the future.

Even if you find yourself in a situation in which you must hire a professional appraiser, you will be able to help guide the valuation effort to ensure optimal results. Regardless of the reason for valuation, type of business, size of operation, geographic location, or any other situation-specific factor, you now have the ability to evaluate practically any business to arrive at its approximate FMV. Whether the subject company is a retail business or manufacturing operation, employs only three people or fifty, is growing or shrinking, is profitable or not, is good, bad, or ugly, you now have the tools to credibly estimate its value.

Using all three components of the ARM approach will help ensure that your final estimate is well grounded both in theory and in practice. Use of cash flow under the income approach provides the most theoretically pure value estimate. Use of the proper rule of thumb will help you to stay in touch with industry practice and generally accepted valuation techniques for each type of company. Finally, tapping into the market comp databases will round off your overall estimate through the use of actual, historical deal prices for the subject company. The reality check or payback method will provide further assurances that you are on the right track.

By averaging or weighting the three ARM-related results, you will base your final estimate on a wide variety of factors similar to those assessed by professional appraisers. Except for extremely rare conditions, your value estimate should be credible and useful in furthering your cause. Whether you are buying, selling, seeking bank financing, settling a divorce or estate tax problem, or just curious, applying the ARM approach will serve you well. Given the subjective element of all valuation methods, do not be alarmed if another valuator reaches a different conclusion. If you are familiar with the key valuation determinants, you can justify your conclusion in the same manner as professionals.

To finish our analysis of the ARM approach, a list of important valuation concepts and commentary might be helpful. As stated throughout the book, it will be advantageous to review the relevant chapters as needed. Don't hesitate to go to one of the key valuation Web sites to investigate a particular issue or locate market comp data.

Words of Wisdom

The following short statements, paragraphs, or quotes are not listed in any special order, nor do they necessarily relate to one another in any particular manner. They should be considered as a summary of key valuation concepts and tips to aid the business valuator in optimizing the use of his or her new skills.

Valuation is and always will be one part art (subjective, normative, opinion-oriented) and one part science (objective, positive, factual).

Valuation ultimately is a prophecy as to the future.

The greater the risk associated with future cash flows, the less they are worth.

A company's ability to generate cash flow or income for its owners is far and away the most influential factor for determining its value (all other factors ultimately are secondary).

Only businesses that are not making a profit or have shut down should be valued heavily based on the asset-based techniques.

Most small businesses with ACF of $250,000 or less sell for 2.3 times ACF on average.

The greater the cash flow, the higher the multiples (all other things held equal).

Businesses with ACF greater than $500,000 sell for higher multiples than those with less than $500,000 in ACF (less than $250,000, one to three times ACF; $250,000 to $500,000, two to four times ACF; $500,000 to $1 million, three to six times ACF).

Purchase contract terms and conditions can affect the deal price almost as much as traditional business valuation factors such as the amount of ACF, asset values, and growth rates.

The ARM approach generates a valuation result based on seller financing (e.g., a valuation result of $400,000 is based on a typical down payment of approximately 35 percent, payback period of three to five years at 8 to 10 percent rate of interest).

Stock sale prices normally are less than asset sale prices because of normally favorable tax treatment for the seller.

Businesses purchased on all-cash terms receive a discount of 10 to 25 percent, depending on the relative motivations of the parties.

When searching for suitable market comps, make sure that they are similar at least in terms of size, type of business or industry served, and geographic location.

Remember that each market comp database is unique, but three of the four major databases use the exact same measure of cash flow as presented in this book, namely ACF (only IBA cash flow differs because it excludes depreciation and amortization).

The BIZCOMPS database backs out inventory from its reported sale prices, so to directly compare with other databases, inventory must be added back into the price and the resulting multiple calculated.

In general, the more valuation methods used, the better, and the more comps reviewed, the better. Never rely on a single valuation method if possible.

For two businesses with equal cash flow, the one with higher valued assets is worth more (all other things held equal).

On average, manufacturing businesses sell for higher multiples than service businesses because of the presence of tangible assets and their role as a barrier to entry into the manufacturing-related industry (service businesses are easier to enter, so competition is greater and the cash flows are riskier and thus worth less).

To compare apples with apples (company to company and market comp database to market comp database), the ACF figure is calculated consistently and on the basis of a single owner working the business full-time (e.g., adjustments must be made for more than one owner, family members, or an absentee owner).

The primary reason people buy businesses is to make money.

The ACF represents the amount of cash-equivalent benefits accruing to a single owner working a business on a full-time basis and is equal to pretax income plus a series of addbacks made up of owner's compensation and perks, depreciation and amortization expense, interest expense, and any one-time, unusual, nonrecurring expenses.

This same ACF figure represents the amount of cash available to a new owner to service debt, pay herself a salary or living wage, and earn a positive return on the invested cash.

Valuation, like beauty, is in the eye of the beholder. The same business can have different values for two different buyers under two different sets of circumstances (i.e., investment value can be greater than FMV).

Fair market value is defined by the IRS as "the price at which the property would change hands between a willing buyer and a willing seller, neither under any compulsion to buy or sell and both having reasonable knowledge of the relevant facts."

There are three basic valuation approaches: income, cost (asset), and market. At least one method from each approach should be used for every valuation effort.

Each valuation assignment and each company is unique, and reasonable people will disagree on what the correct value is for a given business.

According to the IRS *Valuation Training* coursebook, "In valuation, there are no absolutes and there are only general guidelines to which individual judgments must be applied." The IRS also states, "There are available substantive aids and/or methods which are generally recognized and accepted by the appraisal profession and the Courts."

IRS Revenue Ruling 59–60 often is cited as a useful overview or introduction to the factors that affect business value. The eight factors (restated by authors) that must be reviewed for tax-related valuations are as follows:

Nature of business or industry and history of the enterprise since inception

Economic outlook in general and for subject business and industry

Book value of company stock and financial condition of company

Earning capacity of the company

Dividend-paying capacity of the company

Goodwill or other intangible asset value

Prior sales of the company's stock and size of block sold

Market prices of stocks for companies engaged in a similar line of business

No single valuation technique is universally applicable to every valuation assignment.

Many valuators believe that the value of any business is the sum of the expected future economic benefits accruing to the owner discounted back into present value (today's dollars).

Forecasting future cash flows (i.e., revenues and expenses) is just as difficult as estimating the proper discount rate (or valuation multiple).

The sum of the parts may not equal the whole; that is, fractional interests in a company (minority interests) are not worth a proportionate share of the entire company's FMV because of a lack-of-control discount.

Minority interests in privately held companies are subject to both a lack-of-control discount and a marketability discount according to tradition and to the courts (such discounts are multiplicative, not additive).

According to modern financial theory, the value of any asset (or collection of assets such as a company) is the present value of all net future cash flows accruing to its owners.

Discounted cash flow analysis is based on the modern financial theory and is increasingly accepted by valuation professionals and the courts as a superior valuation technique.

According to Shannon Pratt, the income approach is the core of valuation theory, but actual market transaction data can provide compelling empirical evidence of value.

Financial statements prepared in accordance with generally accepted accounting principles (GAAP) are presented in a manner that reflects primarily the historical cost principle, which can and does often differ from FMVs.

A company's FMV is almost always greater than its book value, which is solely a function of accounting entries.

The "excess earnings" method, originally created by the IRS and called the Treasury approach, has evolved from being the core of IRS valuation methods to being applicable for IRS purposes only if no other acceptable method exists. Despite this condemnation by the IRS, this method often is used in cases of divorce for professional companies such as medical practices or dental offices (at the request of the courts, which have grown comfortable with this technique over the years).

Location is key (for retail businesses, anyway).

Capital-intensive manufacturing companies typically have very high ratios of hard assets to gross revenues, with the value of each asset driven by its contribution to gross revenue and net profits. Thus, the ideal valuation approach is some acceptable multiple of net cash flow (as opposed to an asset-based valuation). (Source: Sam Stapley, designated broker for the VR Business Brokers office in Scottsdale, Arizona [Roth & Associates; phone 480-949-8612]).

Valuing businesses is very different from valuing residential homes because business owners are not required to report or disclose selling prices and businesses differ dramatically in numerous material ways. Thus, entrepreneurs should rely on professionals to assess FMV, and no company sells more businesses than VR Business Brokers (thousands of businesses sold since 1979). (Source: Jim Roth, owner and broker for the VR Business Brokers office located in Scottsdale, Arizona [Roth & Associates; phone 480-949-8612]).

If available, local market comp data are preferable because of pricing variations across regions of the United States; for example, in Phoenix, Arizona, the Valley Board of Business Brokers collects and presents statistical data related to reported sales from their approximately eighty-member group (see *www.vbbb.org* for more details). Florida Business Brokers Association (FBBA) gathers statewide comp data from its members and has quite a large database also. There are also state business broker associations in California, Colorado, Georgia, and Texas that could have stats available, as well as the United States Business Exchange (USBX).

"If there is an area in the field of taxation where uncertainty is the hallmark, it is the area of valuation of an interest in a closely held business." (Source: Irving Blackman, author of *Valuing Your Privately Held Business,* revised edition, published by McGraw-Hill, New York, 1992).

An appraisal is "a supportable opinion as to the value of something" according to Ray Miles, director of the Institute of Business Appraisers and author of *Basic Business Appraisal* (published by Southeast Business Investment Corporation in Boynton Beach, Florida, 1984).

According to the 2000 edition of the BIZCOMPS Small Business Studies, the average sale price during 2000 was approximately $230,000 (business brokerage market segment as opposed to middle-market).

Approximately 5.5 million businesses with at least one employee exist in the United States according to the SBA.

Approximately 1 million of these businesses are for sale at any given time, with only one out of these four actually being sold over the course of a year.

Valuation results in a vacuum are meaningless; they matter only in the heat of the battle.

To the extent that every known valuation technique contains at least one major subjective component, the ability to confidently and convincingly defend your assumptions is critical for prevailing in a valuation dispute. It is essential to tailor your presentation to the intended audience or relevant decision maker (whether a buyer, seller, judge, or jury).

"Valuation is an art to be learned, not a science to be practiced." (Source: Dr. Ken Ferris, author of *Valuation: Avoiding the Winners Curse,* Prentice Hall Financial Times, Upper Saddle River, NJ, 2002.)

Glossary

The following definitions were taken primarily from the *International Glossary of Business Valuation Terms,* developed jointly by the American Institute of Certified Public Accountants, American Society of Appraisers, Canadian Institute of Chartered Business Valuators, National Association of Certified Valuation Analysts, and Institute of Business Appraisers (IBA).

This user-friendly glossary was jointly developed to enhance and sustain the quality of business valuations for the benefit of the business valuation profession and clients of its practitioners. Each of these organizations has adopted this glossary for both educational and professional needs. Such a cooperative effort is further evidence of the continuing standardization of the business valuation process, which has contributed to the improved usefulness and credibility of the valuation profession. In short, adoption of similar terminology and concepts facilitates communication between valuator and customer.

This glossary was developed to provide guidance to business valuation practitioners who are members of the listed societies, organizations, and others performing valuations of business interests or securities by further codifying the body of knowledge that constitutes the competent and careful determination of value and, more particularly, the communication of how that value was determined. Obviously, it is beneficial for the entrepreneur as well, whether one is attempting to estimate value on one's own or simply reviewing and interpreting the results contained in a professional appraisal.

Please note that additional terms were added to match the unique vocabulary developed in this book. Such entries (e.g., "ADJUSTED CASH FLOW") are entered in capital letters to avoid confusion. In addition, a few of the original entries in the *International Glossary* were deleted because they were beyond the scope of this book.

Adjusted book value: the value that results after one or more asset or liability amounts are added, deleted, or changed from their respective financial statement amounts.

Adjusted cash flow (ACF): the primary measure of earnings used in the ARM approach. It is equal to pretax income plus addbacks including owner's compensation, owner's benefits, interest, depreciation, and amortization. It is calculated based on a single owner working full-time and further represents the amount of pretax benefits available to a new owner to service debt, pay an owner's salary, and earn a positive return on the invested cash.

Appraisal: see *Valuation* (*appraisal* and *valuation* are used interchangeably in the glossary).

ARM approach: a simplified routine or process used to estimate the value of small businesses based on the application of three distinct valuation components: ACF, rules of thumb, and market comps. The valuator can use a mathematical average of the three results or apply a weighting scheme to reflect each component's strengths or weaknesses.

Asset (asset–based) approach: a general way of determining a value indication of a business, business ownership interest, or security by using one or more methods based on the value of the assets of that business net of liabilities.

Benefit stream: any level of income, cash flow, or earnings generated by an asset, group of assets, or business enterprise. When the term is used, it should be supplemented by a definition of exactly what it means in the given valuation context.

BIZCOMPS: one of the four major sources of market comparable sales results as used in the market approach to business valuation (others include Pratt's Stats, IBA Database, and VR Business Brokers BizStats).

Blockage discount: an amount or percentage deducted from the current market price of a publicly traded security to reflect the decrease in the per share value of a block of those securities that is of a size that could not be sold in a reasonable period of time given normal trading volume.

Business: see *Business enterprise.*

Business enterprise: a commercial, industrial, service, or investment entity, or a combination thereof, pursuing an economic activity.

Business valuation: the act or process of determining the value of a business enterprise or ownership interest therein.

Capitalization: a conversion of a single period stream of benefits into value.

Capitalization factor: any multiple or divisor used to convert anticipated benefits into value.

Capitalization rate: any divisor (usually expressed as a percentage) used to convert anticipated benefits into value.

Capital structure: the composition of the invested capital of a business enterprise; the mix of debt and equity financing.

Cash flow: cash that is generated over a period of time by an asset, group of assets, or business enterprise. It may be used in a general sense to encompass various levels of specifically defined cash flows. When the term is used, it should be supplemented by a qualifier (for example, "discretionary" or "operating") and a definition of exactly what it means in the given valuation context.

Comparable sales method: the most applicable market-based valuation method used in the ARM approach to business valuation. This method relies on strength through numbers such that the average price to ACF and price to gross revenue multiples can be used in comparison with the subject company. If the subject company has above-average characteristics (e.g., rising sales and profits, exceptional lease, minimal importance of owner to business success), then a multiple above the average should be applied.

Control: the power to direct the management and policies of a business enterprise.

Control premium: an amount (expressed in either dollar or percentage form) by which the pro rata value of a controlling interest exceeds the pro rata value of a noncontrolling interest in a business enterprise, which reflects the power of control.

Cost approach: a general way of estimating a value indication of an individual asset by quantifying the amount of money that would be required to replace the future service capability of that asset.

Cost of capital: the expected rate of return (discount rate) that the market requires in order to attract funds to a particular investment.

Discount: a reduction in value or the act of reducing value.

Discount for lack of control: an amount or percentage deducted from the pro rata share of value of one hundred percent (100%) of an equity interest in a business to reflect the absence of some or all of the powers of control.

Discount for lack of marketability: an amount or percentage deducted from the value of an ownership interest to reflect the relative absence of marketability.

Discount rate: a rate of return (cost of capital) used to convert a monetary sum, payable or receivable in the future, into present value.

Earnings before interest and taxes (EBIT): a commonly used measure of income made up of pretax income plus interest expense. The usefulness of a measure such as EBIT is that it allows meaningful comparisons from one business to another based on similar capital structures (no debt or interest expense).

Earnings before interest, taxes, depreciation, and amortization (EBITDA): another common measure of earnings used in business valuation; for example, middle-market manufacturing companies might sell for six to ten times EBITDA (same as EBIT, but depreciation and amortization expense are also added back to pretax earnings).

Economic life: the period of time over which property may generate economic benefits.

Effective date: see *Valuation date.*

Enterprise: see *Business enterprise.*

Equity net cash flows: those cash flows available to pay out to equity holders (in the form of dividends) after funding operations of the business enterprise, making necessary capital investments, and reflecting increases or decreases in debt financing.

Equity risk premium: a rate of return in addition to a risk-free rate to compensate for investing in equity instruments because they have a higher degree of probable risk than risk-free instruments (a component of the cost of equity capital or equity discount rate).

Excess earnings: that amount of anticipated benefits that exceeds a fair rate of return on the value of a selected asset base (often net tangible assets) used to generate those anticipated benefits.

Excess earnings method: a specific way of determining a value indication of a business, business ownership interest, or security determined as the sum of a) the value of the assets obtained by capitalizing excess earnings and b) the value of the selected asset base. Also frequently used to value intangible assets. See *Excess earnings.*

Fair market value: the price, expressed in terms of cash equivalents, at which property would change hands between a hypothetical willing and able buyer and a hypothetical willing and able seller, acting at arm's length in an open and unrestricted market, when neither is under compulsion to buy or sell and when both have reasonable knowledge of the relevant facts. (NOTE: In Canada, the term "price" should be replaced with the term "highest price".)

Forced liquidation value: liquidation value at which the asset or assets are sold as quickly as possible, such as at an auction.

Going concern: an ongoing operating business enterprise.

Going concern value: the value of a business enterprise that is expected to continue to operate into the future. The intangible elements of going concern value result from factors such as having a trained work force, an operational plant, and the necessary licenses, systems, and procedures in place.

Goodwill: that intangible asset arising as a result of name, reputation, customer loyalty, location, products, and similar factors not separately identified.

Goodwill value: the value attributable to goodwill.

Guideline public company method: a second market-based valuation method that relies on the share prices of publicly traded companies as a basis for estimating the value of similar yet smaller businesses. Use of this method almost always requires adjusting the average multiple (price/earnings) of the comparable companies to reflect the size effect, which is based on the proposition that smaller businesses are riskier and therefore investors require and receive a higher rate of return (i.e., the multiples for the smaller companies are significantly smaller than for their larger counterparts because of the increased risk).

Income (income-based) approach: a general way of determining a value indication of a business, business ownership interest, security, or intangible asset using one or more methods that convert anticipated benefits into a present single amount.

Intangible assets: non-physical assets (such as franchises, trademarks, patents, copyrights, goodwill, equities, mineral rights, securities, and contracts as distinguished from physical assets) that grant rights, privileges, and have economic benefits for the owner.

Invested capital: the sum of equity and debt in a business enterprise. Debt is typically a) long-term liabilities or b) the sum of short-term interest-bearing debt and long-term liabilities. When the term is used, it should be supplemented by a definition of exactly what it means in the given valuation context.

Invested capital net cash flows: those cash flows available to pay out to equity holders (in the form of dividends) and debt investors (in the form of principal and interest) after funding operations of the business enterprise and making necessary capital investments.

Investment risk: the degree of uncertainty as to the realization of expected returns.

Investment value: the value to a particular investor based on individual investment requirements and expectations. (NOTE: In Canada, the term used is "value to the owner.")

Key person discount: an amount or percentage deducted from the value of an ownership interest to reflect the reduction in value resulting from the actual or potential loss of a key person in a business enterprise.

Liquidation value: the net amount that can be realized if the business is terminated and the assets are sold piecemeal. Liquidation can be either "orderly" or "forced."

Liquidity: the ability to quickly convert property to cash or pay a liability.

Majority control: the degree of control provided by a majority position.

Majority interest: an ownership interest greater than fifty percent (50%) of the voting interest in a business enterprise.

Marketability: the ability to quickly convert property to cash at minimal cost.

Marketability discount: see *Discount for lack of marketability.*

Market (market-based) approach: a general way of determining a value indication of a business, business ownership interest, security, or intangible asset by using one or more methods that compare the subject to similar businesses, business ownership interests, securities, or intangible assets that have been sold.

Minority discount: a discount for lack of control applicable to a minority interest.

Minority interest: an ownership interest less than fifty percent (50%) of the voting interest in a business enterprise.

Multiple of cash flow: the first component of the ARM approach calls for calculating ACF and then estimating the proper multiple to apply to arrive at a preliminary estimate of business value. For example, all businesses sold in the VR Business Brokers network have consistently sold on average for around 2.3 times ACF. However, as the amount of cash flow rises, the applicable multiple also rises (e.g., for ACF of around $500,000, a range of two to four would apply as opposed to a range of one to three for businesses with $250,000 or less in ACF).

Net book value: with respect to a business enterprise, the difference between total assets (net of accumulated depreciation, depletion, and amortization) and total liabilities of a business enterprise as they appear on the balance sheet (synonymous with "shareholder's equity"); with respect to an intangible asset, the capitalized cost of an intangible asset less accumulated amortization as it appears on the books of account of the business enterprise.

Net cash flow: a form of cash flow. When the term is used, it should be supplemented by a qualifier (for example, "equity" or "invested capital") and a definition of exactly what it means in the given valuation context.

Net tangible asset value: the value of the business enterprise's tangible assets (excluding excess assets and non–operating assets) minus the value of its liabilities. (NOTE: In Canada, tangible assets also include identifiable intangible assets.)

Non-operating assets: assets not necessary to ongoing operations of the business enterprise. (NOTE: In Canada, the term used is "redundant assets.")

Orderly liquidation value: liquidation value at which the asset or assets are sold over a reasonable period of time to maximize proceeds received.

Premise of value: an assumption regarding the most likely set of transactional circumstances that may be applicable to the subject valuation; e.g. an going concern, liquidation.

Rate of return: amount of income (loss) or change in value realized or anticipated on an investment, expressed as a percentage of that investment.

Redundant assets: (NOTE: In Canada, see *Non-operating assets.*)

Replacement cost new: the current cost of a similar new property having the nearest equivalent utility to the property being valued.

Report date: the date conclusions are transmitted to the client.

Reproduction cost new: the current cost of an identical new property.

Residual value: the prospective value as of the end of the discrete projection period in a discounted benefit streams model.

Risk-free rate: the rate of return available in the market on an investment free of default risk.

Risk premium: a rate of return in addition to a risk-free rate to compensate the investor for accepting risk.

Rule of thumb: a mathematical relationship between variables based on experience, observation, hearsay, or a combination of these, usually applicable to a specific industry.

Rule of thumb/ARM approach: the second component of the ARM approach calls for the valuator to determine whether one or more specific rules of thumb apply to a particular type of business; if so, each rule must be evaluated in the context of the subject company. Many rules simply offer a range of multiples (e.g., 1 to 2 times ACF for small gift shops) or a combination range of multiples plus assets (e.g., 1 to 1.5 times ACF plus assets for small retail businesses).

Special interest purchasers: acquirers who believe they can enjoy post-acquisition economies of scale, synergies, or strategic advantages by combining the acquired business interest with their own.

Standard of value: the identification of the type of value being utilized in a specific engagement; e.g. fair market value, fair value, investment value.

Sustaining capital reinvestment: the periodic capital outlay required to maintain operations at existing levels, net of the tax shield available from such outlays.

Terminal value: see *Residual value.*

Terms and conditions: any component or feature related to the purchase or sale of a business that is placed in a purchase contract (e.g., training period, down payment, amount of inventory included in sale). Every term and condition can affect the final deal price and should be considered in this light when negotiating a deal price (which ultimately becomes a market comp when reported as a closed transaction to one of the major databases). For example, a study of the BIZCOMPS database found that businesses sold with seller financing (promissory note from buyer to seller) sold for approximately 25 percent more than businesses sold for all cash, (i.e., an approximate 20 percent discount was received for all-cash offers).

Valuation: the process of estimating business value. Although *valuation* and *appraisal* are used interchangeably in this glossary, a working difference between the two is found in the fact that completion of appraisals requires certification on the part of the valuator, whereas anyone can complete a business valuation. For example, Certified Business Appraisers can complete appraisals and valuations, but noncertified parties can complete only valuations.

Valuation: the act or process of determining the value of a business, business ownership interest, security, or intangible asset.

Valuation approach: a general way of determining a value indication of a business, business ownership interest, security, or intangible asset using one or more valuation methods.

Valuation date: the specific point in time as of which the valuator's opinion of value applies (also called "effective date" or "appraisal date").

Valuation method: within approaches, a specific way to determine value.

Valuation procedure: the act, manner, and technique of performing the steps of an appraisal method.

Valuation ratio: a fraction in which a value or price serves as the numerator and financial, operating, or physical data serve as the denominator.

Value to the owner: (NOTE: In Canada, see *Investment value.*)

Weighted average cost of capital (WACC): the cost of capital (discount rate) determined by the weighted average, at market value, of the cost of all financing sources in the business enterprise's capital structure.

Index

Scott Gabehart

Mr. Gabehart began his business career as a corporate auditor for Fortune 100 corporations Motorola and Schering-Plough. As a Certified Business Appraiser, currently associated with VR Business Brokers in Scottsdale, Arizona, he has listed, valued, marketed, and sold literally hundreds of businesses of all types and sizes, from retail and manufacturing to distribution and service, and for all types of reasons (ESOP, straight sale, SBA loan, divorce, buy-sell agreement, etc.)

Mr. Gabehart is the author of *The Upstart Guide to Buying, Valuing, and Selling Your Business*. He is listed as the Industry Expert for the valuation and sale of accounting/tax practices in the 2002 *Business Reference Guide* and is a regular columnist covering business valuation issues for the *Journal of Real Estate and Business* in Scottsdale, Arizona. In addition, he has taught business valuation at the American Graduate School of International Management.

He is an active member in the Valley Board of Business Brokers, the Institute of Business Appraisers, and the National Association of Certified Valuation Analysts, among other organizations. Mr. Gabehart holds degrees in economics, German, and business administration, including his MBA from the American Graduate School of International Management (Thunderbird). Mr. Gabehart can be contacted at (888) 347-2811.

Richard Brinkley

Richard Brinkley's background brings together a wealth of experience in business sales, real estate, appraisal, franchising, brand development, marketing, operations, and organizational strategy. He has worked as a licensed real estate and business broker, consultant, and franchiser since 1986, focusing recently on the development and implementation of sound principles related to business ownership transfers, conceptual and strategic planning, marketing, and performance improvement of privately held businesses and franchises throughout North America. He has served as CEO of a leading U.S. business broker franchise network, president of a large real estate franchise network in Canada, in addition to personally acquiring and selling several businesses over the years.

Mr. Brinkley has assisted business owners not only to valuate their privately held companies but has also successfully structured transactions with both public and private acquirers. He has earned the designations of CBI, Certified Business Intermediary, from the International Business Brokers Association; CBC, Certified Business Councilor, from The Institute of Certified Business Councilors; and he is a member of the Florida Business Broker Association, Business Brokers of Florida, and is a lifetime member of the Institute of Business Appraisers

He has been recognized for his achievements in franchising by *Entrepreneur* magazine and has been quoted in *The Wall Street Journal* and many other publications as an expert on privately held business sales in North America. Mr. Brinkley can be contacted at (800) 690-0059.